# Making History Mine

# Making History Mine

Meaningful Connections for Grades 5–9

Sarah Cooper

Stenhouse Publishers
Portland, Maine

Stenhouse Publishers
www.stenhouse.com

Library of Congress Cataloging-in-Publication Data
Cooper, Sarah, 1975-
  Making history mine : meaningful connections for grades 5–9 / Sarah Cooper.
    p. cm.
  ISBN 978-1-57110-765-7 (alk. paper)
 1.  History--Study and teaching (Middle school)--United States. 2.  History--Study and teaching (Secondary)--United States. 3.  History--Methodology.  I. Title.
  F1219.73.C676 2009
  372.89'044--dc22
                                                                2008055385

Cover design, interior design, and typesetting by Designboy Creative Group
Manufactured in the United States of America on acid-free, recycled paper
15 14 13 12          9 8 7 6 5 4 3 2

v

*For
Jane Schaffer,
master teacher*

# Contents

# Acknowledgments

Teaching is a profession that thrives on collaboration. I could not have written this book without the mentorship, inspiration, and guidance of so many people, many of whom I do not have room to name here.

Holly Holland is a writer's editor: sensitive, kind, and challenging. This book owes so much to her tireless work.

In ten years of teaching, many have epitomized the middle school ideal for me. Ellen Howard, Alison Fleming, and Midge Kimble have shown how much young adolescents matter. Richard Geib, Tammy Shpall, and Kristina Kalb spent countless hours sharing history curriculum ideas in my first three years and beyond.

Librarians are the often-unsung heroes of a history department and a school. Those I have been fortunate enough to work with include Sue Hodge, Reggie Ursettie, Meryl Eldridge, Sarah Lucy, Kathy Snyder, and Pam Force.

After a summer of intensive writing about teaching, it was a joy to return to real kids in the classroom. Thanks to all of my students at Milken Community Middle School, Peak to Peak Charter School, the Bishop's School, and Flintridge Preparatory School for your willingness to think hard and be engaged.

The Flintridge Prep history and English departments, not to mention the rest of the faculty, continually remind me of the power of intellectual conversation and easy camaraderie among colleagues. Thanks also to Peter Bachmann and Peter Vaughn for nearly a decade of thoughtful guidance.

Melinda Hennessey has been a mentor to me since I was fifteen years old and she switched me into her AP European history class. Her passion and commitment to teaching inform every page of this book.

Before my parents retired, my dad taught social studies and my mom taught English. Now I teach English and history. My debt to them is incalculable, in teaching and in life.

My sons, Noah and Sam, remind me each day of what's important. And my husband, Ken, supports me in every way, even when I don't realize I need it. I could not have written this book or had such a fulfilling past fourteen years without him.

# Introduction

At the end of every year, like so many history teachers, I regret simply skimming the surface of the past. Three weeks, and there went India. We spent half a day on Emperor Ashoka, and I completely glossed over the Mauryan Empire. Should I have devoted more time to Andrew Jackson and less to Abraham Lincoln? And how can my students possibly go through their teenage years, let alone adulthood, without fully processing the achievements of women such as Jane Addams and Hildegard of Bingen?

I think I've perfected the "oh well" half smile and apologetic shoulder shrug in response to my students' desire to dive deeper into history.

"Will we get to the Byzantine Empire this year? We never get to the Byzantine Empire," says Jackson, an especially eager ninth grader who is looking at the world history syllabus with mild skepticism.

"We will, for a couple of days in March," I say, smiling and shrugging, mentally robbing Rome to pay Constantinople. Maybe we could carve out one class period to create mosaics that imitate the stags and ostriches of Byzantine art.

Another year, in an eighth-grade U.S. history class, Gianna asks, "How does Thomas Jefferson's Democratic-Republican Party relate to politics today?"

What a great question—and what a thoughtful invitation to veer from my lesson plan on Hamilton and Jefferson. My students need to know the history of American political parties, but they also need to make relevant connections to contemporary issues. Our weekly current events discussions only hint at the intricacies of today's government. Could I squeeze in a modern-day political debate at the end of the Early Republic unit?

As we discuss modern political systems in a seventh-grade global cultures class, Camilla wonders why Communism was so appealing, anyway. This I can answer succinctly—"Wouldn't you like everything to be equal, at least in theory?"—before moving back to our conversation comparing capitalism, Communism, and fascism. But when I catch my breath after school that day, I kick myself for giving so little time to such a grand question. Maybe we could do a ten-minute simulation of what it might be like to live in a land where the government gives everyone a job and an income.

The bane of the history teacher's existence is coverage. The middle grades social studies curriculum is invariably a mile wide and an inch deep, making it difficult to do justice to the subject and to our students. So we trudge on, moving like exhausted soldiers determined to keep up with the general's plan for advancement. We are dedicated, but many of us wonder if there is a better way. Can we tap into our students' curiosity about the world around them without dulling their senses through content overload? Can we probe more of the mysteries and miseries of global cultures and still prime our students' passion for activism and their hope for the future? Yes, we can. The solution, I believe, lies in the search for meaning through personal connections to history.

# Goals: Finding a Personal Connection

Four years into teaching middle school world and U.S. history, influenced by the ideas of *Understanding by Design* (Wiggins and McTighe 2001), I started asking myself at the beginning of a chapter: what do I want my students to know and be able to do with this information? Such a big-picture approach helped me create more meaningful assignments that generated measurable knowledge. Instead of just putting together interesting bits of material, I began to understand how to visualize the beginning, middle, and end of a unit.

After several years of these small steps, I felt comfortable expanding this emphasis on specific goals to an entire course, asking myself two guiding questions: (1) who are my students now? and (2) what do they need to learn to become conscientious and knowledgeable adults?

## Who Are My Students Now?

In all teaching, but especially in the identity-forming crucible of middle school, the student is as important as the material; human development parallels academic development. Middle-schoolers focus on themselves, wanting to know how their studies relate to their lives. Passionate people, they want to harness their enthusiasm to change the world for the better. They crave movement and physical expressions of learning. Joyful and humorous human beings, they pride themselves on seeing the fun in most any situation. Like all of us, they want to feel appreciated and competent and useful. The history we teach reaches them best when it involves novelty, humor, meaning, a sense of self, and a connection to the real world.

## What Do They Need to Learn to Become Conscientious and Knowledgeable Adults?

The vast majority of our students will not become professional historians. In their careers, however, they will need to know how to find valid information, analyze it from multiple perspectives, and communicate it clearly. In a world that *New York Times* columnist Thomas Friedman reminds us is increasingly "flat" (Friedman 2006), our students also will need to distinguish themselves with creative approaches and critical thinking. Such abilities stretch far beyond traditional expectations of memorization and regurgitation. Students will need qualities that business writer Daniel Pink calls *symphony*, "putting the pieces together" so they encompass more than the sum of their parts; *story*, crafting tales that influence people; *empathy*, sensing what others are feeling; and *meaning*, connecting to deeper values that underlie our everyday lives (Pink 2006, 66–67).

When working with students who may not immediately see the value in becoming historians, how can we guide them toward exciting discoveries and meaningful relationships while still focusing on academic standards and curricular mandates? The best answer I've found is to teach under the shelter of broad themes and global concepts, conveying ideas that connect content across topics and grade levels. With this approach, students are not focusing on the tiny details of history, although facts remain crucial to effective argumentation. Instead, adolescents see history through the eyes of individuals and then move outward to larger implications and patterns. One of the best places to begin is with the personal, for who isn't interested in learning why and how we have come to live as we do?

# Starting with the Standards

All of the chapters are rooted in state and national standards, and detailed descriptions of those links open each section of the book. Here I want to emphasize the larger goals of teaching middle school history.

## 1. The Role of the Individual: Assessing Who Makes History

I begin my history classes each year by telling students, "You will *all* make history." Focusing on notable individuals of the past helps students envision how they, too, can influence the future and use their burgeoning power effectively. Such strategies personalize the content.

## 2. How Opinions Become History: Analyzing Point of View

Recognizing point of view can be as simple as flipping through an eighth grader's diary entry or as complex as deciphering a New Deal historian's sanitized treatment of Franklin Delano Roosevelt. By examining a variety of primary and secondary sources, including textbooks, students can understand the motives of historical and contemporary people. Considering perspective also helps students come to terms with the complexities of history: nothing is as simple as the textbook might have you believe.

## 3. Fighting Words: Examining Rhetoric, Reasoning, and the Role of Language in History

History comes alive most vividly through the words of people who lived it. Writing is a source of inspiration and power. By inspecting speeches, letters, and diaries, students can explore the power of literature to move people—not to mention their own ability to effect change through a letter to the editor or a political poster. Fictional sources also can engage students' emotions and encourage intuitive leaps.

## 4. A Broader View: Finding Patterns in the Past

After students have examined personal connections, point of view, and the role of language in history, they can move beyond an individual's scope to the wider blueprints of the past. This category evokes more traditional history teaching about chronology, geography, government, and economics. However, starting with a personal reference and then expanding the discussion, such as presenting Theodora's speech to Justinian during the Nika rebellion before investigating Byzantine politics, can help students understand global relationships on an approachable scale. They can ask themselves, where do my ancestors and I fit into these patterns?

## 5. How Historians Think: Writing as a Way of Understanding

Students can examine and further understand what they think about history by pulling together their ideas into analytical paragraphs and essays. Such high-level synthesis goes to the core of what real historians do: examine primary sources and make a case for a point of view.

## 6. Current Events: Connecting Past to Present

With a foundational knowledge of analytical writing and the broad patterns that link historical events, students can compare the past to the present in greater depth. Teachers can build students' understanding by forging strong, personal ties to the curriculum. Individuals and institutions intertwine: just as students' grandparents affect their lives, society's past actions shape today's domestic and foreign policies.

## 7. The Power of Information: Igniting Passion Through Research

We can plant the seeds of historical research early on in a course, such as when we ask students to consult biographical sources to understand the motivations of historical figures. Later, after students have integrated the first six goals of *Making History Mine* into their mental framework, we can introduce more expansive projects. Guided, independent research helps students become creators of knowledge, not simply receivers or manipulators of information, and shows them how to explore the world and their potential role in shaping it.

## 8. Global Citizenship: Learning to Evaluate Ethics and Solve Problems

Moving from the individual's role in history, as defined in Chapter 1, we can show our middle-schoolers how to use this knowledge to take action. Encouraging students to direct their passions toward civic activism is the essence of character development. It gives young adolescents a chance to make their own history.

History at all levels and in all units poses moral questions to students. Sometimes such inquiries can kick off a chapter in the textbook or the school year, while at other times these dilemmas require students to plunge into additional research. This final goal strives to foster engaged citizens who are ready to lead and equipped to direct their newfound skills toward local, national, and global change.

# Planning the Sequence: Where Do I Start?

History in the middle grades often throws too many ingredients into the soup. Depending on the particular state standards involved, teachers may be expected to address ancient, medieval, and modern world history; early and modern U.S. history; geography; current events; economics; and often state history as well. Mindful of this potential hodgepodge, I've structured *Making History Mine* to show you how to use these goals and lessons within any secondary grade span or subject. It might seem confusing to change topics frequently, such as when I mention the cattle herds of Theodore Roosevelt in the same chapter as the sculptures of China's Zhou dynasty, but I want to make these ideas appealing and applicable to all levels and all subjects.

Many of this book's goals are recursive: they come back again and again within a particular unit and throughout the year. I've often found it a good rule of thumb to begin with the first three goals, focusing on the individual, before building up to the larger patterns and connections of the last five themes. Introductory hooks at the beginning of a lesson or a unit will grab students' attention because of the personal relationships established. However, a unit will work just as well if we start with the big ideas, such as geography or chronology, and then zoom in toward the people affected by these larger trends. Much depends on your students: their background knowledge, their attention span, their interests, and their skills.

In the past decade, I have taught both middle school and high school classes, from geography and current events to world and U.S. history. I've used the lessons and strategies mentioned throughout the book at all levels, including the time-crunched space of an AP U.S. history class. Appealing to skills-based and identity-related standards can work for any student in any grade. Every year I try to learn more and reach more students. Thank you for coming on this journey with me.

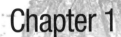

Chapter 1

# The Role of the Individual: Assessing Who Makes History

## What's Inside?

### Skills and Strategies

- Analyze poetry for historical meaning
- Understand connotations of words
- Organize a history binder
- Write conversations among historical figures
- Read and write historical narratives
- Create graphs, posters, and comic strips to show comprehension
- Understand why humans explore
- Interview a relative
- Draw a map or time line

Standards

✔ Storytelling
✔ Biography
✔ Economics
✔ Citizenship
✔ Identity formation
✔ Social norms

# Setting the Tone: A Poem for Day One

On the first day of the new school year with my middle school history students, after introductions and a review of class procedures, I like to share a poem dedicated to the unnamed individuals who brought glory to the famous figures of history. Bertolt Brecht's "A Worker Reads History" urges us to recognize ordinary people whose contributions made great events possible. The poem begins with the question and answer, "Who built the seven gates of Thebes?/ The books are filled with names of kings." Through this brief pair of lines I hope to set the stage for the deeper inquiry that will ideally define our year together, asking students not to accept easy answers or single interpretations but to critically examine evidence, bias, and motivation. Later in the poem, Brecht asks who helped Alexander the Great achieve his many triumphs, who supported Julius Caesar when he came and saw and conquered, and who shared Philip II's grief when England wrecked his Spanish Armada. "A Worker Reads History" leaves us wondering about the star-studded stories of history with a short stanza at the end: "So many particulars./ So many questions."

Although just a fifteen-minute activity, this lesson scaffolds instruction so that everyone can feel successful walking out of class on the first day. Some students might understand every word of the poem from the beginning, while others can use more guidance; I try to balance their needs by providing small steps leading from literal to metaphorical meaning.

First I read the poem aloud so everyone can hear the words and think about their definitions. As I do, I ask students to underline words that confuse them or sound especially powerful. Giving students this choice differentiates instruction by allowing the strongest readers to focus on the text's intensity rather than its literal meaning. Typically, students have questions about terms such as *masons* and *bellowed*. I ask them to circle these words and write a short definition supplied by me or other students during our discussion. If the class seems engaged and not overwhelmed by this task, I also introduce the literary concept of connotation, the feelings or associations that a word invokes. Then Katharine can suggest that *masons* implies sturdiness, while Jonathan can say that *bellowed* suggests anger or sadness.

After we've discussed unfamiliar or unusually vivid words, I ask the students to stand up, with poem in hand, playing into the middle school love of novelty and physical movement.

"We are going to read aloud the poem as a class and use your best slow-reading voice," I say. "No shouting, though."

This direction usually elicits some tentative smiles and frantic looks at friends that silently ask, "What's going on? This is a little crazy."

"Up, up," I say, and the room rustles with their new height. I usually circle the classroom as we all read the poem together. This way, I can begin to see students' personalities and make sure everyone is giving the choral reading their best effort. Some of the boys will slump as they read; some of the girls will giggle. After all, this is the first day of sixth or seventh or eighth grade, and image is paramount among one's peers. At the end of the first rendition, I'll usually praise the fine initial effort but then urge them to try another round and this time really give it our all. The second reading runs better because students are more comfortable reading aloud and more familiar with the text. By focusing on the words and sounds of the poem, we are showing the importance that reading comprehension will have in everything we do in history this year.

After we've finished reciting the poem twice, I ask the students to sit down and mark two lines or phrases that they liked and to write down why in five to ten words per phrase. If some students complete only one reason, that's fine, but I want to challenge those who can do more. If many students struggle to explain their choices, I might ask them to pick one phrase and illustrate it briefly in the margin of their papers. Offering options can play into middle-schoolers' desire to use their growing responsibility in whatever productive ways possible.

We share several responses. Naomi loves Brecht's image of the men of Atlantis calling for their servants on the night that mythical city fell because she says it shows their dependence on the "little people." Bobby enjoys the poem's literal and figurative questions about the price of victory—who paid for all these accomplishments?—because such reflections make us think about the challenges that history books don't always address. These responses are unusually full, especially for the first day of class. To elicit the "because" part of their answers, I often push students to probe their initial reactions, even two or three times, and then say, "Yes, that's it, that's real thinking. I can see your brain working." In this way, I let students know that they cannot get away with sharing only the first thought that pops into their heads.

Now that we have translated some of the difficult words, recited the poem aloud, and discussed the most compelling phrases, I ask students the big question, the one that cuts to the heart of how historians think: "What is the author's point in this poem?" Or, to make the activity more immediately relevant, "Why do you think we're starting with this poem in history today?" Again I ask students to write down their ideas; I usually give a minimum word count so they know what to expect, about ten to twenty words or one to three sentences. By this point, most students can build on their classmates' responses, and our discussion of particular phrases evolves into a reflection of the poem's larger meaning: "It reminds us of all the people who did the icky work in history," "It shows us that our textbook doesn't tell us everything," or "It tells us that unnamed people can have a huge effect on the world." I write the ideas on the board and also ask students to jot down their favorite summary of the poem so that they have it for future reference in their binders. (See Figure 1.1 for more about student binders.)

This kind of activity—combining reading comprehension, literary awareness, historical context, and critical thinking—enables us to view the nuts-and-bolts details of history through a longer lens. We can zoom in to get a closer look at the lives of individuals and pan out to assess the impact on the society or the historical period under review. I decided to use this poem on the first day of school after many Septembers of trial and error. In previous years, I had asked my middle school students to write about their stake in history. Where do they enter into the story? What grabs their attention? Alex's hook was the weaponry used throughout the world's military campaigns. Jordan was fascinated by the power and influence that women have held, however briefly. But many students couldn't connect to the past or understand why they should care about events that happened so long ago.

Figure 1.1

## Organized Student Binders

Part of a student's job in middle school is learning how to organize materials for many different classes at once. Compiling a history binder helps students keep their coursework in order and gives them a wealth of sources and handouts to supplement the textbook. I ask students to keep everything from the unit we're studying in a one-inch, three-ring binder or a section in a larger binder in the order that they received or created it, with page numbers and a student-created table of contents. I got the idea for a table of contents and title page for each unit from Teachers' Curriculum Institute's Interactive Student Notebooks. (For more information about how these notebooks encourage students to respond interactively to information, see http://www. teachtci.com/forum/isn.aspx.)

Everything goes in the notebook, from class handouts to lecture notes to homework responses to creative activities. I tell students that the binder is like a parallel textbook: everything on one topic is in one place rather than being spread out in sections such as homework and class notes. When we encounter a theme or idea relevant to an earlier topic in the unit, students can immediately pull out the appropriate piece of paper. I have assessed the binders in different ways depending on my class sizes and goals for student learning: by collecting individual assignments and returning them, by grading all the binders at the end of the unit for completion, or by looking at some assignments in class and collecting others. The use of binders can be flexible depending on your and your students' needs.

Other times I searched for readings that expressed a similar sentiment about the individual's role in shaping memorable events. However, "A Worker Reads History" has the advantage of being easily accessible because it repeats the same concept in many different ways. If students do not know any of the places or people mentioned in the poem, they still can understand that Brecht is praising the unsung heroes of history. And if they do not comprehend all of the questions the poem asks, they can usually latch onto at least one. In addition, Brecht's poem addresses a key thematic strand identified by the National Council for the Social Studies: "How can the perspective we have about our own life experiences be viewed as part of the larger human story across time?" (NCSS 1994). Finally, unlike some lesson plans that wind up boring the teacher, this bold and open-ended poem never feels dated or repetitive. Every time I read it, I notice a new phrase or think of a different response to the author's plaintive queries. As a result, I enter every class on the first day energized to discover what my new students think.

# Why Start with the Individual?

Examining the lives of real people makes my job easier. In the past, other introductory activities proved less than inspiring:

- A discussion of what students already know about the syllabus landed like a lead balloon ("Oh yeah, we learned about chivalry in sixth grade; that was cool/boring/a long time ago").

- Leading with a question of "Why is it important to study history?" generated a few engaging but predictable answers and much more telling than showing ("so we can learn from the past; so we don't make the same mistakes").

- A discussion of any summer reading assignment usually prompted nervousness ("When will we have a test on this?") and showing off ("Remember when the main character sailed across the Atlantic on page 32?") that ended up shutting down less knowledgeable students. Such assessment is better left for a quiz or writing assignment later in the week.

Recent research has shown that students "learn more when the concepts are personally meaningful to them"; a personal link gives students a framework within which to understand and approach the history we teach (Bransford, Brown, and Cocking 2000, 11). Entering the minds of real figures from history is one of the most interesting ways to board a time machine to the past. It's hard not to be curious about those who lived a long time ago when you can hear their voices and feel their passions expressed in primary source documents.

In addition, middle school students are fascinated by identity formation, which involves noticing others' actions and deciding which ones fit with their developing system of values. Viewed through the lens of the individual, history is really a form of glorified gossip.

- Do you think Anna Comnena of the Byzantine Empire idolized her father as much as her history, *The Alexiad,* implies? What drove her to write her recollections at a time when most women were not literate or encouraged to contribute to the canon? Let's study the introduction to her epic and read between the lines.

- What about the relationship between John Adams and Thomas Jefferson, stormy for years after Jefferson bested Adams in the election of 1800? What do you think allowed them to put aside their differences and reconcile in the years before their deaths (which, incidentally, both occurred on July 4, 1826, the fiftieth anniversary of the commemorated signing of the Declaration of Independence—how amazing is that)?

The psychology of history appears writ large in biography. We don't have to stretch the truth too much to cast history as the longest-lasting soap opera or interactive video game ever told. (See Figure 1.2 for tech-savvy activities that build on these stories.)

## Figure 1.2

### Modern-Day Takes on Historical Figures

Ask students to:

- Create a fake Facebook or MySpace page for Anna Comnena or Thomas Jefferson that they will share with the class but not actually post. Who are their friends? What do they say about their daily activities? What is their "away message"?

- Write the script for a soap opera or reality TV episode, create a page of a graphic novel, or choose another medium to reflect the drama of John Adams's and Thomas Jefferson's political reconciliation and same-day death.

- Produce a talk radio panel or documentary focusing on the acrimony of the Election of 1800. Use real quotations where possible.

As you read this chapter, please keep in mind that the suggested activities are just samples of the many possibilities for making history personal to young adolescents. You might prefer a different scene-setting poem, or you might ask your students to role play instead of read on day one. You might favor discussion rather than document analysis during the first few weeks of school. Instead of emphasizing the individual's role in history through an introductory unit, you might decide to sprinkle the focus throughout the year, providing a hook for each major topic. All of the activities in this book are designed to give you concrete plans to work with as well as creative ideas to spark your imagination. Nothing is set in stone because we must respond to our students—and go with our passions, guided by the standards—every day that we teach.

In seeking to build a foundation for understanding the substance of the times we study, I've adopted a range of strategies to help every learner comprehend the important ideas conveyed in historical writings. (For more on primary sources, see Chapter 3 and Appendixes B, C, and D.) Before I discuss the many benefits of using primary source documents in middle school history classes, however, I also want to share some pitfalls. Too often, in my desire to move quickly through material, I have inadvertently sacrificed understanding for coverage. A blank, glazed, pained look on the faces of even my best students is a sure indicator of this mistake. At other times I have chosen sources that proved too challenging or too dry for middle schoolers—or maybe for just about anyone. I still remember when

I tried to read the entire 1832 "South Carolina Ordinance of Nullification" from Andrew Jackson's presidency because I was so excited about the way it showed the strong will of a bellwether state in the years leading up to the Civil War. Unfortunately, my students did not share this passion, and the document's arcane language stunned them into silence. Sometimes a better way to tell the story, I realized, is simply to tell the story. When I discover during class that a historical document is not provoking the response I had hoped for, I might stop and return to the story behind the facts, or I'll ask students to pick one phrase from the piece and illustrate how it makes them feel. Then I'll jettison that selection and choose a better source for the future.

## Chatting with Kings and Presidents: My Dinner with George Washington

At times, we can present primary documents not as decipherable texts but as conversation starters. On the entertainment television channel E!, students often see quotations from modern celebrities plastered across the screen. Why not invite students to have conversations with historical figures as well? By writing such dialogues, based on historical people's own words, students can consider how personality affects leadership, how leaders make decisions, and how rulers show their people what is important to run their country. This activity can be done anytime during the year when you have a unit with rulers who recorded many of their thoughts, or even who left many artifacts behind, as with Emperor Shi Huangdi's terra-cotta soldiers during the Qin Empire in China. (Judy Chicago's "Dinner Party," a famous art installation from the 1970s whose place settings on a table represent famous women from history, can provide additional inspiration for this activity. To see photos of and information about the piece, go to the Brooklyn Museum's website at http://www.brooklynmuseum.org/exhibitions/dinner_party. The page also has a link to a teacher packet on the exhibit.)

To provide grist for their conversations, my eighth-grade U.S. history students read quotations by George Washington, John Adams, and Thomas Jefferson during a unit on the Early Republic. Next to each quotation, they write an adjective describing how the comment makes the person sound. For instance, Washington seems "dignified" and "formal," they say, when he intones at the end of his life, "Doctor, I die hard, but I am not afraid to go." Adams strikes them as "dutiful" and "pessimistic," and Jefferson "fashionable" and "witty."

"Which person would you like to invite over for dinner?" I ask.

Rachel chooses Washington for his straightforward judgments, and Matt likes Jefferson for his suave way with words. Some students worry about sitting down with any of them, concerned that they would be intimidated in the presence of such learned men.

"Would you feel intimidated by talking to today's presidents, such as George W. Bush or Bill Clinton?"

No way, the students respond, because these modern leaders seem much more approachable. The exercise might seem lighthearted, but the focus on personality delights middle school students who are deep into discovering their own identities. In our discussion we have also touched on thematic standards of "power, authority, and governance" and "individual development and identity," to name just a few (NCSS 1994). From here, students can select an event from the president's life, such as the Alien and Sedition Acts from John Adams's tenure, and create a conversation between, say, the president and a newspaper reporter who disagrees with him.

The changes in communication during the past two hundred years raise other interesting questions that students can address in their imaginary tête-à-têtes. After we look at Abigail and John Adams's "Remember the Ladies" letters from 1776 (accessible on the Massachusetts Historical Society website at http://www.masshist.org/adams/manuscripts_1.cfm##), I ask if this couple would have written in the same style if they had used Instant Messenger instead of writing in longhand. These eighth graders say no, and they suggest that the frequently separated Adamses might have corresponded more often because they would not have had to wait for postal delivery. After this reading, students can create two written conversations between the Adamses, one using Instant Messenger and one through traditional correspondence. Then we compare the impact of these different modes of communication.

For ancient world history, students could consider the words or portraits of the emperors or philosophers of the early Chinese dynasties, the speakers of ancient Greece, or perhaps the architecture and trading goods of ancient Africa. For societies without copious written records, we can encourage students to use material sources, such as a photo of the Great Zimbabwe or a drawing of a Buddhist shrine, to insert themselves into history. I often look to online images for these photos, citing the source if I reprint it for classroom use. Many textbook websites also feature compelling images.

After looking at a quotation or a portrait relating to a historical figure, students can create a range of products:

- A poster with side-by-side pictures of people in history, followed by a written comparison of personality, decision-making skills, speaking ability, or other qualities chosen by the students

- A fictitious conversation with one of the historical figures, using his or her actual words as dialogue

- A scrapbook "compiled by" a historical person with several of his or her favorite quotations, portraits, and/or events

Such activities encourage students to enter into the minds of people from the past while also requiring them to draw from the public record. Through written and spoken conversations, students discover how society worked long ago, how crucial primary sources are for our understanding of that society, and how historical figures solved problems. I often assign such dialogues at the end of a unit, when students have enough sense of the characters of history—through textbook readings, primary sources, and photos and artifacts—to ground these conversations in fact.

# Tell Me a Story

Sometimes primary sources, fascinating as they are, can seem like just another piece of paper if you use them too often. Some weeks, I've copied mounds of speeches and documents, only to realize by Thursday that I simply cannot ask my students—or myself—to slog through another piece of text written in old-fashioned language that will require intense concentration to decipher. We've had enough "spinach" for a while; now we need some "pizza" to lighten our historical diet. One way to do this is to ask students to become the storytellers of history, imagining that they live in the times about which they are reading. They become the individuals of history, building empathy and understanding of these real characters—this is a way of inviting students "to explain self in relation to others in the society and culture" (NCSS 1994).

Deft authors of historical fiction can help us with such time traveling. Ann Rinaldi is a master of the genre in works such as *Nine Days a Queen: The Short Life and Reign of Lady Jane Grey* and *A Break with Charity: A Story About the Salem Witch Trials*. Laurie Halse Anderson brings the Early Republic period alive in *Fever 1793*, which my students have enjoyed both as pleasure reading and as summer reading. Kamala Markandaya's *Nectar in a Sieve*, about the monsoon's torturous effect on modern India, helps students view a single country through contemporary and ancient prisms. Tracy Barrett's *Anna of Byzantium*, about historian Anna Comnena's relationship with her family and ultimate exile to a convent, is another compelling account.

Other fine sources of historical narratives for middle-schoolers include the magazines produced by Cobblestone Publishing: *Cobblestone* for American history, *Calliope* for world history, *Faces* for world cultures, and *Dig* for archaeology. (To order back issues of these publications, go to the publisher's website at www.cobblestonepub.com.)

The best storytelling often emerges after we read an excerpt of a page or less from one of these books. Then I set students free to craft their own imaginative tales. Wonderful responses emerged from a lesson based on a *Cobblestone* article about the writing of the U.S. Constitution. "It Almost Didn't Happen" (Barton 1982) communicates the uncertainty surrounding the Constitutional Convention and the drafting of the new nation's charter. The assignment: Pretend you are sitting in a restaurant in Philadelphia during the Constitutional Convention and overhear two delegates talking about their day. Write down what you hear, based on the article you read.

Here is how Toshie, an eighth grader with a talent for writing and a flair for whimsy, put herself back in time. Note that she deliberately includes anachronistic details, such as the blended coffee she orders, which help make the piece her own. I have included her original draft, including spelling errors.

Figure 1.3

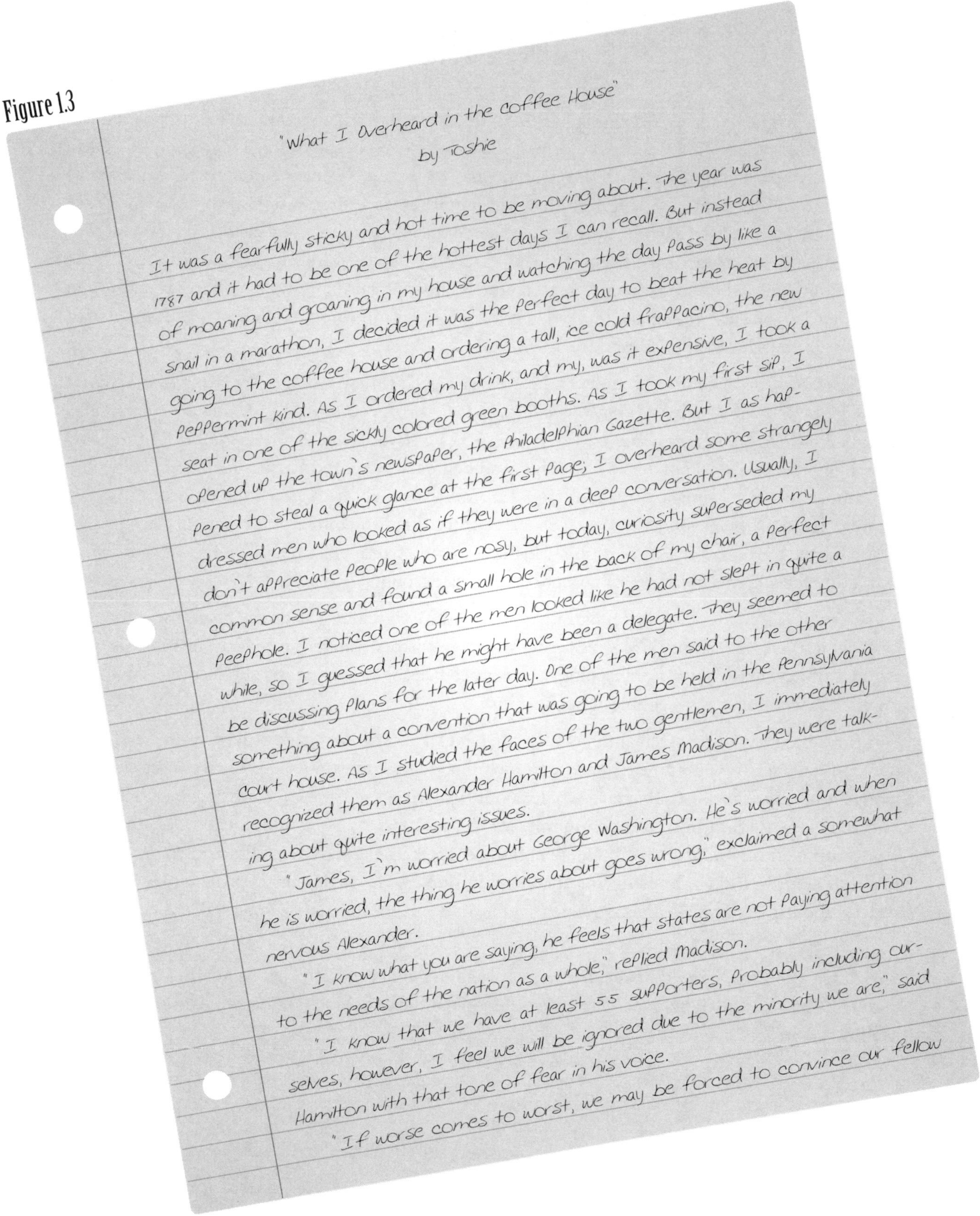

"What I Overheard in the Coffee House"
by Toshie

It was a fearfully sticky and hot time to be moving about. The year was 1787 and it had to be one of the hottest days I can recall. But instead of moaning and groaning in my house and watching the day pass by like a snail in a marathon, I decided it was the perfect day to beat the heat by going to the coffee house and ordering a tall, ice cold frappacino, the new peppermint kind. As I ordered my drink, and my, was it expensive, I took a seat in one of the sickly colored green booths. As I took my first sip, I opened up the town's newspaper, the Philadelphian Gazette. But I as hap- pened to steal a quick glance at the first page, I overheard some strangely dressed men who looked as if they were in a deep conversation. Usually, I don't appreciate people who are nosy, but today, curiosity superseded my common sense and found a small hole in the back of my chair, a perfect peephole. I noticed one of the men looked like he had not slept in quite a while, so I guessed that he might have been a delegate. They seemed to be discussing plans for the later day. One of the men said to the other something about a convention that was going to be held in the Pennsylvania court house. As I studied the faces of the two gentlemen, I immediately recognized them as Alexander Hamilton and James Madison. They were talk- ing about quite interesting issues.

"James, I'm worried about George Washington. He's worried and when he is worried, the thing he worries about goes wrong," exclaimed a somewhat nervous Alexander.

"I know what you are saying, he feels that states are not paying attention to the needs of the nation as a whole," replied Madison.

"I know that we have at least 55 supporters, probably including our- selves, however, I feel we will be ignored due to the minority we are," said Hamilton with that tone of fear in his voice.

"If worse comes to worst, we may be forced to convince our fellow

Figure 1.3 (continued)

supporters to write a constitution. For that I thought of a new idea, we would have men come up with their own ideas and present them," suggested Madison.

"That is so scary because I thought of the exact same thing. I feel that those federalists should call for a vote to write a constitution at the beginning of today's convention," replied Hamilton.

"As much as I love your ideas, I feel that that may not be the best approach. Not to offend you or anything, but you have a past of angering your audiences with your somewhat arrogant manner," said Madison in a matter-of-factly tone.

"I'm going to have to admit that you probably are the better at this, due to the fact that you a respected scholar and I admire your honesty. Thank you. Well, I best be off to hope that this convention goes well," a respectful Hamilton replied.

"And so shall I, friend."

They both vacated the booth and walked out into the outside world. I wasn't so sure what exactly happened, but for their sake, I hope their constitution will go well.

To appeal to students with varied learning styles, we could differentiate the assignment in a number of ways. Suggestions for activities include:

- Create a bar graph based on four major issues that the writers of the Constitution sought to resolve, such as the refusal by some states to support the fledgling country financially. For each issue, the height of the bar can show how difficult the obstacle was to overcome. Then put your graph on a transparency or a PowerPoint slide and explain it to a partner or to the class. This activity could also lead to a debate about the relative importance of the issues.

- Act out a dialogue between Madison and Hamilton in the coffeehouse, referring to at least five facts from the *Cobblestone* article in your presentation.

- Create a comic strip that explains how the Constitution was approved. Each panel could show a controversy and its solution.

Whichever presentation you or your students choose, the result should be a deeper understanding of the difficult decisions made by the Founding Fathers. From storytelling to press conferences, we can design assignments that incorporate key skills, such as the idea that "students thoughtfully read the historical narratives created by others," and content, or the requirement that students "[e]valuate the major debates that occurred during the development of the Constitution and their ultimate resolutions" (NCHS 1996; California State Board of Education 1998, 34). Activities based on a historical narrative that brings the past to life can also be used at any point throughout the year: to pique students' interest in a topic, to develop their narrative writing skills in conjunction with the language arts standards, or to communicate a content standard that might otherwise seem dry.

# Exploring Versus Settling: Discovering Your Values

Poems, primary sources, historical fiction—many texts can help students become their own tour guides to the past. Sometimes, though, it is intriguing to start with the ideas and questions inside their heads. The most personal topics let them imagine what they would do given the power to affect history. One thought question that carries students from the personal to the political concerns the value of exploring versus settling; this issue can inspire units as varied as the Age of Exploration, the journeys of Marco Polo or Christa McAuliffe, or the travels of Lewis and Clark. Through a full-class conversation, students relate their personal challenges to those of the people in the past.

To prime the pump, we briefly discuss the problems and joys of exploring. Students cite the danger, uncertainty, and fear that come with venturing into new lands as well as the excitement and anticipation of striking out for somewhere new. Similarly, we consider the advantages and disadvantages of establishing roots. Catie points out that settling down can be boring and take a long time, while Mike says that staying in one place can help people build a sense of community and make family connections. At this point, we carry the conversation to a personal place: think of one instance of "exploring" in your life and one instance of "settling down." This can be a difficult question to consider from a blank page, so I often ask students to discuss some ideas in partners or groups and then spend ten to fifteen minutes writing about their ideas in class or for homework. Later, during that class or the next day, we collect stories and answers on the board:

| Exploring | Settling Down |
|---|---|
| - Trying gymnastics for the first time | - Making good friends after I'd been in my neighborhood for a year |
| - Going on a hike with my dad up a "fourteener" in Colorado | - Doing my homework every night |
| - When I found bugs behind my house when I was seven | - Building a tree house |
| - Walking around the mall with my friends without my parents around | - The community garden at school |
| - Coming to the United States from Taiwan when I was three years old | - Moving to our new apartment last summer |
| | - Cleaning my room when my mom told me to |
| | - Cooking dinner, doing dishes |

This activity can be especially powerful for immigrant or refugee students, who are truly modern-day explorers. Their personal experiences add concrete examples to our abstract discussion of exploring and settling. For an interdisciplinary connection to language arts, students could read a nonfiction book such as Ishmael Beah's *A Long Way Gone: Memoirs of a Boy Soldier,* detailing his experiences as a child soldier in Sierra Leone and then as a refugee in the United States, or a fictional piece such as a story from Jhumpa Lahiri's *Interpreter of Maladies,* about Indian immigrants' adjustment to life in modern America.

After we make a list, which can stretch for a dozen entries per side if students are excited about the connections to their lives, I ask them to talk to a partner about what the items have in common. This activity requires a cognitive leap, and some partnerships will discover commonalities more quickly than others; we all take notes so that everyone can learn from the insights.

"The ones on the exploring list are adventurous and scary," Debbie and Jane determine.

"The settling down list is kind of repetitive, but it also creates something, like a garden or a tree house," observe Brendan and Christine.

At the end of the discussion, I ask students to jot down which they would rather do, explore or settle down, or both, and explain why. Now we have a personal foundation for a study of conquistador Hernando Cortés in the 1500s, westward pioneers in the 1800s, or astronaut Sally Ride in the 1980s. Consider just two examples of state content standards that such an activity could address: "Describe the expansion of Muslim rule through military conquests and treaties, emphasizing the cultural blending within Muslim civilization and the spread and acceptance of Islam and the Arabic language" for a medieval and early modern history course, or "Cite the significance of the trans-Eurasian 'silk roads' in the period of the Han Dynasty and Roman Empire and their locations" for an ancient history class (California State Board of Education 1998, 26, 28).

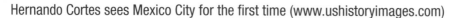

Hernando Cortes sees Mexico City for the first time (www.ushistoryimages.com)

The possibilities are vast for other guiding questions that can carry through a unit or a year. Some that can be applied to many historical units are as follows:

- If you ran a country, what might lead you to govern well or become corrupt? Is corruption an inevitable consequence of power?

- If you were a ruler, how would you ensure that people would respect you?

- Would you make a lot of laws or not many laws at all if you ruled a civilization?

- How would you maintain order if you ran a government or a dynasty?

Figure 1.4

## Exploring New Horizons

For more expansive applications of the ideas of exploring and settling, try these options with your students. Ask them to:

- Interview a parent, grandparent, or others in the community (possibly refugees) about their experiences coming to this country, moving around, or settling down. Students could present their interviews through an oral history recording, a written transcript, a biographical essay, a podcast, or a PowerPoint presentation.

- Draw a map and time line to support the experiences of two groups, people with long local histories and people who've moved to the community more recently. For the former, are there buildings, schools, or streets named after their ancestors? For the latter, whose family has come the greatest distance or explored the greatest number of countries? Trace the migration patterns. You could also contact a local historical society or library to see if they could help with research and, possibly, archive the work that your students do.

- On a field trip to a museum that covers local, regional, or national history, look for examples of primary sources that show the perils or benefits of exploring and settling. When you return to the classroom, create a video or write a letter to the editor describing the importance of these people's experiences. (As examples of videos, the teacher could show brief excerpts from Ken Burns's documentaries *The Civil War*, *The West*, or *The War*, which all give life to people from long ago.)

- Which form of government would you most like to live under, and why?

- How does religion or ethnicity affect your life? How has it affected governments in the past or today?

- What would you have done to stop the decline of the Roman Empire (or the Song Dynasty, the Umayyad caliphate, the presidency of Andrew Johnson)?

- What do you think is most important for a government to focus on: military defense, artistic accomplishment, or economic strength?

One caution: I've seen three or four students dominate class conversations more times than I care to remember. The rest of the middle-schoolers are gazing at the leaves on the trees outside; tapping their pencils; writing their homework in their planner, wondering where they left their planner, or wishing they *had* a planner; doodling in the margins of their notebooks, doodling in the margins of their friend's notebook . . . does this sound like your classroom on a dull day, too? Every time I ask students to consider a thought question, I do a few things to encourage them to participate fully:

- *Write it down*: Give students eight to ten minutes to write the question and a solid response. Incorporating "wait time" into a lesson can result in more developed and more thoughtful responses (Rowe 1987). I often suggest a word count so that they give a thorough answer. Ten words per minute is reasonable, so I'll usually request fifty-plus words, which gives slower writers time to complete the assignment.

- *Look over their shoulders*: After the first few minutes, I'll walk around the room to see what students are coming up with, urging those who have not yet thought of ideas to write whatever they're thinking of. I'll also ask a question of those who have written copiously to help them expand their thinking. I can't make it around the room to every student, but I do try to give this one-on-one attention to a good fraction of the class. In the next such activity, I'll focus on different students. At the beginning of the year, I think some students feel strange about having me look at everything they write; however, when they realize I will tell them what I like about their ideas and help them come up with more, they relax.

- *Cold-call students*: If I've given adequate wait time—and I'll extend the period for writing if I find that students need more minutes to think—then everyone will have a response by the end, if only a sentence or two. Students then feel comfortable if I call on them because they can simply read what they wrote. This technique shows reluctant speakers that they have something to say.

- *Require students to take notes*: Depending on the class, I will either write down students' major points on the board or I will ask students to write down one major idea from each person's statement themselves. At the beginning of the year, I will often write most of the summaries; as the year progresses, I expect students to write down more themselves. Asking for notes has two purposes: It keeps students focused, and it gives them a record of our class's ideas. It also shows students how much grander our ideas can be when we put them together.

- *Ask students to synthesize*: At the end of such a discussion, I will ask students to write a two- or three-minute response to one of the questions under consideration: What did you learn that you hadn't thought of before? What additional questions or ideas do you have now that you've heard your classmates' thoughts? What else would you like to learn about what we've discussed? Students can write their answers on an exit card or in their notebooks, which I will sometimes collect. I don't tell them until the end of class whether I will collect the notes, which keeps them on their toes and also helps manage the paper load. Sometimes, too, I just walk around the classroom and eyeball their responses, verifying that students have taken sufficient notes but not adding to my homework, especially during weeks when my take-home bag is already filled with assignments waiting to be graded.

- *Encourage students to apply their knowledge*: The abstract thinking behind thought questions leads well into the concrete realities of primary sources. For the activity on exploring and settling down, strong sources include Marco Polo's account of his visit to the court of Kublai Khan and Thomas Jefferson's directions to Lewis and Clark for what he would like them to explore in the Louisiana territory. We can ask students to label sections where the authors show fear or confidence, success or failure. They can then write a journal in the voice of a Mongol courtier or Meriwether Lewis.

# Pulling It All Together

In this chapter, we have looked at a sampling of ways to consider the individual's role in history: poetry, primary sources, dinner-table conversation, storytelling, and thought questions. These methods only begin to approximate the impact one person can have. Put together, they address historical analysis skills as well as content standards and spark questions that can guide an entire year:

- How much influence can an individual have on history?

- How can individuals prevail against overwhelming social, political, or economic forces?

- Do you notice individuals in your lives who are as powerful as those we have studied?

With these questions at the fore, we can move on to an examination of what other individuals—historians—have to say about the events of the past, and why their interpretations are important for students to grapple with and critique.

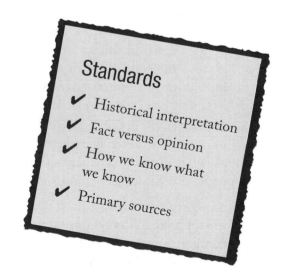

Chapter 2

# How Opinions Become History: Analyzing Point of View

## What's Inside?

### Skills and Strategies

- Analyze artifacts
- Consider the "history of history"
- Synthesize secondary sources
- Deconstruct historical narratives
- Infer from a map
- Imitate a famous historical poem

### Standards

✔ Historical interpretation
✔ Fact versus opinion
✔ How we know what we know
✔ Primary sources

# Start Locally to Think Globally: Personal Primary Sources

Looking around the room during the second week of school, my students notice a variety of objects on their classmates' desks: a soccer ball for Eric, a pink pencil case for Emily, a tennis shoe for Patrick, and a picture of a family picnic for Ali. Yesterday we spent five minutes defining *primary source*, a term many of them already understood from previous history classes.

"It's something written by someone who was there," says Tom.

"It's an eyewitness account," says Rachel.

The assignment for today was to bring in a personal primary source for discussion, making sure not to tell anyone why the artifact is important.

As I look around the room, I realize that some students have forgotten about the homework until the last minute—thus Patrick brought his shoe, one of the pair he is wearing on his feet, and Emily just pulled out her pencil case from her backpack. However, this is part of the fun of the assignment. I told students they could offer anything that tells something about them, and I'm curious to hear what Patrick and Emily will come up with on the spur of the moment.

The first year I tried this activity, I simply asked students to share their "source" with a partner and explain the significance. The exchange served as an icebreaker and a brief introduction to the study of history. Afterward, however, the exercise seemed little more than show-and-tell, which has its occasional place in middle school classrooms but does not hint at the deeper level of analysis I expect throughout the year. In addition, in my early years of teaching—when I was more nervous, shared less humor with students, and tried to account for every detail in my march toward instructional perfection—I sometimes gave students a hard time (and fewer points) if it was clear that they had grabbed the first thing they found in the hall before class. Now I figure that students will be turning in so many homework assignments during the first six weeks (some of which I'll grade, but many of which I'll just look at and acknowledge completion) that this one can be a chance for laughter at the more, shall we say, unusual choices. As a teacher, I always have to remind myself that the teachable moment often is the unexpectedly humorous moment, so I try to seize the chance to laugh together as a class. And I well remember the day *I* forgot my own personal primary source that I had intended to use as a model and grabbed a mini candy bar from the teacher's lounge instead.

Once each student has a personal primary source on his or her desk, I place students in pairs or groups and ask them to pass their own source to the person on the left. "You are historians one hundred years into the future," I say seriously. "Imagine that you know little or nothing about the culture of middle-schoolers in the early twenty-first century and are attempting to understand our society from this object alone."

For each object, students have three to five minutes to complete the following:

a)  Write one or two guesses of what this source tells you about the life of the person who owned it.

b)  Write one or two observations that this source tells you about the life, society, and/or culture of students in your town in the early twenty-first century.

To model this activity, I've held a jade lion figurine from China and asked students to imagine what this says about me and the time in which I live. Some actual responses from students, creativity encouraged:

### Thoughts About the Person

- This person was a zookeeper or a lion trainer.
- He or she used this figurine to scare away mice.
- This person had an entire collection of animals, like Noah's ark, with two of each kind for good luck.

### Ideas About the Society

- The society had the capability of carving gemstones.
- The society worshipped lions.
- People placed these figures on their car hoods.

Sometimes a student suggests a more common answer: that the lion is a souvenir from a trip, which it was, and shows that this person (me) liked to travel. I emphasize that the zany hypotheses are just as valid, though, and that historians need to be creative, especially when serving as archaeologists investigating an unfamiliar culture. The Snickers bar, though an impulse choice, also produced some intriguing guesses:

- The candy bar is small, which meant that people couldn't carry much.
- The society's members liked encasing everything in chocolate because their stomachs were sensitive.
- The people in the society were futuristic and ate only items wrapped in plastic.

This activity can take as little or as much time as you like. With three or four students per group, they generally will spend fifteen to twenty minutes analyzing their "data" and five minutes sharing their individual ideas with the group. Students love to discuss their responses with each other.

"I didn't know you liked to sketch pictures of your sisters," Erin says when she learns the real reason Emily chose the pink pencil case.

"Hey, I'm doing soccer right now too," David responds when he hears why Eric brought in his favorite sport's equipment. If we have time, I ask students to share the stories behind their objects in front of the class as well as mention their classmates' unusual guesses. To wrap up the discussion, I bring the entire class together and ask students to talk about the benefits and problems of using artifacts as primary sources.

"You can really touch and feel what it was like for someone living back then," says Alex.

"Yeah, but who knows what these things were actually used for?" Kristi argues. "Like with Eric's soccer ball—if we didn't know what it was, we might have thought it was a spherical game board, like a checkerboard, or an early map of the world."

The students' off-the-wall guesses have shown them that primary sources can just as easily be used to misinterpret as to correctly identify habits of the past—and that the interpretations depend on who is doing the viewing.

Much as each of the National Geographic Society's "Five Themes of Geography" relates local to global geographic features (Joint Committee on Geographic Education 1984), I like to get my students thinking about personal primary sources at the beginning of the year because it enables them to become historians and consider the importance of their own lives. If they all will make history, as I tell them on day one with the "Worker Reads History" poem, then these artifacts are the building blocks of their impressive future biographies.

# From "You Are There" to "You Decide What Is Important"

In Chapter 1, we watched students jump into the heads of history makers by empathizing with their plights, disagreeing with their tactics, and wrestling with their challenges. Chapter 2, on the other hand, looks at history from the perspective of the people who chronicled it, rather than the people who made it. In the activities that follow, I encourage students to become historians themselves and to assess how and why we write history. The National Center for History in the Schools asks students to "examine the interpretative nature of history" in this way by "comparing, for example, alternative historical narratives written by historians who have given different weight to the political, economic, social, and/or technological causes of events and who have developed competing interpretations of the significance of those events" (NCHS 1996).

By entering into such historiographical discussions—conversations about the history of history—students can understand that interpreting the past is a somewhat subjective enterprise. One person's narrative often includes details that another's leaves out. With the meta-cognitive thinking required, such conversations about the history of history can raise some of the most interesting questions of the entire year about knowledge and power: "How do we know what we know?" and "Who decides what is history?"

# Where Does History Come From? Material Culture During the Shang Dynasty

When students read a textbook, it can seem as if the words on the page are as immutable as stone, penned by an omniscient mind. Within the first month or two of school, I like to extend the "personal primary source" activity to an examination of artifacts from a real society. In this way, students can understand how historians composed the accounts of the times in which they lived. This activity can be done anytime, with any civilization rich in material sources. (See Appendix B for suggestions of where to find such artifacts online.)

"Let's mix things up today," I begin. "We've been reading a lot in our textbook about the Shang and Zhou dynasties in China: now let's look at some pictures of art from these ancient cultures." In pairs, students examine a handout featuring photographs and brief descriptions of a Shang jade buffalo, a Zhou bronze wine container, and a Zhou bronze bell from the Metropolitan Museum of Art website (http://www.metmuseum.org/toah/ht/03/eac/ht03eac.htm and http://www.metmuseum.org/toah/ht/04/eac/ht04eac.htm). Then they look at each artifact and underline key facts from its description. To catapult students into the history, I ask them to discuss these questions as a group and write brief responses:

- *How would you have felt holding this artifact?*
  "Royal and rich," Naomi says of a ritual wine vessel.

- *Do you like this object? Do you think it is beautiful or ordinary? What do you like/not like about it?*
  "The buffalo is awesome," Peter says. "Really 'Home on the Range.'"
  "But it's in China, Peter," Doug ribs him good-naturedly.
  "Yeah, but you see how it shows that nature was important to the society? Just like in America with the midwestern prairies."

- *List two adjectives to describe the society's values.*
  Kelly suggests "down-to-earth" and "civilized" for the Zhou, while Ryan offers "religious" and "natural" for the Shang.

Once we have discussed the feel and importance of the artifacts, we look at two passages in the textbook's China chapter that describe the art of the Shang and Zhou dynasties. "What kinds of primary sources do you think the historians used in this section to compile the text?" I ask. By this point, students can hazard some guesses: bronze bells, jade figurines, and royal tombs. The textbook's stone wall, so seemingly monolithic, has started to crumble. (One important note: When I first did this activity, I distributed the photographs in black and white and showed the original color photos after students had completed the activity. Only when Doug said, "Wow, I really didn't like or understand the objects as well until I saw them in color" did I kick myself for not giving the more visual learners a rich entry point into the material. The next time, I put the photographs into a PowerPoint presentation and showed them onscreen at the outset.)

You can broaden this artifacts assignment to include our own time, or to fit into a journalism or language arts class, by asking students to find an article from a newspaper or reliable website. First, they can identify all the primary sources and eyewitness accounts the reporter might have used when researching the article. Then they do the same for secondary sources. Going further, you might ask students to pretend that they are historians one hundred or two hundred years into the future: How useful would this article be as a primary source if you were researching a book about American sports or American society in the early 2000s? Why or why not? Write an explanation or tape a video interview in which you pretend to be the historian. Figures 2.1 and 2.2 suggest additional activities and resources that you may wish to consider.

A funny coda to this activity: I initially used this newspaper lesson during the first week of a journalism class, bringing in an article about a blue whale off the California coast. When I asked students who would be good sources to interview for this piece, they offered up "a lifeguard," "a park ranger," "a zoologist," and "an environmental activist." And then I called on Danny, a witty eighth grader whom I barely knew at the time. His answer? "The whale." He kept me laughing—and pulling out my hair—all semester.

## Figure 2.1

### Going Beyond Personal Primary Sources

Some other ways students can think about the ambiguity of primary sources are:

1. **Primary Source Walk.** Lead your students on a walk around campus for five minutes and ask them to take notes silently the whole time about what they see happening. When they return to class, ask them to spend five minutes writing down what they thought were the two to four most important sights on their walk and why. The class can vote for the most important events or observations and then discuss what these facts would reveal—or not reveal—to a reader about the school's history on this day. As a follow-up, students can write a reflection or talk to their parents about the similarities and differences among the various reports, suggesting how this process relates to the usefulness of primary sources for historians.

2. **Brainstorm Questions.** Ask pairs of students to make a list of several questions that would be helpful when analyzing primary source documents. Then collect the questions on the board and make a class list for future use. Examples might include: "What do you think this was used for?" and "Do you think this is a decorative or a functional object?" DoHistory.com has an excellent list of questions to ask about primary sources at http://dohistory.org/on_your_own/ toolkit/primarySources.html. The site was inspired by Laurel Thacher Ulrich's impressive *A Midwife's Tale: The Life of Martha Ballard, Based on Her Diary, 1785–1812* (1991; see Appendix C for the complete list).

3. **Still Life or Collage.** Ask students to create an artistic representation of primary sources from their own lives and photograph them or glue together a collage of photos showing important events. Then tell students: "Write two accounts of the still life or collage—one real account describing why the objects and scenes are important to you, and one imagined narrative that is as skewed as you can make it while still relying on the same sources. You can also ask a relative, classmate, or friend to write the second account." Spread the real or false narratives around the classroom and have students pair the accounts with the still life or collage they describe.

4. **Rate Your Stuff.** Ask students to list or photograph half a dozen primary sources from their own lives and categorize them on a scale of importance, ranging from "important only to me" (such as a seashell from a solitary beach walk) to "important to the city or nation" (a crayon rubbing of part of the Gettysburg Address from the wall of the Lincoln Memorial in Washington, D.C.).

Figure 2.2

## Summer Workshops for Using Primary Sources in History Classrooms

Many wonderful summer institutes ask teachers to dig into archives, museums, and libraries to find primary sources for their classrooms. Keep in mind that seminars are often competitive and deadlines can fall early in the year. Here are just a few:

- The Gilder Lehrman Institute of American History Summer Seminars, held at universities and other sites across the country and taught by college professors and other luminaries (http://www .gilderlehrman.org/teachers/seminars1.html)

- Monticello-Stratford Hall Summer Seminars for Teachers, a three-week seminar for social studies teachers focusing on Virginia during the American Revolution (http://www.monticello.org/ education/stratford.html)

- National Archives, Primarily Teaching Summer Workshops, at National Archives facilities across the country. In these, teachers find sources in the archives that would help their teaching and put together lesson plans based on their findings (http://www.archives.gov/education/primarily-teaching)

- National Gallery of Art, Summer Teacher Institute, a weeklong workshop on a particular topic (http://www.nga.gov/education/teacinst.shtm)

- National Endowment for the Humanities, Summer Seminars and Institutes for School Teachers, with workshops ranging from two to six weeks (http://www.neh.gov/projects/si-school.html)

- UCLA History-Geography Project, Summer Institutes, on local, U.S., and world history (http:// centerx.gseis.ucla.edu/HGP/events1.php)

# Telling History: Compelling Historical Narratives

Once we have discussed how historians transform primary sources into narratives, I introduce students to secondary sources—those written by someone who did not witness the events he or she is describing. One four-page excerpt that captivates me every time I read it is a gut-wrenching passage by Edmund Morris in *The Rise of Theodore Roosevelt* (1979, 363–366). In it, Morris describes Teddy Roosevelt's herd of cattle dying on the plains of the Dakota Territory's Badlands during the bitter winter of 1886–1887. Morris writes sentences such as, "last summer's drought, aggravated by overstocking, had reduced the grass to stubble. The starving cattle were forced to tear it out and eat the frozen, sandy roots" (364).

The passage ends with, "Patiently they began to sort and stack the skeletons of what had been one of the greatest range herds in the world" (366). When I read these descriptions to my students, their jaws literally drop as they consider the enormity of the loss. By thoroughly investigating this selection, whether or not your curriculum includes an in-depth look at Theodore Roosevelt, your students will gain a new understanding of these historical skills and themes:

- The impact of climate upon history

- The power of story to take us back to a place and time

- The force of strong imagery in telling history

- "The role of chance, oversight, and error in history"

- "The credibility of primary and secondary sources" (California State Board of Education 1998, 21, 22)

Badlands National Monument, South Dakota (Photo by W. H. Raymond III. Figure 26, U.S. Geological Survey *Bulletin 1493.*)

One caution: The first time you show your students a secondary source from a "real" history book written by a "real" historian, make sure it is compelling to young adolescents. I've made the mistake of picking a text that I liked, then finding that it bombed in class because it featured more analysis than storytelling. I do include excerpts from analytical books in my curriculum, but not at the very beginning. (See the following sections for suggestions on presenting analytical sources.)

After years of trial and error, I've developed some strategies to attack narrative passages in class. I usually use a variety of these techniques to ensure that every student understands the story. Then we can have a discussion about the importance of the historian's work.

# 1. Provide Enough Context

Because I've usually read other parts of the book besides the excerpt I'm sharing, I know what is happening in the passage, but my students don't. In past years, I've too often relied on a rushed, several-sentence description, verbal or written, of the backstory or context. What about a student who is daydreaming while I give the background, or someone who doesn't find the description compelling enough to really understand it? These days, I spend five or ten minutes doing any or all of the following to provide context:

a)   Going back to a textbook passage that students have read and asking them to reread it

b)   Finding a short encyclopedia entry about the topic

c)   Showing some photos from the time or of the events I'm describing

# 2. Give Students a Personal Stake in the History

As with all history and all stories, if students cannot imagine themselves in a situation like the one that the protagonist faces—and there is, I would argue, a protagonist or antagonist in every good piece of historical narrative—they will tune out. It's what I call the "who cares?" factor: why should we care about this person? One strategy I've used is asking a thought-provoking question about the topic. For the Theodore Roosevelt passage, such questions could be as follows:

• Have you ever experienced a loss of a personal possession? How did the loss make you feel?

• Has your family ever been affected by a natural disaster? Describe your story. (Of course, be sensitive to the emotional impact of recent natural disasters in your area if you ask this question.)

These questions can also develop historical themes in addition to analysis, such as the effect of climate on communities and the year-to-year nature of farming, whether in Myanmar's delta or America's Midwest.

# 3. Cut Up the Text

Before you read the narrative, take a half-dozen sentences from the passage, cut them up into strips, and ask students to put them in the most dramatic order. The Theodore Roosevelt passage is not completely linear, so students often have different answers and different reasons for their ideas.

# 4. Read the Text Aloud, Twice

Sometimes I tell students that, if they are aural learners, they can put their heads on their desks while I read aloud a passage for the first time. To keep them involved, I ask students to make mental images of the descriptions in the text as I go. Also, I might interrupt the reading, asking students to turn to a partner and briefly describe what is in their heads. The second time through, students underline especially powerful passages or phrases. "Just mark the ones you like," I say. "You don't even have to know what they mean, as long as they sound good to you." Then we discuss the phrases, which helps bring out students' questions about the narrative.

## 5. Use Visuals Whenever Possible

In addition to showing photos relating to the text, sometimes I ask students to illustrate a scene that they think is most important. "I'm a terrible artist—can I do stick figures?" Jeremy asks. Absolutely, I say, as long as you get the point across. I usually ask students to label their drawings with at least three phrases or sentences from the text so that their artwork will be factually based. For instance, if they were drawing the bodies of cattle rushing down the river, they could label that part of the picture with this phrase: "and still the carcasses jostled and spun" (365–366).

## 6. Talk Up the Mystery

The Theodore Roosevelt passage holds fantastic mystery and foreboding; it unfurls slowly, almost painfully. As you read aloud, students can mark especially dramatic points. Ask them: When did you know what was going to happen? Why is the passage still compelling after that? You can also explore the language in more depth, which is an effective way to keep students underlining and marking up the text as they read. One way is to ask students to circle strong verbs or action words, such as "escape" (364), "invaded," and "hurtling" (365). Students could even make a poem or write a story with these words to show their power.

## 7. Consider Creative Extensions

To ensure that students have understood the text, they could respond to the following prompts:

- Write a letter from Theodore Roosevelt or his herder telling what they found and how they felt after the snows melted.

- If this were a movie, how would you film it? Opening and closing shots? Voice-overs?

- Write a short textbook account, several sentences, of this event. How is it different? What do you like about this source that the textbook does not have room to include?

- You are there: consider Roosevelt's perspective on hearing about this bitter winter loss. Why do we not see his perspective in this interlude when we do throughout the whole rest of the book?

## 8. Imagine the Sources

Ask students to get into pairs or groups and make a list of a half-dozen sources that Morris might have used in his research. Then compare their ideas with the actual list of endnotes from the book to discover that Morris consulted newspapers (such as the *Dickinson Press* in North Dakota) and magazines from the time, Roosevelt's personal diaries, and secondary sources. You can ask students: What does this passage say about the importance of writing down descriptions of events as they happen? How do you think this narrative is different from the newspaper stories? How do you think historians will write about our Internet society, with newspapers laying off reporters and shutting down bureaus all the time? Generally I've found that students do not have to understand or look up every endnote; in fact, their doing so would probably doom your quest to sweep them up in narrative. One well-chosen note can work wonders in showing them that history comes from someplace real.

## 9. Appeal to Students' Sense of a Challenge

Whenever we do something "hard," such as examining a secondary source written for adults, I like to tell students, "People might think you couldn't do this, but I know you can." Then, with the appropriate scaffolding, they generally do. Middle-schoolers can understand just about anything adults do, I believe, if the passage is short enough and we spend enough time on it.

## 10. Supplement This Reading with Another Source

As much as one marvelous source can spark a student's interest, sometimes creating an interplay between two complementary pieces can create unexpected synthesis—much as two children playing together can generate more energy than two playing alone. For instance, you could use an excerpt from Theodore Roosevelt's *Ranch Life and the Hunting Trail* to give students a sense of how difficult the "primitive" ranching life was, and then compare its tone to the Morris passage. (For the "Winter Weather" chapter from the Roosevelt autobiography, go to http://www.bartleby.com/54/5.html.) You also could find an article about farming subsidies today and debate whether it is beneficial for the government to support farmers during difficult seasons.

～ ❧ ～

The discussion on Edmund Morris's Roosevelt excerpt produces a very labor-intensive class or classes, but I've found it to be well worth the time. My goal during this initial investigation of historical narratives is to keep my students talking and writing, to each other and to the entire class, so that they are engaging with the historian's work. If, as Brittany once said after class, "I had no idea that snow could be so interesting," then I've achieved one goal: eliciting enthusiasm. If students translate that enthusiasm into an understanding of historians' motives and challenges, so much the better, as Tom discovered when he said, "Theodore Roosevelt was a powerful man, but even he couldn't fight back against midwestern winters." But we have to keep in mind that such understanding is a layered process, begun with one source and continuing with others throughout the year. Appendix A includes other resources that you can use to supplement the textbook's account of historical periods.

# Shock Students with Fascinating Facts from History

When do I use secondary analytical texts? When the textbook is so disjointed, with so many bits and pieces that I am bored or confused while reading it and I know my students will lose interest as well. When I want to show students that history doesn't just appear; it is explained by historians who help us impose order upon and make sense of the past. When I want to return to a key standard, such as the idea that "interpretations of history are subject to change as new information is uncovered" (California State Board of Education 1998, 22). With many historians' work, I certainly don't read an entire book at once because I don't have time within a unit to do so. Often, I simply scan for relevant passages or base my choice on a librarian's or colleague's recommendation. If I enjoy a book, I'll return to it in more depth during vacation.

One of the most compelling analytical sources I've found moves from mystery to understanding in a way that young adolescents can appreciate. It is Jared Diamond's description of packrat middens in his excellent *Collapse: How Societies Choose to Fail or Succeed* (2005). *Collapse* describes vexing problems that historical and modern-day societies, from the Vikings and the Maya to Rwanda and China, have struggled to solve. An excerpt on the Anasazi appears in a chapter about the settlement at Chaco Canyon (Chapter 5, "The Maya Collapses," 143–147). The preceding section lists different methods of sustaining agriculture in an area plagued by irregular rainfall.

Scientists did not know for sure that this currently dry area was originally well forested until they discovered an ingenious repository of history: packrat middens. No, you're not supposed to know what this term means! At the time of the California Gold Rush in the mid-nineteenth century, some prospectors on their way West discovered what looked like sticky balls of candy on a cliff in the Anasazi region. Unfortunately, the sweet-tasting gobs made the miners feel sick to their stomachs. The substances were not candy, after all, but "hardened deposits made by small rodents, called packrats, that protect themselves by building nests of sticks, plant fragments, and mammal dung gathered in the vicinity, plus food remains, discarded bones, and their own feces" (Diamond 2005, 145). Yes, feces—the gross-out factor looms large. Through radiocarbon dating, scientists realized they could tell when the plant and animal remains in the middens were digested; thus, they could find out when Chaco Canyon was lush with vegetation (145–146).

Anasazi pueblos

"No way," said Evan. "I can't believe he was using rat poop to figure out where those people went."

Rat poop to study history? No way! Let's start at the beginning. (And thanks to history teacher John Ruch for suggesting that I use Jared Diamond's books in class.) Diamond's work is appealing to middle school students because he pulls in unusual artifacts and obscure facts to pique readers' sense of intrigue and weave a compelling narrative.

With middle-schoolers, and even with high-schoolers, I often start to get tired of my own voice after too many teacher-led discussions. So, by this point, I'm happy to put students into groups to examine the excerpt. For analytical sources, I like groups rather than partners because there are more eyes and brains looking at the passage.

At times, if the paragraphs vary greatly in difficulty, I will assign them to homogeneous groups based on reading comprehension skills. More often, though, I'll form heterogeneous groups and ask students to assume roles: a person with a fine speaking voice can read aloud, someone who loves the sounds of words can underline neat-sounding phrases, a student with a more mathematical or logical bent can circle unknown words, a global thinker can list the major ideas of the paragraph, and a visual learner can draw a symbol or picture that describes the passage. Figure 2.3 includes additional ways that students can show what they know.

After the group has read through the paragraph twice and each person has completed his or her assigned task, I ask the group members to write a summary and check it with me. This is probably the most important step to make sure that their interpretation is accurate and, even more crucial, that they feel confident enough to present it well to the class. It is fine if their first explanation is completely off the mark, as long as they are thinking hard and know that they will rethink and revise. If groups finish early, I ask them to guess what the "punch line" is of the historical argument that Diamond is making—what might be his surprise at the end? Once I've approved the group's one-sentence summary (and picture, if they like), I ask them to put the sentence on the board. Sometimes I call this sentence the "thesis" of the paragraph, especially if language arts classes are concentrating on this idea.

Figure 2.3

**Jumping In:
Entry Points to Analytical Documents**

- Read aloud and define key words from the passage while students annotate in the margins. Then students can illustrate a major point from each paragraph.

- Ask students to construct an outline of the author's argument, perhaps in a jigsaw with one sentence, paragraph, or page per group.

- Make a time line of the events described in the piece.

- In groups, ask one person to draw the scene described. Ask another to think of a caption and a third and fourth to write dialogue.

- Perform skits of archaeologists arriving on the scene and describing what they're finding.

- Create a diorama of the historian's article (this only for a topic on which you really want to spend time).

- Assign each group a key term to teach to the class using a visual aid, such as *packrat middens* or *water management*.

- Draw a diagram or flowchart showing the historian's argument.

- Find pictures on the Internet and tell the historian's narrative through a graphic novel (drawn or cut-and-pasted).

Now comes the fun part, in the last five to ten minutes of class. "What is so amazing about this argument and/or the way Diamond tells it?" I ask. Usually the students are excited enough about "history through rat dung" that some do think his writing is incredible.

"He's telling a story about doing research, and it's really interesting," says Robbie.

"He's using pee to make history!" says Ryan.

"He really keeps you interested by making it a mystery," says Maria.

"Yes, all of that," I say. History can be fascinating if you find the mesmerizing parts and weave them into a story.

I have to come clean and admit that I've had considerably less success with other snippets of analytical documents, especially those that were not as straightforward as *Collapse*. One year, I started our study of historical narratives in a world history class with another excellent book by Jared Diamond, the bestseller *Guns, Germs, and Steel: The Fates of Human Societies* (1999). We were studying Africa, and Diamond has a fascinating passage about the role of "glottochronology," or "calculations of how rapidly words tend to change over historical time": in other words, the development of African languages provides clues to when different African societies incorporated various plants and animals into their agriculture (391, 390–397). Without experience reading other, similarly sophisticated history texts, however, the majority of my ninth graders were lost when I foolishly assigned this difficult reading as homework. These students were used to doing well, too, so it took five minutes of prodding—some "confusion analysis," if you will—to figure out just how perplexed they were. As often happens with skilled students, they will give a smile and nod if they don't understand something, not always acknowledging that they don't get it.

With the *Guns* excerpt and other tricky pieces that I've asked students to read on their own, I've found that they will do any or all of the following because I haven't given them enough structure:

- They're baffled, so they ask their friends what they wrote and copy their answers.

- They write short phrases that don't make sense.

- They feel as if they're doing something wrong because I haven't provided enough guidance. As a result, they get frustrated and turn off.

- They do not understand that the historian is making an argument.

- They do not understand the vocabulary well enough to comprehend the excerpt.

For homework the night before we looked at *Guns, Germs, and Steel* in class, my world history students were supposed to read the excerpt, underline a key idea from each paragraph, and write a several-sentence summary. Most did this, but they still didn't have a clear idea of what the author was saying. I realized the depth of their frustration only when I asked them what they thought of the article and they said the author was hard to understand and they didn't know why I'd assigned it.

At this point I regrouped, deciding to spend the entire class period on the article rather than just the first ten minutes. I used the technique I later employed with the *Collapse* excerpt: divided it into sections, asked each group to decide on and write the "thesis" of the section on the board, and then discussed it. Only then, after twenty-five minutes of sustained work on the meaning of the passage, did we start to talk about the argument Diamond was making. Only then did Tara say, "It's hard to tell what's fact and what's opinion because he's such a good writer." And Alex said, "He's making an argument, but you can't really tell because he weaves the facts together so well with his opinion." Finally, I felt that the class recognized what he was trying to do, even if not everyone appreciated it. And when I brought in the Anasazi passage from *Collapse* later in the year, I referred to "our friend Mr. Jared Diamond" with a wink and a smile to acknowledge my earlier missteps.

The moral of these stories? We need to pick passages carefully. Nothing too complicated at first and nothing too hard to get through with some help. Otherwise, quiet students will smile and nod, and more vocal students will express their confusion, but neither group will understand.

To finish with the big picture—I was striving to do the following with both Diamond excerpts:

1. Teach content standards about the Anasazi and the Bantu to supplement the textbook's descriptions.

2. Teach an analytical standard about understanding historians' views: students can "detect the different historical points of view on historical events and determine the context in which the historical statements were made (the questions asked, sources used, author's perspective)" (California State Board of Education 1998, 21).

3. Help students see what real historians do: gather evidence to make an argument that often doesn't sound like an argument. They're almost fooling you. I sometimes continue the conversation by asking, "What else fools you in your life?" Answers could be commercials or the media, leading to a discussion about what we can trust and what we can't.

# Africa Analysis: Pulling Together Many Sources for Deeper Understanding

Usually I don't use analytical sources more than once or twice a unit. Students see the point with small doses, and the labor required is enough that I can't justify spending class time on these pieces every week. However, one year, when we were starting a unit on African history, I felt that the textbook was simply not conveying the fascination behind the topic. "Why do we study African history?" and "How do we know what we know about it?" were the big questions on my mind. Yet the textbook focused mainly on the geography, crops, and governmental structures of a dozen different societies—important, yes, but where was the synthesis? I wanted to convey the messages that African history has not always been studied and that there are interesting new ways to learn history when we don't have conventional sources. After we thought about the reasons behind the history—the historiography—we could put in context the multitude of facts about Mali and Ghana, Kush and Zimbabwe by considering standards such as "Students analyze the geographic, political, economic, religious, and social structures of the sub-Saharan civilizations of Ghana and Mali in Medieval Africa" (California State Board of Education 1998, 28).

Remembering my unsuccessful lesson plan with *Guns, Germs, and Steel*, I picked a more accessible excerpt to begin with: Basil Davidson's defense of African history in his *Lost Cities of Africa* (1959). It describes how little we know about the culture of Meroë, an iron-making site in the Kush region that boasts one of the earliest known African civilizations. Davidson makes the case that Meroë thrived at the same time as ancient Greece—that the African society also "traded widely with many nations, developed its own traditions of art and literacy, [and] implanted its seminal influence far beyond its frontiers" (50). This brief excerpt was published in 1959, long before many scholarly works on African history appeared, such as the breathtaking *Africana: The Encyclopedia of the African and African-American Experience,* edited by Anthony Appiah and Henry Louis Gates (1999). Davidson asks intriguing questions that inspire global connections, such as "What did these citizens know of China, whose bronzes they copied and whose silks they bought; of India, whose cottons they wore; of Arabia, whose cargoes they purchased?" (49). In addition to the previously mentioned techniques for using narrative and analytical sources, we can pose these challenges to students:

- Imagine that you are a detective: What are the "clues" to unlock the mystery of Meroë? Which sources would you use if you were a historian (sculptures and iron smelting ruins, for example)?

- Why must Meroë's "western and southern frontiers . . . be guessed at" (49)? Why didn't we know more in 1959, when Davidson was writing?

- Which of the historian's questions do you find most interesting? What answers might you give?

- What is Davidson's point of view? Can you imagine an alternate point of view?

- Which strong words and phrases does he use to make his point? What do you like about them?

- If Davidson were standing in front of you, what would you want to ask him?

Great Zimbabwe: Modern photo of medieval ruins

The *Lost Cities of Africa* excerpt is a short, fairly accessible one that repeats the same point many times: the magnificence of African culture was severely underappreciated. Other sections in Davidson's book are similarly fruitful for discussion, such as his account of some European travelers' not believing that the Great Zimbabwe was built by Africans but rather by the Queen of Sheba, because the construction was so fine. My students really laugh at that one.

To accompany this introductory work, which students read on the first day of the Africa unit, I included several pieces that enhanced but did not repeat the textbook. I found them by visiting our library's section on Africa, talking to a colleague who teaches an African history elective for seniors, and searching ProQuest Platinum Periodicals for articles on fossils and Ghana's independence. Keep in mind that I am no expert on Africa—I just looked around to find passages that would engage different kinds of learners. Each day, I went over one of the following works in class for ten to fifteen minutes to supplement what students had read the night before in their textbook.

- "Kinship corporations" in Bill Berkeley's *The Graves Are Not Yet Full: Race, Tribe, and Power in the Heart of Africa* (2001). This excerpt is difficult—I read the entire three pages aloud with my students—but it gives a fine overview of how foreign powers capitalized on the idea of "tribes" when coming into Africa.

- Rex Dalton's "Awash with Fossils" (2006). This piece follows a variety of foreign paleoanthropologists to Ethiopia.

- A primary source about Ethiopian king Zar'a Ya'kob that describes the opulence of the Solomonid court (Brummett et al. 2000, 237).

- Two articles from modern newspapers on Ghana's fiftieth anniversary of independence in 2007, found on ProQuest Platinum Periodicals: Tiffany Harness's "An Inspiration for Independence" (2007) and Simon Robinson's "The Saga of Ghana" (2007). The first piece gives a brief overview of Ghana's history, and the second portrays Ghana's history through the eyes of one family.

- Leon P. Spencer, "Free Trade Will Not Help Africa," and Thompson Ayodele, "Free Trade Will Help Africa," in *Africa: Opposing Viewpoints* (1992).

The first time I stitched together this patchwork of analysis, I wasn't sure how much my students comprehended. They were taking notes, thinking about the arguments behind the pieces, and participating in discussion, but I didn't know if they understood the big ideas. As a result, I asked them to spend half an hour in class at the end of the week writing about the sources. I told them they could use their class notes and that the grade would be worth only a little more than a normal homework assignment. I didn't want to penalize them for any lack of understanding that I might have caused. The assignment read: "Pick three or more sources from those we've read this week that share a similar theme, idea, tone, etc. Include a topic sentence in your paragraph that tells what the similarity is, and include at least one fact or quotation from each of the sources relating to your theme."

I gave the students a variety of themes to start with, including the economy, American colonialism, the rise of civilizations, how we know Africa's history, and why Africa is important to study. It didn't matter which theme they picked, as long as they now had a framework on which to hang all the disparate facts in their textbook. And I was glad to note that, yes, they had been paying attention to at least some of what we had been discussing. I took away from this experiment the idea that students don't need to understand every word of every article—though some will, and such depth is appropriate for their level of reading comprehension—in order to understand the big themes that shape our study of history. Figure 2.4 shows some of their responses.

# Biography 360°: Approaching Individuals from All Sides

*Listen my children, the tale is at hand*

*Of a traitor betraying our British command*

*The eighteenth of April, as darkness did fall*

*A messenger traveled—his name 'twas Paul.*

*Revere sent a warning—"The British doth land!"*

Figure 2.4

## Two Africa Synthesis Reflections

### Kelly's Africa Synthesis

Here is Kelly's synthesis, which touches on different ways to understand African history. Kelly wrote this one-shot draft in twenty-five minutes with the articles and notes in front of her; she did not have time to add a concluding sentence. If I were doing this assignment again, I would give students an entire class period to write (forty-five minutes) and might also have them revise their drafts based on peer response. I thought this was a fine stab at the assignment given the limited time; with more minutes, Kelly would have likely included more analysis. The assignment is reproduced just as she wrote it. My annotations are in italics.

Guns, Germs, and Steel by Jared Diamond, the ProQuest articles on Ghana's independence, and Emperor Zar'a Ya'kob's coronation Primary show how we know about African history. In the Guns, Germs, and Steel article, we learned about how to date the Plants and to find out where they originated by using the technique glottochronology. This was interesting because it isn't a very "advanced" [yes—explain] way to look and learn, which is very uncommon these days. In the ProQuest article, we learned about Ghana's history through People who describe what they have heard from their ancestors. This might not be the most accurate way, but by using the method of oral traditions, you get to understand the People's way of thinking. And finally, the Zar'a Ya'kob Primary source tells us of civilization back then and how the social classes and religion were handled. Since this was a Primary source, it is Probably the most accurate and tells us about Zar'a Ya'kob's strengths and weaknesses from one Point of view. [relate back to other ideas]

Figure 2.4 (continued)

**Maria's Africa Synthesis**
Here is Maria's synthesis, which looks at the economy of Africa then and now. Maria's analysis was interesting for the brief time she had. I would like to have seen a few more specific facts to back up her ideas, but the creative connections were excellent. The assignment is reproduced just as she wrote it.

From the excerpt on Zar`a Ya`kob to Jared Diamond's Guns, Germs, and Steel and the ProQuest articles on Ghana, the struggle and maintenance of the economy has been a key factor since the origins of Africa. In the 2nd ProQuest article, the plumeting economy is not only a national burden, but a personal one as well. Because of its deep poverty, Ghana is stuck in a hole of violence and hardships, and must work twice as hard as many to build themselves back up. The bad economy has led to limited education which then affects the future of Ghana's economy. In Zar`a Ya`kob's coronation, the economy at the time was flourishing with extensive shrines. Gold was abundant and the nation was grateful during this rich time. However just like any other area, the economy is an unsteady balance that can be thrown off at any moment. In Guns, Germs, and Steel, the Bantu were able to expand that territory because of their economical advantages. The iron tools and wet farming techniques were modern aspects that lead to a comfortable economy, stable with food production and trade. Yet . . . . [She ran out of time]

So begins a "revised edition" of Longfellow's famous poem, written by eighth grader Simone after we finished "Paul Revere Week" in our U.S. history class. When I have time, I try to read books by current historians to find memorable stories, intriguing images, or new approaches—such as statistical studies or social histories—that can enliven the history in our textbook. That year, I had just finished reading David Hackett Fischer's astounding *Paul Revere's Ride* (1994). The book looks at the famous night of April 18, 1775, in intricate detail and makes Revere's journey pulsate with every gallop. *Paul Revere's Ride* epitomizes the importance of examining well-known history through multiple lenses.

As I made my way through the book, I referenced illustrations and quotations that might be useful for my eighth-grade history class. After I finished, I culled the many resources to just a few—as much as I wanted to expand the unit to "Paul Revere Month," I knew the standards and curriculum requirements were too crowded with other important people and events to give Revere additional space on the school calendar. The handouts I chose included the famous portrait of Revere by John Singleton Copley; a map of the Boston area that showed the locations of ports and commerce; a list of words that Bostonians pronounce differently than people in other regions of the country, such as "Bast'n" for "Boston" and "chattaer" for "charter" (Fischer 1994, 4–5); and the poem by Longfellow that schoolchildren have memorized for more than a century.

By choosing such a variety of sources, I aimed to follow a standard of historical thinking described by UCLA's National Center for History in the Schools: that students should be able "to consult documents, journals, diaries, artifacts, historical sites, works of art, quantitative data, and other evidence from the past, and to do so imaginatively—taking into account the historical context in which these records were created and comparing the multiple points of view of those on the scene at the time" (NCHS 1996). I would save such an in-depth unit for at least a month into the school year, when students have established the skills and concentration they might need to pull together so many disparate sources. The unit would build on techniques students had learned in other activities featuring the role of the individual—primary source interpretation, visualizing personalities, and highlighting the importance of vocabulary—to understand Boston's milieu in the late 1700s.

On the first day of this weeklong unit, we focused on geography to give context. I showed pictures of the Freedom Trail on a Microsoft PowerPoint presentation so students could imagine what the buildings looked like, asking if anyone had been to Boston.

"It was so hot!" Jonathan said of a recent summer visit, and we discussed what the weather might have been like in April 1775.

When I handed out copies of the map "Boston in 1775" from Fischer's *Paul Revere's Ride* (1994, 11), I asked students to jot down "three things you can tell about this world or society from the map itself." They listed elements as apparent as the many churches and as subtle as the crowded streets. We decided that this was a city in which people couldn't easily get away from each other and thus had to know each other well, a community that valued religion and tradition. At the end of class, I had extra time and so asked students to color in the water on their copies of the map. Suddenly they saw even more how isolated Boston was and how simple it would have been for the British military to cut off the city's access to the rest of Massachusetts and beyond. The students imagined themselves there and saw the threats they might have faced from the British.

On the second day of the unit, we focused on personality by looking at the Copley painting of Revere, represented in both black and white on their handouts and in color on a PowerPoint slide.

"What do you think Mr. Revere was like to know?" I asked. "Would you like to have dinner with him?"

"He seems smart," Maggie said, "from his hand on his chin."

"Why is he holding a teapot?" Matt asked. We read a short biography of Revere and learned about his work as a silversmith.

"Do we still have silversmiths today?" Doug wondered.

"Yes, but we do much more by machine," I said.

We went on to talk about why Revere was portrayed half in shadow (The mystery of his midnight ride? His courage in facing the British at night? Many answers seemed plausible) and what the smooth texture of everything in the painting might tell us about his world (neatly ordered, clean, at least in this picture).

"Then that world blew apart," said Matthew.

"Exactly—this painting shows Revere in a world that was in the throes of revolt. How would you feel?"

We also looked at the language of the time, and students enjoyed putting on a Boston accent. They noted that it helped give a sense of the atmosphere of the time to imagine Revere speaking in this unusual vernacular.

Days three and four brought us to documents: to Longfellow's admiring poem, which we read aloud chorally, and to an account of the Battle of Lexington by the Provincial Congress at Watertown, Massachusetts, on April 26, 1775. (For this source, see the excellent *Cooperative Learning Basics: Strategies and Lessons for U.S. History Teachers, Grades 7–12,* published by Jackdaw Publishing, www .jackdaw.com.) Students compared the tone of phrases from the poem and words from the deposition. Longfellow portrays Revere as saintly, while the government documents are much more understated. "Would you have testified before the committee, or would you have been terrified of the British reaction?" I ask, leading to a discussion about when courage is smart and when it is foolhardy.

On day five, I hoped to synthesize the lessons from the week: inferring the particulars of Boston society from a map of the time, imagining Paul Revere's personality from the Copley painting, and comparing the tone of the Longfellow poem and the citizens' depositions immediately after the midnight ride. I knew our coverage of Revere had been inadequate, even with spending so much time on him. We could have looked at his early life, at other accounts of his ride, at more photos of Lexington and Concord, at other historians' views. But this week, I wanted them to construct their biography of Revere from a variety of sources, to feel the Revolutionary War fervor and the pace of colonial life. They focused on a key figure using real documents of history: court testimony, a painting, a map, and a poem.

On this last day of the unit, I gave them a choice: write a paragraph arguing whether Revere was a hero, or try to reimagine Longfellow's poem from the British perspective. Such an assignment could easily tie in to a language arts persuasive essay requirement. Throughout the unit, you could also work or team with other teachers to make interdisciplinary connections, perhaps comparing the size of Boston then to your city today for a math class, or contrasting Boston in the 1700s with Boston today, after much of the water has been filled in by land, for an earth science class. For a computer science, science, or math class, students could also use Google Earth to zoom in and out; investigate the role of the Atlantic Ocean in the East Coast's tidal patterns; or figure out the fastest way to get from Boston to Lexington today, both as the crow flies and on human roads.

Simone concluded her poem with a lament from the British about their defeat, a reflection on who loses when one side triumphs:

> *The message succeeded, for the colonists tried*
>
> *To help Revere, and several cried—*
>
> *"The Redcoats are coming, the Redcoats are coming!"*
>
> *All through the villages, hooves pounded, drumming*
>
> *Though our marvelous soldiers defied its flight*
>
> *The shouts continued all through the night.*
>
> *As the sun rose in the morning bright*
>
> *America was ready, ready to fight*
>
> *And Britain was defeated that terrible night.*
>
> *God Save the Queen!*

At the end of class we looked at a quotation from the conclusion of Fischer's book: "The next generation, the children who heard the Lexington alarm but were too young to fight, grew up to be the statesmen of America's silver age. Their experience on the day of Lexington and Concord made a difference in their lives" (1994, 289). For example, John Quincy Adams was eight years old on the night the American fighters passed his house. "What big events have made a difference in your lives? What people?" I wondered aloud. The week had focused on Paul Revere, but I hoped we could continue the lessons into the next month and beyond. (See Figure 2.5 for more approaches to draw students into secondary sources.)

# Why Study Secondary Sources?

So why spend all this time with historians' sources? In addition to showing students that history is far more individual and interesting than the pabulum that can appear in their textbooks, the applications are far ranging and interdisciplinary. By understanding historians' arguments, students can develop a critical eye toward the media and toward people who are trying to sell them a bill of goods. The ability to discern fact from opinion, to see that seemingly unbiased accounts can still have an agenda behind them, serves students well in any humanities discipline. Finally, these sources show that history can be compelling, just as with their own lives and their own primary sources. By imagining how historians chronicle the past, our middle-schoolers can picture themselves becoming part of the world's story.

Figure 2.5

## Additional Ways to Make Historians' Work Come Alive

Once students have read small excerpts by "real" historians about the period they are studying, you can ask them to bring these views to life with some of these activities that tap into multiple learning styles:

• Watch a five-minute video clip of a historian on C-SPAN's *Booknotes*, a TV show that ran from 1989 to 2004 and interviewed hundreds of authors. Then read an excerpt of his or her work and talk about how the historian's personality might have affected his or her scholarly interests. (Go to www.booknotes.org for more than five hundred shows available to teachers and other interested parties.)

• Create a Venn diagram comparing and contrasting different accounts of a topic, such as the Bantu migration from northern to southern Africa. Your textbook's account and a historian's excerpt would be good sources to consider. Which facts or interpretations do both sources include, and which facts or interpretations are only represented in one account or the other? Illustrate the diagram.

• Using two different-colored highlighters, mark the facts in a historian's excerpt in one color and the opinions in another. Then do the same with a paragraph on the same topic from your textbook. Compare your highlighting with a partner or another group (it will likely not be exactly the same). Which source has more opinion in it? Which source is more interesting? More reliable?

• Draw a map of the world, a continent, or a country. Write a caption for a relevant place on the map for each historian you have read, with a fact and opinion relating to his or her work.

Chapter 3

# Fighting Words: Examining Rhetoric, Reasoning, and the Role of Language in History

## What's Inside?

### Skills and Strategies

- Analyze point of view
- Understand rhetorical techniques
- Consider speaker, audience, and purpose with Aristotle's rhetorical triangle
- Ponder moral dilemmas

### Standards

- ✔ Primary sources
- ✔ Citizenship
- ✔ Political rhetoric
- ✔ Critical thinking
- ✔ Historical writing and analysis

# A Shower of Sparks: Language Comes to Life

When I introduce the first primary source of the year, I often tell my students that the document is like a firecracker, possibly a sparkler. At first, it doesn't look like much, just a dull paper tube. Then, as we dig into the language—as we "light the fuse"—the source opens for our understanding in a shower of sparks. The kids laugh at my clunky metaphor. But in all seriousness, I measure the success of a primary document by how well we have ignited the language, whether we have authentically cast ourselves back in time so we can imagine the impact those words had on the original listeners and readers.

All primary documents tell a story, but some are crafted so carefully that they deserve sustained time and attention. Ideally, at least one such source in a unit will affect all students intimately and passionately.

Why should we look closely at the language of political and social documents in a history class? Isn't such sentence dissection largely the job of our fellow language arts teachers? Yes—to some extent. Often, American literature classes study the phrasing of Patrick Henry's "Give Me Liberty, or Give Me Death" speech from the Revolutionary period or Sojourner Truth's "Ain't I a Woman?" oration from the mid-nineteenth century, tracking rhetorical style and noting repetition or dialect. With such nuanced scrutiny of language, students begin to understand how the structure of a revolutionary's words can sear the pages of history books. As a result, students might decide to use their own words to inspire, perhaps writing a letter to the newspaper or leading a rally after school.

However, if we leave most or all of such language analysis to English teachers, we miss out on a crucial element of our own history curriculum: identifying with the motives of famous people by analyzing speeches, proclamations, and eyewitness accounts. When our students unpack language, they often understand the content better. By looking closely at *how* a historical character speaks or writes, we can perceive more clearly *what* they were trying to say, *who* they were addressing, and *why* they were trying to influence this audience. If we take note of such elements as repeated words, the tone or feeling behind documents, or the choice of one phrase over another, we get to know the authors better, blurring the boundaries between modern cultures and the past. By studying documents for their language choices as well as their content, our students can make history their own in the following ways:

- Understanding that we share common motivations and dreams with people who lived long ago

- Sympathizing with the mistakes and regrets of those from the past, and striving not to repeat them

- Stepping into the heads of historical figures and speculating that they may have felt as we do today

- Analyzing how politicians of the past created logical arguments or made specious claims so we can replicate their techniques in our own work—or know when our modern elected leaders are trying to fool us with rhetorical flair

We can use such rhetorically rich primary sources for topics in political and social history. (We can also seize the opportunity to collaborate with our colleagues from the English department, linking history, literature, and language with authenticity.) When the textbook becomes overwhelming with long lists of names, dates, and accomplishments, we can step back to examine a speech from a president or another key figure so students can deepen their perceptions of the period. For instance, nearly every U.S. history textbook cites Thomas Jefferson's famous quotation from his first inaugural address, "We are all Republicans, we are all Federalists." When we investigate the entire paragraph where the quotation first appeared, we can ask questions about the nature of power and politics, based on the following excerpt: "I believe this, on the contrary, the strongest Government on earth. I believe it the only one where every man, at the call of the law, would fly to the standard of the law, and would meet invasions of the public order as his own personal concern."

"Why does Jefferson sound so confident about this government?" we can ask. "Is he just trying to bluff his way through the aftermath of the bitter and prolonged election of 1800, attempting to placate the American people into accepting his Democratic-Republican Party victory over the Federalists? Or does he really believe the nation is as strong as he makes it out to be?"

When I discussed this passage with a group of eighth graders, Rebekah asked, "What does it mean to 'fly to the standard of the law'?"

"It means to protect your country and uphold its laws at all costs," I say.

"Would people do that today, protect their country so strongly?" David wonders. "*Do* they do that today?"

His question opens a natural segue to the relevance and resonance of historical texts. By beginning with a famous quotation, easily found in textbooks, and selecting features from the original speech for our students, we can make Thomas Jefferson seem more human than his granite head on Mount Rushmore. With such personal connections to the past, students can better empathize with the decisions Jefferson made later in his presidency, such as the risky purchase of the Louisiana Territory from France.

# Nail-Biting Decisions: What Would You Have Done?

Connections to history build easily when students read the words of individuals who lived it, such as Ben Franklin's speech at the 1787 Constitutional Convention, Theodora's speech on the occasion of the Nika rebellion, and Booker T. Washington's "Atlanta Exposition Address." In addition, such close reading enables students to "examine the historical record for themselves" (NCHS 1996). In my middle school world and U.S. history courses, regardless of the students' skill level, I use small or large pieces of primary documents at least once a week; in my eleventh-grade regular and AP U.S. history classes, I use them daily. Students groan and grumble at first, complaining that their binders are bursting with papers. Eventually, though, most start to see the relevance of such sources.

## Ben Franklin: Wise Statesman or Political Waffler?

*Imagine that you are Ben Franklin. You are sitting at the Constitutional Convention in September 1787. You have been an architect of the governmental structure for this new nation, and your opinion is as respected as anyone's in the American colonies. You know your words are being recorded for the future and will affect the next hundreds of years of the United States. And yet you hesitate, you couch your words in uncertainty as you urge the assembly to endorse the document: "Thus I consent, sir, to this Constitution, because I expect no better, and because I am not sure that it is not the best" (Franklin 1906). How can you say this, Ben Franklin, you waffler? What purpose do you have in admitting your own frailty as a human being while discussing a question affecting the entire nation?*

For the Franklin excerpt, I would reference only part of the three long and difficult paragraphs it contains. In a class that includes many struggling readers or English language learners, I would pick only the quotations that are essential to understanding Franklin's admission of "fallibility." For a class with a wider variety of learners, I might reprint the entire document, but I would ask the class at the beginning to underline or highlight the sentences we will discuss. Figure 3.1 shows some useful passages and suggested exercises for deepening understanding.

### Figure 3.1

### Getting Inside Ben Franklin's Head

| Ben Franklin's Quotations | Ways Students Can Build Understanding |
|---|---|
| 1. "I confess that I do not entirely approve of this Constitution at present; but, sir, I am not sure I shall never approve it, for, having lived long, I have experienced many instances of being obliged, by better information or fuller consideration, to change opinions even on important subjects, which I once thought right, but found to be otherwise." | • With a partner, mime what it looks like to "confess" something. What is the feeling behind the word?<br><br>• Discuss why Franklin says he is "*not* sure I shall *never* approve it." Why does he use the double negative? Do you speak a language at home that uses the double negative (e.g., *No tengo ningún dinero*)? Where in math do you find double negatives, and why? (One possible response: a negative of a negative number.) What effect does this sentence construction have on his words?<br><br>• Take turns reading the sentence until a punctuation mark. For instance, one student would read, "I confess I do not entirely approve of this Constitution at present"; the next would read "but"; the next would read "sir"; and so on. Do this twice. Mark two or three phrases you think are most important. Discuss. |

Figure 3.1 (continued)                                    Chapter 3 ■ Fighting Words    47

| | |
|---|---|
| 2. "I doubt, too, whether any other convention we can obtain may be able to make a better Constitution;" | • Freewrite for five to ten minutes about a decision in your life that you doubted. Why did you doubt it? What ended up happening? Were your doubts justified?<br><br>• Form groups, each one representing a different state at the convention: some from states with many slaves, some from states with few slaves, some from states with large populations, and some from states with small populations. After each group discusses its position, one person can represent the views of each state and explain to the class. Discuss: Do you agree with Franklin that another convention wouldn't produce a better Constitution? How difficult was it to achieve a compromise in your class groups? |
| 3. "Thus I consent, sir, to this Constitution, because I expect no better, and because I am not sure that it is not the best. The opinions I have had of its errors I sacrifice to the public good. I have never whispered a syllable of them abroad. Within these walls they were born, and here they shall die." | • Discuss: Why did Franklin "expect no better" than the current Constitution? How could he say this, given that so many great minds are assembled in one place?<br><br>• Think of a time when you kept a secret for the good of your family, your school, a friend, or another institution or person that is important to you. You do not have to share the secret, but you will talk with a partner or write the reasons why you kept it a secret. As a class, make a list of these good reasons on the board. Then talk about which reasons might have applied to Franklin. |
| 4. "On the whole, sir, I cannot help expressing a wish that every member of the convention who may still have objections to it, would, with me, on this occasion, doubt a little of his own infallibility, and, to make manifest our unanimity, put his name to this instrument." | • Circle the word *infallibility*. Which familiar word is in the middle of it (*fall*)? Draw or describe what a person might look like who consider himself or herself infallible—unable to ever fall or be wrong. Do you want to know this person? Do you want this person running your government? How do you feel about Franklin that he "doubts a little of his own infallibility"—that he sees himself as human and imperfect?<br><br>• If you were a delegate at the convention, what would have been your biggest fear about signing the Constitution? Discuss with a partner or group, and write on the board the most powerful fear you imagined. Then the class can discuss which fears were valid and which did not come to pass.<br><br>• Look at a painting of Benjamin Franklin. How would you describe his personality? Does he seem like a humble man, or does his appearance belie his words? |

## Empress Theodora: A Thespian Makes a Civic Appeal

*Put yourself in the place of Empress Theodora, wife of Emperor Justinian during the glory days of the Byzantine Empire, in the sixth century CE. Your tranquility in the gorgeous peninsular city of Constantinople has been shattered by an attempted coup from the Greens and the Blues, the city's political groups who now threaten your family's future. Your husband would be willing to abdicate the throne and flee, you suspect. You, on the other hand, deliver a speech in which you insist that you will stay in the city until death, that "the royal purple is the noblest shroud" (Safire 1992). What kind of personality do you have that allows you to stand so firm in the face of disaster? Did your earlier life as an actress have anything to do with your impressive confidence?*

Theodora's speech contains many vocabulary words that are useful not only for history but for life, such as "indomitable" and "shroud." To provide some context for our discussions, I often ask students to research the meanings of eight or ten selected words two nights before we look at the speech (see Figure 3.2). The next day we go over the words in class, making sure that everyone has appropriate definitions. Discussing vocabulary gives students a chance to talk about the power of words and to participate in a nonthreatening, easy way. In addition, I often act out some of the fun words—stomping my foot while I intone "indomitable," or shaking like a mouse while I whisper "timorous," and then ask students to do the same.

Theodora

To further preview the speech the next day, and to help students sense Theodora's dignity, I often ask them either to write a creative description of what they think the speech by Theodora might be about, given the words they've defined, or to draw a picture of what kind of person might use these words. The next day, when we discuss the speech, we can compare their ideas with the actual text. Katelyn thought that the speaker would be "awesome." "Why?" I asked. "Because she wouldn't let anyone stand in her way—check out 'indomitable.'"

In my early years of teaching, I assigned the words for homework and then gave a quiz the next day, without an in-class discussion of the words beforehand. This method did not sufficiently engage every student, and many failed to grasp the speech's impact. Another technique I tried that did not work well was to ask students to circle unfamiliar words during class and write the definitions in the margins before we discussed the text. Nice idea, but by the time we had completed this task, the speech was dead in the water from boredom. By examining the words ahead of time, students can try to deduce the meaning of the speech, rather than labor over the meaning of individual words, and feel a sense of accomplishment when they encounter words that they now know.

Figure 3.2

### Sample Vocabulary-Building Activities for Theodora's Speech Before the Nika Rebellion

Students fill in the definitions on this sheet for homework. The related sentences are designed to show them the terms in context. The next day in class, we go over their definitions to make sure they have found appropriate explanations, and they can add to or change their definitions as needed.

1. **shroud (n, v):**

   Her burial <u>shroud</u> was covered with gold threads.

2. **timorous (adj):**

   He was a <u>timorous</u> person; he never went out alone at night.

3. **galley (n):**

   "Ahoy, mates!" cried the captain on the <u>galley</u> as the boat cut through the choppy sea.

4. **indomitable (adj):**

   Theodora was an <u>indomitable</u> woman; she would not be swayed by the opinions of others.

5. **intolerable (adj):**

   "This summer heat is <u>intolerable</u>," thought Eliza as sweat dripped down her nose.

6. **yonder (adj):**

   Over <u>yonder</u> are the sheep; right in front of you are the chickens.

7. **adage (n):**

   "Don't cry over spilled milk," the old <u>adage</u> advises.

After we analyze the language of Theodora's appeal, students can comprehend the nature of political power, as described in a curriculum standard on "Power, Authority, and Governance": "Through study of the dynamic relationships among individual rights and responsibilities [the emperor versus his people], the needs of social groups [the Blues, the Greens, and the people of Constantinople], and concepts of a just society, learners become more effective problem-solvers and decision-makers when addressing the persistent issues and social problems encountered in public life" (NCSS 1994). Theodora, in other words, serves as a touchstone for students to ponder what is right and wrong when ruling a society.

"Should rulers stand their ground, no matter what?" I ask about the royal couple. "Yes," says Justin, "because they are setting an example, like when Bush said we should stay in Iraq." Rachel's hand waves in the air. "No way," she says. "Sometimes you just need to get out before it's too late." Miri pipes in, "Wouldn't you be scared of the Greens and the Blues if you were Theodora? I'm impressed she was willing to stay. I would have followed her anywhere after that."

Not every class discussion leaps to current events and emotional appeal so quickly. When I hear too many kids muttering to each other, "Who were the Greens and the Blues again?" and "Why were Justinian and Theodora important?" then I know it's time to go back to the facts of the revolt, to place Theodora's words in context once more.

Booker T. Washington

## Booker T. Washington: Straddling the Divide

*In the late nineteenth century, stand with Booker T. Washington as he addresses the Cotton States and International Exposition in Atlanta, Georgia, in 1895. He urges African Americans across the country to "'Cast down your bucket where you are'—cast it down in making friends in every manly way of the people of all races by whom we are surrounded" (Washington 1901). Three decades after the end of the Civil War and the passage of the Emancipation Proclamation, which freed the slaves but did little to change cultural biases and restrictions, what leads you to encourage blacks to separate from whites socially but not economically? How do you stand up for your convictions knowing that other prominent African Americans, notably W. E. B. DuBois, disagree with you, so much so that DuBois will call your outlook "submission and silence as to civil and political rights" in his treatise* The Souls of Black Folk *(1903)?*

Booker T. Washington's speech works well for more literal learners because it has such a visual image of independence: "Cast down your bucket where you are." Here is an excerpt:

*A ship lost at sea for many days suddenly sighted a friendly vessel. From the mast of the unfortunate vessel was seen a signal, "Water, water; we die of thirst!" The answer from the friendly vessel at once came back, "Cast down your bucket where you are." A second time the signal, "Water, water; send us water!" ran up from the distressed vessel, and was answered, "Cast down your bucket where you are." And a third and fourth signal for water was answered, "Cast down your bucket where you are." The captain of the distressed vessel, at last heeding the injunction, cast down his bucket, and it came up full of fresh, sparkling water from the mouth of the Amazon River. To those of my race who depend on bettering their condition in a foreign land or who underestimate the importance of cultivating friendly relations with the Southern white man, who is their next-door neighbor, I would say: "Cast down your bucket where you are"—cast it down in making friends in every manly way of the people of all races by whom we are surrounded.*

To allow the words to sink in, I read aloud the first paragraph like a story before even handing out the speech, and then I read it again while the students look at the text. Then they briefly illustrate in the margin what it might look like to "cast down your bucket where you are." Nicole draws a man who looks like Popeye, with strong muscles and feet firmly planted into the ground, while Jesse sketches a big bucket with water sloshing hard.

After this illustration exercise, I ask them to suggest at least two ways this quotation is symbolic so they can develop metaphorical thinking. This activity works well with partner or small-group discussions where students can cross-pollinate their ideas. At times I've had to walk around the room several times, urging students to think beyond the literal. Sometimes, when the ideas are not yet flowing, my voice becomes repetitive even to myself: "Cast down your BUCKET . . . what might that mean?" If the figurative connections are not coming, then I'll resort to more dramatic tactics, such as asking students to come up and show us what it looks like to cast down their buckets. Then I'll hoist a pretend or real bucket and plop it down on the ground. After this levity, students return to their partners and usually can brainstorm some ideas: "you keep your head down," "you accept what you have in life," "you don't strive for more," and "you don't want anyone looking at you too much." With this combination of language and image, students are more prepared to examine the societal implications of this complex metaphor for African Americans in the late nineteenth century.

"Why would anyone tell people to act this way?" asks Brittany.

"It was a different time, come on," says Alex. "People had to be careful—remember that the Civil War had just happened—and Reconstruction had been a disaster."

Such conversations enable students to "explain the central issues and problems from the past, placing people and events in a matrix of time and place," an analysis skill reflected in California's state standards, as well as "analyze the character and lasting consequences of Reconstruction," a specific history content skill (California State Board of Education 1998, 22, 38).

# The Rhetorical Triangle: An Inside Angle on Learning How to Read History

We don't have to be linguists to appreciate the grounding simplicity of Aristotle's teaching about rhetoric: that a speaker's influence stems from his ability to target his audience through *ethos* (ethical connections), *pathos* (emotional appeals), and *logos* (logical reasoning). These principles provided the foundation for what is now known as the rhetorical triangle. Aristotle believed that the best argumentation was balanced, with all sides of an equilateral triangle represented.

Many writing programs have adapted this theoretical base to help students dissect text as they read and build effective structures as they write. The Northern Arizona University Writing Program has published a concise explanation of this modern format that can serve as a useful model for middle school teachers and students (jan.ucc.nau.edu/~dem22/Rhetorical%20Triangle.doc). In this design, the three sides of the rhetorical triangle include the *author* (or speaker), the *audience*, and the *purpose*. Figure 3.3 shows the two versions.

## Figure 3.3

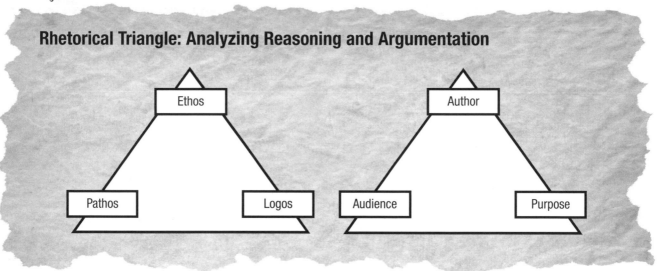

**Rhetorical Triangle: Analyzing Reasoning and Argumentation**

Ethos / Pathos / Logos

Author / Audience / Purpose

Each of the sides of the modified triangle gives us a straightforward way to frame historical texts for students and deepen our classroom discussions. For example:

- **Author/Speaker:** Who is speaking? Why does he or she care enough to write or speak? What makes this author or speaker a credible source? What does this text tell us about his or her personality or intentions? Which events in history might have shaped or influenced the author/speaker's message?

- **Audience:** Who is the intended or actual audience? What is the author/speaker's relationship to the audience? How do you think the speaker's awareness of this audience affects his or her choices of language? How are we different from the original audience? If we pretend to be the original audience, how do these differences affect our understanding of the speech?

- **Purpose:** What is the writer's intent—to persuade, inform, entertain, shock, something else? What are clues in the text that suggest the purpose? Which rhetorical tools does the writer use to make her case? Do the arguments still carry weight today? How does the writer's appeal influence your thinking?

We can expand on these principles in many different ways (Figure 3.4 suggests some additional lenses through which we can view primary sources), but the three-point design gives us a good place to start and return to whenever we examine historical documents. The symbolic representation also benefits visual learners, who can analyze text from another perspective.

Figure 3.4

## Looking Deeper into Primary Sources

These perspectives on primary documents give students specific tools with which to unpack the language. For earth-shattering documents, I might ask every student to respond to all of these elements so that they immerse themselves in the text; for other pieces, I will often divide these criteria among groups or pairs in a jigsaw and then ask students to share their responses with the class.

- **Diction or Word Choice:** Circle strong words, especially verbs (such as those in the "Declaration of Sentiments" from the 1848 women's rights convention in Seneca Falls, New York). Why did the author pick these specific words? How are they more vivid, persuasive, or interesting than other words the author could have used? Also, find odd words, such as Andrew Jackson's appalling references to "extinguishing" the Indian populations in the Southeast by moving them to Indian Territory under the Indian Removal Act of 1830. Is the author trying to hide something or express something distasteful with unusual word choice?

- **Voice:** Is the writing formal, informal, confiding, distant? Do you want to sit down and chat with this author, or would you rather keep him or her at arm's length? Is the voice typical of the time period, or is it more or less flowing, more or less

Figure 3.4 (continued)

impassioned than other documents? How do you feel when you hear this author's words? Diaries such as Mary Chesnut's account of Southern life during the Civil War or Thomas Jefferson's "fire bell in the night" reflection on the Missouri Compromise (http://www.loc.gov/exhibits/jefferson/159.html) are rich resources to analyze for voice because their authors are relatively uncensored in these private moments.

- **Impact:** What moves you in the speech? What do you want to remember for your own life? These questions apply especially to documents of change and inspiration, such as chapters on "The Right to Be an Individual" and "How Everyone Can Take Part in Politics" in Eleanor Roosevelt's appealing and readable *You Learn by Living* (1960).

- **Currency:** What is similar to today in the document's themes or expressions? Presidential speeches and proclamations often suggest contemporary comparisons because the structures of the executive and legislative branches of government have remained, for the most part, unchanged.

- **Form:** How does the author choose to express his or her ideas—in prose, poetry, or song lyrics? How does the form affect the meaning? For early America, famous sermons give a sense of the rich metaphors embedded in society's daily language, such as Jonathan Edwards's frightening "Sinners in the Hands of an Angry God." For foreign cultures, poetry can offer a new view into common living, as with Chinese poetry of the Song and Tang dynasties and ancient India's epic *Rig Veda*. Pulling in actual songs to understand a period can also inspire students, such as the lyrics to the "Erie Canal" for a unit on the Industrial Revolution.

- **Connections Among Multiple Sources:** The teacher can create a "mini-DBQ" (*document based question*, a term from the history Advanced Placement exams given by the College Board) that pulls together a few sentences from three or four sources on the same topic, such as Manifest Destiny in U.S. history or the Qin Dynasty in China. You can assign a group of students to review each document and present it chorally or perhaps ask students to draw the most important ideas of each document on paper.

The triangle of ethical connections, emotional appeal, and logical reasoning also serves as a useful framework for assessing students' grasp of these documents. I hope that students will understand and be able to imitate the speaker's influential tactics, as Aristotle's rhetorical triangle describes. The assessments that follow can apply to all manner of controversial documents. Some are formative, used as checks for understanding in class or for homework; others are summative, used at the end of a unit to see progress; and many can function as either formative or summative assessments. You can assess for all three elements of Aristotle's triangle for a speech that is particularly gangbusters, or you can focus on one element that is particularly relevant to one speech. By the end of the year, students will have examined a range of documents through these lenses and will be better equipped to judge the intentions, impact, and rationality of speakers and writers, past and present.

# Assessments Based on Aristotle's Rhetorical Triangle

## A. Ethos (Ethical Connections; Author/Speaker)

The following assessments help students link the words a speaker uses with the historical events that shaped the time period in which he or she wrote. As a result, students can understand that the era in which people live affects the way they think, write, and behave—as it does for us, although we may not always realize it.

a) Write an imaginary diary entry from the speaker's perspective explaining why he or she wrote the document and what he or she hoped to communicate. Include references to historical occurrences that influenced the person's thinking.

b) Compare several sentences from two speeches or documents, either written by the same person (such as Lincoln's Gettysburg Address and Emancipation Proclamation) or written during the same historical period on similar themes. Which words are similar? Which are different? What tone does each speech have, based on the words the speaker chooses? Make a chart or write an analytical paragraph comparing the two, bringing in historical evidence from the time period to make informed guesses as to why the speeches are different or similar.

c) Pretend you are a member of an opposing political party or intellectual group, and write a rebuttal to the speaker's words, choosing one or two major points on which to focus. Use historical evidence from the time to ground your assertions in fact.

## B. Pathos (Emotional Appeal; Audience)

Once students have entered into the heads of the historical figures who penned these words, they can imagine themselves listening to or reading the document and then judge its emotional impact.

By doing so, they can be more sensitive to people in their own lives who are playing on emotion to convince them of an idea or sell a product. In addition, they can consider the role charisma plays in creating successful politicians.

a) Write a journal entry about a time when you tried to persuade a friend or parent of something that was important to you. In your writing, discuss whether showing deep emotion during your argument helped or hurt you. Why or why not? Then look at a document you have studied as a class that includes emotional appeals. How does your journal entry affect how you see this document? Discuss this question with a partner, and then create a class list of the pros and cons of showing emotion in private and public life.

b) Read a speech or document from your perspective, and write down your immediate reaction to the ideas proposed. Then, as a class, decide who the original audience might have been. Reread the speech and write down your reaction as someone in that original audience. Share both responses with a partner and discuss whether your reactions are similar or different. If they are different, why do you think that is? Come back together as a class to list the elements of society back then that made the audience's reaction opposite to or the same as our reaction today.

c) Bring in two brief examples of your writing: a formal assignment from English or history class and informal writing from an email, a note to a friend, an instant message, or a social networking page. In small groups, read and pass along each person's two writing samples so that everyone sees everyone else's work. Then, as a group, make a list of the conventions and content for formal and informal writing, and put the lists on the board. (As an alternative to compiling a list, students could also choose two of the writing samples to present to the class in the tone in which they were written, and then the class can make a list of the conventions.) Finally, respond to these questions on your own: Why do we write differently for different audiences? Why do words that sound perfectly acceptable in one context sound ridiculous in another?

## C. Logos (Logical Reasoning; Purpose)

a) Find a modern politician's speech or statement from a website such as C-SPAN (www.cspan.org), PBS Online News Hour (www.pbs.org/newshour), or the *New York Times* (www.nyt.com). Briefly outline the speech, and then compare the structure of his or her argument to a speech you have studied in class on a similar topic, such as sending troops to war or passing a social welfare law. Does the contemporary politician refer to more specifics or fewer? Why or why not? What are the strengths and weaknesses of his or her argument? Create a Venn diagram or chart of the similarities and differences, and then write why you think the speeches are similar or different.

b) Identify one "language trick" that a historical figure uses in a speech, such as Martin Luther King's repeated use of "One hundred years ago" in the middle of his "I Have a Dream" speech. Then write a persuasive paragraph or speech of your own on a topic you care about. In your speech, imitate this language trick and/or the argumentative structure of a document you have studied in class. (Students usually enjoy writing their own speeches modeled on another person's structure because they get an immediate leg up in sounding presidential or professional.)

c) Study the words of a political speech from the past fifty years, such as John F. Kennedy's inaugural address in 1961 or Ronald Reagan's inaugural address in 1981. Then watch a clip of that speech. How important is the written language compared to the delivery? Does the language play second fiddle to the politician's personal magnetism, or is it still important? Make a chart or Venn diagram comparing the impact of the written and the spoken word. Such an activity can lead to a discussion about the power of personality versus the power of words: how important are words if someone is a persuasive public speaker?

In the next part of this chapter I'll discuss two more examples of using primary source documents to guide students' understanding of the language of U.S. and world history: first, looking at political and national goals through the Gettysburg Address, a document that students think they know inside and out but that bears closer investigation through repeated words; and, second, understanding the power of rhetoric to challenge and resist a government through Demosthenes' Second Philippic from Greece in the fourth century BCE.

# Breaking Open the Gettysburg Address to Understand Lincoln's Values and Priorities

Some documents communicate the ethos of a time so well that they beg for students to analyze them, not once but multiple times throughout their academic careers. In this way, they are like classic novels or movies, giving us new insights about the characters and themes at different stages in our lives.

Many students will have read, perhaps memorized, the Gettysburg Address by the time they arrive in middle school. Yet engaging in a deeper investigation of this important document—peeling its layers like an onion—can help our ten-to-fourteen-year-olds grasp the profound challenges that Lincoln and the young nation confronted in the middle of the Civil War. Like so many pivotal documents in history, the address sets the tone and mood of the country, hinting at the nation's emotions and priorities at a time of internal turmoil.

Preassessment is critical, particularly when we are dealing with documents that students might have seen before. The first year I taught the Gettysburg Address to my eighth-grade history students, however, I did not sufficiently determine their knowledge beforehand. On the day I intended to teach it, I realized that they all knew Lincoln delivered it after the turning point of the battle of Gettysburg. Many remembered that he supposedly dashed off the words on the back of an envelope, and a few recalled that Edward Everett, the speaker who preceded Lincoln, droned on for nearly two hours.

What, then, could I salvage from the day's lesson? That day, I didn't accomplish much. We read the speech and talked about why it was important to the Civil War. I asked students to discuss quotations they liked. A few raised their hands to ask if they could recite bits of the address, since their fifth-grade teacher made them commit it to memory. At the end of the period, I felt that I had simply reminded students of things they already understood, rather than inspiring them to look deeper—at a level appropriate to thirteen- and fourteen-year-olds rather than to ten-year-olds. Looking back on that lesson, I wished I had asked students the day before to write down three things they knew about the Gettysburg Address and at least one question they had about it, perhaps in the structure of a KWL chart (what students Know, what students Want to know, and what they have Learned). Then I could have structured my lesson to address their curiosity and build on their background knowledge rather than repeat what they already understood.

The next year I was determined to do more with the text. The speech came up first that fall in my eleventh-grade U.S. history classes, where I went in with a lesson plan that investigated a Library of Congress photo of Lincoln at the battlefield, maps of the battle's three days, and diaries from people who had been there, all found online with a simple search. It was an interesting day spent with a variety of primary sources. Yet I still felt we were simply talking *about* the speech, rather than letting the power of the words move us and make us feel that we were standing on the battlefield on a clear November day.

When we came to the address later that year with my eighth graders, I decided to try something different. They already knew the context of the battle from a textbook reading and a short clip in Ken Burns's *Civil War* miniseries; we also had read accounts by the wounded of wartime hospitals. With such sources, I had hoped to bookend the speech with other elements of the time period, helping students imagine what it would have been like to stand on Little Round Top or to suffer the amputation of a leg in a battlefield hospital. Now I wanted the speech to stand on its own so that students could step into the head of Lincoln at this moment, late in the war. To prompt such empathy, we needed to look carefully at the 286 words he chose.

To begin, I asked my students to put everything away except the speech itself: "Pretend you're seeing it for the first time, or

Lincoln at the Battle of Antietam

at least with new eyes." I read it aloud to them once, urging them to imagine they were standing on the battlefield, straining to hear Lincoln's eulogy. Then I read the passage again, this time asking students to underline words or phrases they liked. I started writing their choices on the board. And then, surprising me, my students identified a pattern in the repeated phrases Lincoln used, which revealed his priorities for ending the war and reuniting the splintered country.

"Hey, a bunch of these quotes in the speech have 'dedicate' in them," Lisa said. "Why do you think Lincoln did that? It's such a short speech that I think he could have thought of different words."

Brendan started looking over his paper with pen in hand. "He uses 'dedicate,' or 'dedicated,' five, no, six times!"

"Really?" I said. "I never noticed that. Let's look through the speech together. Brendan, can you tell us where you found each instance of 'dedicate'?"

The first use of "dedicate" appeared immediately: "dedicated [devoted] to the proposition that all men are created equal." We continued, looking for the other examples and writing an informal definition of "dedicate" for each to show that Lincoln was using the same word deliberately, in many different senses. Here are the definitions we decided upon:

- "whether that nation or any nation so conceived and <u>dedicated</u> [intended] can long endure"

- "We have come to <u>dedicate</u> [set aside, commemorate] a portion of that field as a final resting-place . . ."

- "we cannot <u>dedicate</u> [officially mark], we cannot consecrate, we cannot hallow this ground"

- "It is for us the living rather to be <u>dedicated</u> [committed] here to the unfinished work which they who fought here have thus far so nobly advanced."

- "It is rather for us to be here <u>dedicated</u> [devoted] to the great task remaining before us."

"Why does Lincoln use this word so many times?" I wondered aloud.

"Well, it's one of those words that has a whole lot inside it," Rachel said. "Look at what we just wrote—'dedicate' can mean anything from setting something aside to devoting your life to something."

Christine waved her hand in the air. "Yes, and think about where Lincoln was at this point in the war. It was November 1863, you said. So the war had gone on for more than two years. He wasn't sure if the Union would win, and it was really tough. Wouldn't it make sense that he would be thinking all the time about the cause he had *dedicated* himself to?"

Thinking aloud, I said, "I wonder if he even knew he was repeating the word that many times." At this point, I really did not know whether he was aware of the repetition, and I'm still not positive, but I wanted to let my students know that I am always a learner with them.

"Ms. Cooper, you're always telling us that great authors don't use words by accident," Matt jumped in. "Do you really think Lincoln didn't realize that he was using this word six times?"

"You're probably right, Matt," I said. "He was rumored to have written the speech so quickly, but still, I'll bet he understood the impact that his words would have. Perhaps he wanted the

Union soldiers and civilians to continue to dedicate themselves to the cause, even when it was getting difficult. . . . Let's see what other words he uses repeatedly." Searching for words that appeared multiple times was an activity that every student, even those who struggled with reading comprehension, could do. Using this tool, all students found an opening for deep and deliberate analysis. After five minutes, we had created a chart on the board listing the speech's repeated words (see Figure 3.5).

Looking at this list, I got goose bumps—always a sign that my students are teaching me something profound. In these words, I realized, lay the underlying themes that we don't always see on a first reading. Lincoln was trying to communicate his values and priorities at this time in the war. To help students understand the thematic connections, I asked them to group the words into different categories, a strategy to guide them from literal to thematic thinking.

"Folks, do you see any of these words that should go together? Any themes?" I asked.

They looked at me blankly for a moment, but then the wheels started to turn.

"What does 'consecrate' mean again?" Maggie asked.

"To make something holy, like 'hallow,' which Lincoln also uses," I said, asking students to write down this definition so that they could understand Maggie's connection more clearly.

"Okay. Then we can put *consecrate, dedicate,* and *devotion* together," Maggie said. "They all have to do with something important or holy."

### Figure 3.5

**Repeated Words in the Gettysburg Address**

dedicate/dedicated

field/battlefield/ground
("ground" not repeated, but similar meaning)

lives/live/living

consecrate/consecrated

here

dead/died

devotion

people

nation

we/us/our

great

freedom/liberty/equal
(none of these is repeated, but they have similar meanings)

"This use of 'holy' is so interesting, Maggie," I said. "Why is Lincoln using this religious language? Have we seen this before?"

"Wasn't there some speech we read?" Elizabeth wondered.

"Yeah, that one about angels," Brent said. "Wasn't it when Lincoln became president?"

"Right, his hope that 'the better angels of our nature' would affect the country, in his First Inaugural Address," I said, referring to another speech we had read the week before. Usually I do not incorporate intense political speeches into the curriculum so often, but Lincoln's writing is so descriptive that it enables students to conjure images as if they were examining photos of the battlefields. "How about other connections?"

We put together the words of place: *battlefield, here.* "They make you seem like you're there, really immediate," said Mark.

After a few more minutes of thought came the words of human beings: *people, we/us/our, lives/live/living, dead/died.* "Lincoln wanted to remind the people listening that this was a war about people, not just bodies or battlefields," Danny said.

Sophie made a connection to the "Battle Hymn of the Republic," which we had listened to earlier in the week. The Civil War period is a rich repository for songs, and the sound track from the Ken Burns *Civil War* miniseries includes a beautiful choral version of the hymn that sears the words into students' memories. "Wasn't there a line about dying and living?" Sophie asked as she flipped through her binder. "Right, here it is: 'As he died to make men holy, let us live [originally "die"] to make men free.' So is Lincoln talking about Jesus?"

"Not directly, I think," I said, treading gently because of the religious content, "but he is certainly appealing to the ethical and moral sense of the people listening, trying to make them believe that there is something higher than themselves that they should continue to fight for. Remember, it can be really hard for us to imagine just how close civilians were to this war. We'll see that more next week, when we look at General Sherman's march through Georgia."

The class was silent for a few seconds, looking at what we'd put on the board. I was quiet, too, thinking about how to connect these words even more. So far we had linked *consecrate/dedicate/hallow/devotion* under the importance of religion, the sense that God was guiding Lincoln in his work; *battlefield/here* under the importance of place, remembering that people fought here; and *people, we/us/our, lives/live/living, dead/died* under the importance of human beings making choices, deciding that they would fight for their noblest ideals. These themes of religion, place, and humanity related not only to the Civil War, but also to many wars fought in the name of religion or country in the past two thousand years. What else could we glean?

"I think there's one more category," Gabriella said, "talking about something more important than ourselves, more important than any one human being, even Abraham Lincoln." At her recommendation, we put together *great, nation,* and *freedom/liberty/equal* because they testified to the freedom that the United States offered slaves through the Emancipation Proclamation. To help students reflect on the connections we had made as a group, I asked them to talk with a partner about the main idea of the speech and to write a brief summary.

Jennifer and Ryan wrote a concise variant on the theme that most students identified: "Lincoln wants to make everyone listening, or reading, feel they have a responsibility to the soldiers who died at Gettysburg. The people standing there are supposed to make sure that this nation of freedom keeps going."

By jumping into Lincoln's head through the language that he found most important, we uncovered a sense of duty and honor that the president wanted to instill in the country's collective consciousness. To cement the idea that words could convey idealism, the next day I asked students to answer this question in a short paragraph: how did the repeated words in the Gettysburg Address show what Lincoln cared about? Their responses solidified Lincoln's values that we had pulled out from discussion the day before.

# Demosthenes, That Demagogue: Exploring Key Rhetorical Concepts Through Political Commentary

A final example of a document that students can analyze for intent and impact comes from world history. Compared to American history, world history can seem like fallow ground for finding primary sources. Some civilizations did not produce many written documents, and other sources may not be available in translation. But searching for political and social commentaries from well-trodden subjects, such as the European Middle Ages and ancient Egypt, Greece, and Rome, can be fruitful.

Ancient Greece is ripe for the picking because the society's intellectuals wrote so much. However, I did not want to use just any document, particularly when we might cover straightforward topics, such as the Athenian *polis* (city-state) or the Homeric concept of *hubris* (overweening arrogance), during class discussions. Instead, I wanted to help students unravel a period with which they often had difficulty because of complex foreign affairs: the middle of the fourth century BCE, a century after the Golden Age, when Philip II of Macedonia (Alexander the Great's father) was threatening the Greeks with his army.

Why was this century important enough to merit studying a document? First, this transitional era marked the beginning of the end of Greek liberty, the point at which the country started to succumb to foreign powers. Philip would win the war he waged on Athens and Thebes. Identifying the precipice where a culture starts to decline is a global concept that applies to many civilizations, from ancient Rome to the feudal Middle Ages to, perhaps, the United States today. Second, the textbook mentioned that the orator Demosthenes agitated against Philip and wrote three devastating speeches, filled with invective, which led to our modern word *philippic* (a speech that points out the flaws of a politician, often with violent language). When I looked up the three Philippics online, I thought that the passion with which Demosthenes spoke would appeal to my students, often full of

The bust of Demosthenes

fiery emotions themselves. Lastly, Demosthenes' description of Philip's leadership, and his own suggestions for Greek action, brought up key issues of leadership and rebellion—again, relevant issues both 2,500 years ago and today. A speech by Demosthenes would not only help students understand why Greece would eventually succumb to Philip (and later Alexander the Great), but it would also give students a personal perspective on cultural decline and political leadership.

More personally, Demosthenes' speeches show that the voice of a maverick can sway public opinion, leading students to ask who our gadflies are today and how seriously we should take their ideas. Students also enjoy hearing a little bit of Demosthenes' background—that his famous oratorical skills were slow to develop, so much so that legend has it he filled his mouth with pebbles to enhance the quality of his voice. In addition, if some of your students have read Orson Scott Card's award-winning sci-fi novel *Ender's Game*, they will immediately recognize the name Demosthenes and will see deeper meaning in the book after they read the speech. Such personal and interdisciplinary connections can give students a stake in the speech before they read one word of it, linking their identity and experiences to this new text.

At times, as with the Gettysburg Address, it is useful for students to parse every word to see themes, especially with short documents. More often, however, students can benefit from gleaning the gist of the document rather than noticing every word; such attention to major ideas can lead them to imagine that they lived in ancient Greece or Civil War America and can help them see the controversial questions hovering in the air.

Once I decided to use one of Demosthenes' speeches, I looked at the first several paragraphs of each of his three Philippics. To go beyond these introductory pages would probably require too much background information to use in class, and browsing only the beginning made my job easier. (You can also find books that do the job for you with other world history documents, organized by time period, such as Ronald Mellor and Amanda H. Podany's *The World in Ancient Times: Primary Sources and Reference Volume* [2005]. This book is aimed toward middle school students with its short excerpts, clear explanations, and definition of terms throughout.)

I knew I wouldn't want more than a paragraph or so of Demosthenes' words because the language was fairly thick, and I intended for the section I chose to focus on one of the global themes from our unit on democracy: leadership or decline. With these goals in mind, I chose an excerpt from the second paragraph of Demosthenes' Second Philippic, delivered in Athens around 344 BCE (see Figure 3.6). It brashly states the case against Philip's desire to seize power, and it speaks to the possibility of changing a government with which citizens do not agree.

After we have read the speech aloud and defined unfamiliar words (I will often put definitions in brackets in the text to make the process faster and easier for students), I start with the following numbered questions. I ask students to answer the questions with a partner, moving their desks side-by-side so that everyone can see the board. As they work, I ask them to read the speech aloud one more time and then discuss which phrases most appeal to them. For middle school students, such interactivity brings enthusiasm that might not build if they simply read the passage silently on their own. If I think that the class could use the guidance of stopping after each question or two to discuss, I will do that, especially because such a step-by-step process can help less confident readers and speakers follow what is happening.

Figure 3.6

## Passage from Demosthenes' Second Philippic

"They who aspire to an extravagant degree of power are to be opposed by force and action, not by speeches; and yet in the first place, we public speakers are unwilling to recommend or to propose anything to this purpose, from the fear of your displeasure; but confine ourselves to general representations of the grievous, of the outrageous nature of his conduct, and the like. . . . And if, on this occasion, it be sufficient that we [the public speakers] speak with a superior force of truth and justice, this may be done with the utmost ease; but if we are to consider how to rectify our present disorders, how to guard against the danger of plunging inadvertently into still greater, against the progress of a power which may at last bear down all opposition—then must our debates proceed in a different manner; and all they who speak, and all you who attend, must prefer the best and most salutary measures to the easiest and most agreeable." (Demosthenes, "The Second Oration Against Philip")

1. Write down two phrases or sentences you find especially strong, interesting, or moving from Demosthenes' speech (use quotation marks):

a)

b)

2. For each phrase or sentence, explain why you find it effective (5–10 words).

a)

b)

This set of questions—what do you like, and why do you like it?—is often an encouraging way to begin because it does not require comprehension of the entire document, and it allows individual students to discuss why they like the sound or intensity of a phrase. Beginning with the *sound* of language is often simpler than starting with the *content* because students can simply think about how the words fall on the ear, not their deeper meaning. For example, Leah liked "superior force of truth and justice" because it sounded "strong," and Danny chose "the outrageous nature of his [Philip's] conduct" because the word "outrageous" reminded him of the exaggerations that he sees on some cable news shows. Following the phrases students prefer with the reasons they are effective forces kids to articulate not only *what* but *why*. Such practice can also encourage them to write strong essays because they see the result of providing evidence to back up commentary.

3. Do you agree that rulers who desire too much power should be "opposed by force and action, not by speeches"? Why or why not? (20–25 words)

This question moves on to the meat of the paragraph. The students' answers to "Should you attempt to overthrow a corrupt leader with violence or with nonviolence?" relate to the twentieth-century principle of nonviolent resistance and can be tied into any number of current events articles, from monks' stand-ins against the Myanmar government to G8 summit protesters' marches against global monetary policy. Students can see that people more than two thousand years ago were as fired up as people are today.

4.  If you had heard Demosthenes' "Second Philippic" in the Athenian agora in 344 BCE, would you have taken him seriously? Why or why not? (20–30 words)

Finally, now that students have located phrases they like, heard their classmates' responses, and thought about one big idea in the speech, they can imagine themselves in a Greek plaza during Demosthenes' lifetime. Such responses often include casual but powerful language, such as, "Was he crazy?" and "You go, Demosthenes!" This authentic expression of the middle school mind gives students the freedom to express themselves while rooting their opinions in fact and analysis.

The class conversation turns first to the words he used. "Did Demosthenes really have to exaggerate with phrases like 'superior force' and 'bear down all opposition'?" Katie wonders. "I think that weakens his case because it sounds like he has to exaggerate to find something to complain about."

"I actually liked that," Devon disagrees. "He's really into his ideas and isn't afraid to express them."

This brief point-counterpoint brings up other questions: Do protesters or rebels have to use extreme language or action to be noticed? Is there a certain personality type that lends itself to being an effective protester or demagogue (a word I teach them on the fly)? Do we know people today who are like Demosthenes—Stephen Colbert, perhaps, or Ralph Nader? Can we think of any women who are like Demosthenes, or are they mostly men? A few sentences by one thinker who lived millennia ago have opened up perennial issues.

This process of unpacking documents starts with the literal—what phrases do you like, and what do they mean? Then it moves on to the analytical—how do his ideas relate to what you think? And, finally, it finishes with the personal—what would you have thought had you been there? Ideally, every student can find a foothold, however small or large, at each point in the process through this scaffolded approach.

# Moving to the Big Picture

A chapter about the language of history, and how to understand it, could run the length of this book. If you are as interested as I am in exploring rhetoric, reasoning, and the role of language in history, please know that you do not have to find documents to pick apart in such detail every day or even every week. As with the historical narratives described in Chapter 2, a little analysis goes a long way in showing students that all documents have real authors who hinted at their motives through their words.

So far, we've examined history on a small scale: the role of the individual, the views of historians, and the impact of writing. In the next chapter, we'll transition to the bigger picture by exploring the broader patterns of history that emerge when we assemble the pieces.

## Chapter 4

# A Broader View:
# Finding Patterns in the Past

## What's Inside?

### Skills and Strategies

- Infer from illustrations, statistics, and dates
- Draw a freehand map
- Take notes
- Create a time line
- Construct a mind map
- Work productively in groups

## Standards

- ✔ Global patterns
- ✔ Government
- ✔ Trade and economy
- ✔ Geography
- ✔ Technological innovation
- ✔ Belief systems
- ✔ The nature of power

As we move from the details of individual stories, historical narratives, and eyewitness accounts to the broad sweep of U.S. and world history, the process can seem intimidating. Terms such as *geography* and *chronology* can loom so enormous in the scope of a middle school classroom that it is often unclear where to start. What I've found is that beginning with the end in mind can make the entry into large concepts easier. The final goal guides our decisions about which skills to emphasize and which activities to include, when to check progress through formative and summative assessments, and how to scaffold the learning so that every student can meet high standards. We can cycle back and forth between big ideas and specific connections, as we might do when gathering materials to build a bridge between a starting point and destination.

In this chapter, I'll start by suggesting strategies that show students how daily activities relate to our long-term objectives. Then I'll describe several larger projects that tap into students' multiple intelligences and honor their ability to create and interpret history.

# The Big Picture Revealed Through Small Details

Needless to say, you and I do not have time to embark upon a major project in every unit. Not every class period needs an infusion of outside materials and creative projects; we'd exhaust ourselves if this were so. Most of our classroom activities will be short and focused on specific people, places, or events. Nevertheless, we can keep the bigger themes in mind, using daily activities to fill in the details that will provide a broader view.

With many of these smaller strategies, students can be teachers as well as learners. If they think about major issues of the time by answering a thought question or tracing a route on a map, they are making key historical connections that they will remember better for discovering them on their own. Once students have solidified these ideas in their own minds, they can teach them to a partner or to the class.

Don't overlook the textbook as a source of good extension activities. Students *and* teachers often view the textbook's maps, drawings, and paintings as items we can skip, when, in fact, these illustrations can inspire meaty observations about history. I've been impressed in recent years by the range of strong primary sources and images featured in the margins of many middle school textbooks. The following ten suggestions go beyond reading and taking notes to inspire students to think about historical patterns.

1. **Draw Themes.** Textbooks often list major themes of history or major elements of civilization, especially in their opening pages. Ask students to jot down a few key words and a small symbol relating to each theme. For "religion in history," for example, students might write "finding meaning" and then draw symbols for each major faith. Throughout the year, they can consult the list and remember their visuals. This technique can also be used as a review: for example, creating an image for each article of the Constitution to remember the key components. The

drawings can be as simple as a house with "Representatives" written on it plus the word "Senate" = CONGRESS for Article 1. Middle school students relish creating organizational systems, whether for their iPod collections or their video games; helping them understand the importance of generating memory devices for tests is an important and age-appropriate life skill.

2. **Infer from a Map.** Many times, I'll flip through a book in our school library to look at thoughtful black-line maps, as with those in H. D. Amos and A. G. P. Lang's *These Were the Greeks* (1982). Then I'll ask students to venture a guess about a culture based on the map. For "Greek Migrations and Dialects" (27), students infer that the Greeks had many variations in language because they were so spread out over islands and peninsulas. This understanding helps them realize that there were many parts of Greek civilization, not simply Athens, Sparta, or the coast of what is now Turkey. For a map of Arabia in approximately 600 CE, students guess that Arabia's coastal residents ate a lot of seafood and that the area was a desirable place to live because of the development of cities. With these initial geographic forays into a culture, we can foreshadow the unit's larger themes, such as the political development of city-states in Greece or the rapid spread of Islam across the Arabian Peninsula.

3. **Color in a Map.** If I have ten minutes at the end of class, I'll often pull out a tub of markers or crayons and ask students to color elements of a map handout we've just discussed, such as bodies of water or areas under one country's influence. Students then write a sentence about how coloring the map has added to their understanding of the time. Often they reflect that certain regions are larger or smaller than they had thought, or that a country was more isolated by water than they had imagined. For a map of the Roman Empire in the second century CE, Tasha wrote, "One city controlled a super-vast area. They controlled places in 3 continents. They must have had a huge army to keep and gain so much land." For a map of Islam in the 700s, she reflected, "I didn't realize there were so many bodies of water around the Middle East and how close they were to Greece. They probably had lots of contact." And for a map of Alexander the Great's travels, Karina wrote, "Alexander was a tireless young man, always traveling, on the go." Such observations give students a chance to imagine they were living in the region on the map and to wonder how they would have coped with geographic, climatic, and military challenges.

Diving into a map can also be as straightforward as outlining the New England, Middle, and Southern colonies in different colors for a U.S. history class. When students go one step beyond coloring to draw this map freehand, the process helps them visualize the relative sizes and harbor access of each of the colonies. Another valuable U.S. map to color is one that shows expansion in the early 1800s, with the Missouri Territory from 1821, the Spanish Territory (still under Spain's control) from 1819, new states such as Illinois (1818) and Louisiana (1812), and the Oregon Territory owned by the United States and Britain together.

4. **Give an Exciting Lecture.** I rarely lecture in middle school history classes, but sometimes the material calls for a teacher's overview so that students can quickly see the through lines of history. When I do lecture, I keep the instruction to ten minutes or break it up with images, movement, and thought questions that students discuss with partners. The best guide I've found for delivering interactive mini-lectures with PowerPoint or traditional slides is Teachers'

Curriculum Institute (TCI), whose units include beautifully paced lectures that encourage student involvement through "act-it-outs" and meaningful questioning. It's no exaggeration to say that just about everything I have learned about effective methods of lecturing to middle school students came from TCI. (For an online primer on TCI's "Visual Discovery" process, go to http://www.teachtci.com/forum/VisualDiscovery.aspx; for information about TCI's content-specific programs, see http://store.teachtci.com/Shopping/Program.aspx.)

5. **Infer from a List of Dates.** Especially when a unit contains many parts and the chronology can be confusing, I write a list of dates on the board and ask students to copy them. Then they write for several minutes on at least one aspect of the society that they understand better because of the dates. For example, "Important Times in Ancient Greece" begins with Greek precursors and ends with a Macedonian conqueror (all dates are approximate to show general patterns):

| | |
|---|---|
| 2000–1400 BCE | Minoans |
| 1600–1100 BCE | Mycenaeans (Trojan War) |
| 1100–800 BCE | Dorians (Dark Ages) |
| 800 BCE | Homer writes |
| 750–400 BCE | Rise of Greek city-states |
| 450 BCE | Golden Age of Athens |
| 350 BCE | Alexander the Great |

In response, students have written that the civilizations lasted for a surprisingly short time and that it took centuries to arrive at the ones we remember really well, like Athens and Sparta. From these observations, we can start to connect the Greeks' ancestors with their Golden Age, noticing how the warrior mentality of the Mycenaeans and the artistic culture of the Minoans filtered through the centuries to the bellicose Sparta and the comparatively "civilized" Athens.

6. **Infer from Statistics.** Population numbers or war deaths can grab students' attention, particularly at the beginning of a unit, because they present a stark and unedited perspective that allows students to draw their own conclusions. When I start teaching about the Civil War, I spend ten minutes asking students to consider statistics about those who died, how much the war cost, and how much the value of Confederate property declined. Young adolescents blanch at the thought that, during the War Between the States, more than 620,000 Americans died, whereas in World War II, "only" 407,000 Americans died (McPherson and Cooper 1998, 1–2).

7. **Make a Chart.** Many textbook chapters contain so much information on cultures or governments that a chart is needed to clarify themes. One such chart included four columns on early African culture, taken from similar subheadings in the text: "Painting and Sculpture," "Music," "Architecture," and "Literature." Students worked with partners and took about twenty minutes to fill in the chart's columns with four or five related bullet points. Afterward we looked at common trends across the arts, such as "creative expression serves religion" and "great variety."

Other useful chart topics include similarities and differences among people or dynasties; this activity helps students see cultural progress over time or compare relative impacts.

8. **Select Important Events.** Sometimes, in the interest of brevity and directness, I like to assign questions from the end of a textbook chapter, especially for material that students simply have to know. Usually I'll pick only one or two thoughtful questions that require students to do more than copy information from the text (or from each other). A similar but more engaging strategy is to ask students to list what they think are the five most important events or people from throughout the chapter or section and write a few sentences explaining their choices. This activity also serves as a ready-made discussion starter for the next day: "What did you think was most interesting?" leads to more exciting conversations than "Who wants to answer number 1?"

9. **Answer a Question to Imagine the Culture.** Ten-minute thought questions can help bridge transitions between cultures or eras, and I often find ideas from a sentence or phrase in the textbook, especially in the broad introductions to each chapter. One such question that I've used after the fall of the Roman Empire, at the beginning of the Middle Ages, asks students to imagine themselves living in a foreign time: what would it look like, feel like, and/or be like to exist between the ancient and the modern worlds? Nuggets from students' responses have included *dangerous, dirty and dingy, exciting and fun, crowded, Christian, gap between rich and poor, fearful,* and *depressed.* After discussing what an uncertain transitional period feels like, students are more ready to hear about how Charlemagne's organizational skills helped Europe stay safe in the ninth century CE because he imposed order on the relative chaos preceding his rule. Middle school students tend to possess both a monumental desire to change the world and an equal pull to remain rooted in the familiar details of their own school and family. Questions that catapult students into the past help them visualize ways of life far different from their own.

10. **Write Adjectives Inspired by a Primary Document.** Students can feel close to a time period by coming up with words to describe the values, priorities, leadership, and emotions reflected in a primary source. For instance, ninth-grade world history students can read aloud a hymn about the creator god Indra from the *Rig Veda,* an ancient Indian text that I found by briefly browsing the Internet Indian History Sourcebook (http://www.wsu.edu:8080/~wldciv/world_civ_reader/world_civ_reader_1/rig_veda.html). Students brainstormed in pairs, and we put their adjectives on the board: *great, powerful, important, controlling, able, conquering, admired, respected, terrible, helpful, first,* and *all-wise.* This list became a basis for our discussion of religion in ancient Indian society. For Tacitus's description of German "barbarians" during Roman times, our adjectives included *hospitable, swift, brave, loyal, hardworking,* and *tough*—not exactly what we thought we would find in an account of these supposedly brutal foreigners. This activity also gives students emotional touchstones to identify with people from the past. "Am I as brave and loyal as these German warriors were?" they might ask. Would I have been so courageous, had I been trained from a young age to fight, as youths were two thousand years ago? Not only do students realize how the chronicler Tacitus saw these soldiers, but they also can speculate how they would have measured up.

# Multiple Ways of Learning Through Thematic Projects

Interactive projects that cover a broad sweep of history have inspired some of the most energetic and productive moments in my middle school classes; such assignments tap into our students' desire for novelty and power while covering important curricular themes and skills. When is it useful to assign projects rather than ask students to engage in daily activities or take tests relating to the textbook?

- When we have looked at so many different sources that stepping back will help students synthesize the material

- When the textbook sections we've read seem disconnected and do not allow students to fully realize analytical standards

- When students need a break from intensive reading and writing

- When students can discern new connections among facts and ideas with activities that appeal to multiple intelligences

After the first experience with a project, I often ask what students thought about it and what I could do differently next time. I remember one November in a ninth-grade history class when I gave less explicit directions than I usually do. I did this deliberately so students would have the opportunity to put their imprint on the project. However, the feedback I received, especially from the less-organized students, was that they really missed the clear guidelines. There is a place for students to feel their own way through a project, but I realized that I needed to provide more modeling of expectations so they could create their own calendar for completion.

Projects that effectively synthesize large themes of history do not have to be complex. Sometimes the best approach is straightforward, as with the projects I'll describe in the next three sections: a time-line review for a midterm exam in ninth-grade world history, a mind map based on the Jacksonian Era for an eighth-grade U.S. history class, and an Islam map project for an eighth-grade ancient civilizations course. I've also found I-Search projects to be productive and high interest, giving students a stake in their learning (Macrorie 1988; Taylor 2006). Let's consider each of these in more detail:

## A Smart Time Line

For almost a decade of teaching, I avoided assigning a major time-line project. I don't know why it seemed so daunting. I worried that its stoic list of dates would be boring, that it would turn off the students to history. But, as I taught a world history curriculum with units whose dates overlapped (ancient China, India, Mesoamerica, and Africa), I realized that I was doing my students a disservice if I did not ask them to make chronological connections *across* rather than simply *within* cultures. How fascinating to realize, for instance, that the inhabitants of China's Shang Dynasty and India's Mohenjo-Daro were rough contemporaries of each other.

As I began compiling a review for the semester midterm exam, I realized that a time line could be as valuable a form of review as any handout I could create. At first, I envisioned a massive physical time line that circled the room, with each student contributing a panel. I'd still like to do that someday, but I wasn't brave enough to figure out the logistics, and I decided I'd rather focus on content than presentation my first time out.

The major content element of the project would, of course, relate to state and national standards about understanding chronology. However, with a project that takes up significant class time, one content standard is not enough. The project itself needs to multitask, bringing in skills as well as content. The skills include researching events, creating an effective graphic representation of a time period, and presenting ideas to the class in a structured and clear manner. As I scratched ideas on a piece of paper, thinking about what I wanted students to know by the end of the unit, I envisioned a project with several components:

- Connections across two or three civilizations in the same time period.

- Brief research in addition to what the textbook included about these events to help students deepen their understanding of the period.

- A small visual to help them remember the content better but not overwhelm them. Also, I wanted to be able to photocopy all of the finished products in a review packet, so everything needed to fit on regular printer paper.

- A brief oral presentation to help the class review and practice speaking skills.

By creating a visual time line and completing the written connections, the library research, and the oral presentation, students would "own" a period and understand it from many different angles. They would become the go-to people for that era in history as their classmates studied for the midterm exam; such a built-in review system also played into many middle school students' desire to socialize as they study.

Frankly, the next step for me was a pain in the neck: trying out project possibilities by modeling what I wanted my students to do. Each time I design a project, I'm tempted to skip this step. However, when I do, I find that the number of procedural questions students ask multiplies by ten. So I began writing a model of the main written component of the project, a connections paragraph that tied together one event from each of three different cultures. The goal of the assignment, as indicated in the rubric, is to "connect all three events through themes and significance." While writing, I discovered that the connections I thought could be described in 250 to 300 words actually needed only about 150 words. I was surprised, and I wouldn't have realized this had I not tried writing the paragraph for myself. (Not incidentally, I also would have needed to grade twice the number of words, and my students would have needed to write those words. Whenever I find that I can justifiably cut down on my students' and my workload without sacrificing content, I jump at the chance. Middle-schoolers are so busy with academic responsibilities, friendships, family commitments, and after-school activities that it is almost an insult to burden them with unnecessary busywork.) I also realized I could include the model on the project directions, giving students a template from which to work. Our textbook publishers helpfully included a list of key world history dates that was a fine starting point (Brummett et al. 2000).

When I presented the project design in class, students had questions about what kinds of events they should choose. A civilization was too broad to count as an event, I said, and I encouraged them to pick an event or person from that era instead. I spent much of my time in the library that first day talking with students, helping them look through sources and indexes, and narrowing or expanding their subjects as needed. As with all research, the choice of topic is only a starting point, and sometimes a wrong path forces us to turn back, regroup, and head in a different direction. (For a teacher model of a sample connections paragraph that included three events, see Figure 4.1.)

After considering what I wanted students to learn from the project and modeling the written portion myself, I wrote the directions. For most projects, I like to give an overview on the first page.

## Figure 4.1

### Connections Paragraph Model 3000–2000 BCE

#### Events

- **AFRICA (c. 3000 BCE):** Farmers start planting *teff,* finger millet, sesame, and mustard in Ethiopia, all crops that fit that specific environment (Brummett et al. 2000, 229). *Add additional information from first research source in your own words, with parenthetical citation (approx. 50 words).*

- **AMERICAS (3000–2000 BCE):** Maize cultivation continues to spread from the Tehuacán valley in Mexico: as far north as the Mississippi River area and as far south as what is now Argentina (Brummett et al. 2000, 324). *Add additional information from second research source in your own words, with parenthetical citation (approx. 50 words).*

- **ASIA (c. 3000 BCE):** In China, the Yangshao area perfects its style of abstract and geometric pottery in the west and jade creations in the east (Brummett et al. 2000, 41). *Add additional information from third research source in your own words, with parenthetical citation (approx. 50 words).*

#### Connections Paragraph

All three events show that ancient society, circa 3000 BCE, was becoming more established and civilized. In Africa, different regions domesticated a variety of different plants, demonstrating the people's ingenuity and adaptability to their surroundings. In the Americas, the staple crop of maize influenced nearly every civilization in the north, central, and southern parts of the region. Maize allowed wide-ranging cultures to move from hunting and gathering to agriculture relatively early on. By this point in history, China already had been growing rice in the south, and millet and wheat in the north, for thousands of years. Such stability enabled the Chinese civilization to venture into the arts with ceramics and jewelry that we still value today. Throughout the world, the agricultural and artistic developments of this early period laid the foundation for the empires and dynasties that would come in the next centuries and millennia.

I'll usually include a model of the written component, a schedule of work, and a grading rubric. Students rarely need help creating visual aids.

I must confess that I was five years into my teaching career before I came up with this organizational structure for projects. Before then, I considered myself ahead of the game if I completed a rubric by the time I had to grade the projects. Even today, I keep an extra copy of the rubric on my desk when grading so I can jot down changes that I want to make the following year. The more time I spend up front, however, the more cohesively the project ensues.

I liked the project enough that I used it again for the final exam at the end of the second semester. The activity met the standard of being able to "construct various time lines of key events, people, and periods of the historical era [students] are studying" (California State Board of Education 1998, 21). More than that, it forced students to think about the relationships between timing and events. With important dates at their fingertips, students exerted control over their writing about history in a way I had not seen before and paid attention to cause and effect.

Figures 4.2a, b, and c provide a few visual examples of this chronological and thematic time-line project by ninth graders Kelly, Maria, and Evan.

## Figure 4.2a

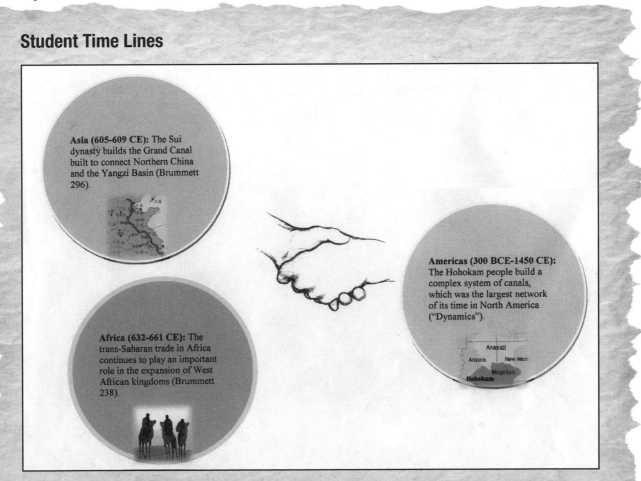

### Student Time Lines

**Asia (605-609 CE):** The Sui dynasty builds the Grand Canal built to connect Northern China and the Yangzi Basin (Brummett 296).

**Africa (632-661 CE):** The trans-Saharan trade in Africa continues to play an important role in the expansion of West African kingdoms (Brummett 238).

**Americas (300 BCE-1450 CE):** The Hohokam people build a complex system of canals, which was the largest network of its time in North America ("Dynamics").

Figures 4.2b and c

The Sophisticated World of 1000-800 B.C.E.

1500-400 BCE          1046-771 BCE          900-700 BCE

The Americas          China          India

The Olmec Civilization created ornate carvings of kings on large pieces of basalt.

During the Western Zhou dynasty, schools for men and women of varied social status were founded in the capital cities of feudal states.

The *Brahmanas*, a Hindu text, was composed to clarify the meanings of various rituals and Vedic songs performed during those rituals.

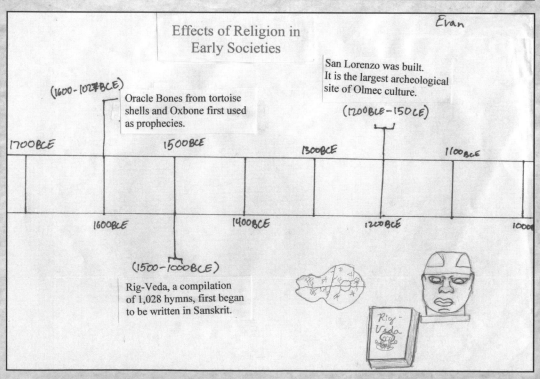

Effects of Religion in Early Societies

Evan

(1600-1027BCE) Oracle Bones from tortoise shells and Oxbone first used as prophecies.

San Lorenzo was built. It is the largest archeological site of Olmec culture.

(1200BCE-150CE)

1700BCE          1500BCE          1300BCE          1100BCE

1600BCE          1400BCE          1200BCE          1000B

(1500-1000BCE) Rig-Veda, a compilation of 1,028 hymns, first began to be written in Sanskrit.

Next time, I would change several elements to make the assessment more interactive and meaningful. After spending several days with students in the library, watching their presentations, and grading their work, I was happy to observe the strong connections they were making, but I wanted to expand those links to include something bigger, perhaps more visual, as with my original idea of a time line stretching across the classroom wall. In addition, using the midterm exam as the presentations' culminating analysis was serviceable but anticlimactic. In class, we did talk about themes that recurred in various periods, such as building military strength at the beginning of a civilization or having the luxury to focus on the arts at a society's apex. But I realized that students would have learned more if they had been able to apply the research their classmates conducted, perhaps by making their own time line from 2000 BCE to 1600 CE based on the various presentations. This way students would have seen the broad sweep of history more clearly, rather than focusing so much on their individual time periods. Instead of asking students to investigate a two-hundred-year span, I might encourage them to pick a theme from the period and then choose events from three or more civilizations based on that theme.

## What's for Dinner? A Mind Map, or Using the Ingredients You Have

Creating a mind map, or a visual representation of what is in your head, is not a new approach to synthesizing material. However, it is an ideal vehicle for giving students the intellectual independence to create their own meaning out of disparate facts and ideas. I like to use this method when we have looked at so many different images and documents that we could stand to impose some order on our thoughts. In fact, I most often choose a mind map when I am not sure whether what I have been trying to teach has gotten across. Like an exit card on which students write what they got out of the day's lesson, mind maps serve as a mirror to my teaching. Have the students learned what I have been trying to teach? More importantly, have they understood the lesson well enough that they can identify themes within the topic? Through reflections of their comprehension, I can plainly see that they have grasped, for example, Jefferson's "wolf by the ears" letter about slavery but not South Carolina's nullification ordinance. Ideally, I will also notice connections in their drawings that I hadn't previously considered and then share these insights with the class. Such was the case with Amber's labeling the parts of her mind map for the years after the War of 1812 "the good, the bad, and the ugly" (see Figure 4.4a). Amber's interpretation gave us a chance to discuss what a nation sacrifices when it gains new lands and holds the conviction that expansion is inexorable: in the case of the United States from 1815 to 1829, a skewed moral compass that allowed slavery to continue for nearly half a century.

Mind maps give every student the chance to interpret history in his or her own way. To encourage this freedom (and also to ensure that every student is doing roughly the same amount of work), I try not to give too many specifications for the historical content of mind maps, but I do give detailed instructions for the format. The directions stipulate how many documents or assignments the map must use, how many visuals it must include, whether it needs a brief explanation of the theme given, and a list of what we've studied on the topic. Such basics might seem to ignore content at the expense of process, but in fact I've found the opposite to be true: as long as I require students to lay out thematic connections among the facts they choose, the level of analytical rigor stays high. See Figure 4.3 for typical requirements I might give for a mind map—in this case, one on modern Europe in a current events/geography class.

Figure 4.3

## Mind Map Requirements

1. ***A theme*** *that applies to the information we have learned about European immigration, the EU, the fall of Communism, etc. Examples: change, progress, courage, tolerance, or any other meaningful word or phrase you can think of.* Such a theme immediately gives students an analytical framework for their ideas. As I walk around while they are working, I can help them assess how well their facts mesh with their themes. For example, in a seventh-grade class, Miruna chose "Fear of Power" as a guiding idea. As I looked over her shoulder, I asked her to expand her notion that the European Union's formation "scared other outside countries." She added that other countries might feel left out economically, a fuller response.

2. ***A creative title that describes your theme.*** Without such a stipulation, I've found that at least half the students forget a title, making their theme less clear to other students, to me, and often to themselves.

3. ***A meaningful fact or quotation from at least seven*** *of the articles/videos/ maps we have looked at. Each should be at least ten to fifteen words and should relate to the theme you have chosen.* I give a list of the articles, maps, and video clips we have read or watched so that students can find the handouts or notes in their binders. Finding facts and quotations is the most labor-intensive part of the process, and I tell students that they can start with the facts and then work their way up to a theme, using inductive reasoning, rather than starting with a theme and moving down toward facts, using deductive reasoning. With induction, they can really own their project because they discover ideas for themselves.

4. ***A source for all information you use.*** With citation requirements, the mind map builds bibliographic skills that students can later use in formal research papers.

5. ***Additional facts or ideas*** *as needed to show your points.* Whenever I forget to include a stipulation that students can include more facts, quotations, or examples, they always ask me whether they can. Middle school students are some of the most literal creatures on the planet, many wanting desperately to know whether they are following the rules and exactly where the boundaries are. Why? So they can test them, of course!

Figure 4.3 (continued)

6. ***Clear, visual connections among ideas and facts.*** Examples could be arrows linking one idea to another, circles relating two facts, or any other relevant graphic organizers. Such representation of analytical connections immediately makes clear how much students comprehend. If students' facts and arrows on a rough draft of the mind map do not show meaningful understanding, then I might ask them to find different facts that support a theme or to reread a paragraph in a helpful article. A mind map, involving several days of class work, lends itself to such individualized attention.

7. ***At least two meaningful illustrations*** *to liven up your ideas. They may be small.* Words with illustrations garner more attention than plain text. When I display mind maps on bulletin boards at the completion of the project, I want the maps to be visually interesting so students will gravitate to them before and after class, informally revisiting the unit.

8. ***Color*** *to give your ideas impact.* If a student is a magnificent black-and-white artist or feels his work would be ruined in color, I will make an exception, but most students' work looks more refined in color. However, over the years I've had several students, mostly boys, whose pencil-and-paper drawings are so intricate that adding color would dissipate their effect.

9. ***A fifty-word explanation*** *(on the back if you like) telling how your mind map shows your theme.* This last requirement gives students the chance to explain why they have put together their themes, ideas, and facts in the chosen manner. During the first few years of doing this project, I did not require such metacognitive thinking at the end. As a result, when I was grading the projects I found myself having to guess at the students' intentions. With such an explanation, students bring their project full circle, returning to the reasons they chose their elements in the first place and showing skills of synthesis and reflection.

I've used mind maps with two very different units—the pre–Jacksonian Era in an eighth-grade U.S. history class and European current events in a seventh-grade geography and current events class. My students constructed their projects with markers and pens, but visual mapping software programs such as Inspiration would be a natural fit. With both topics, I have watched middle-schoolers make creative, global connections: explaining "the central issues and problems from the past, placing people and events in a matrix of time and place" (California State Board of Education 1998, 22). However, both times I encountered pitfalls that I needed to fix. One caution is that the mind maps cannot focus on one topic at the exclusion of all others, especially if we are not having a test on the unit. For example, with the European mind map, many students honed in on the fall of Communism, a fine topic that thematically related to what we had studied. However, many of their projects did not tackle the European Union (EU) or modern immigration, which I realized too late that I also wanted them to include. The next year, I included more articles and sources on those topics and also mentioned the importance of Communism, the EU, and immigration as I introduced the project. Such prescriptive directions meant that very few students stepped outside these guidelines to pick a theme of their own, and many stuck to the subject of politics or the economy rather than the ideas of freedom or population movement. In a U.S. history class, for a mind map on events leading to the Jacksonian Era, many students also picked the same themes—sectionalism and expansion—but these ideas are so broad that the maps showed more range and diversity of thought. My goal in future years is to provide information about enough topics that students will be able to imagine plenty of themes. Figures 4.4a and b show examples of two mind maps of the years before Andrew Jackson took the presidency (1815–1829): Amber's straightforward Venn diagram and Michelle's give-and-take between two themes.

## Figure 4.4a

### Jacksonian Era Mind Maps

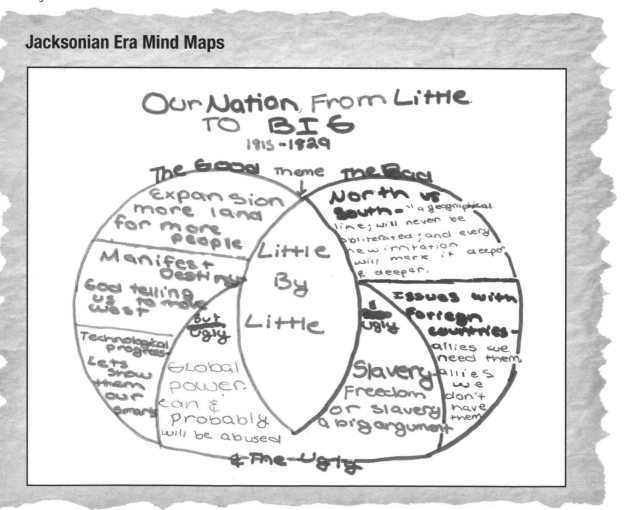

Figure 4.4b

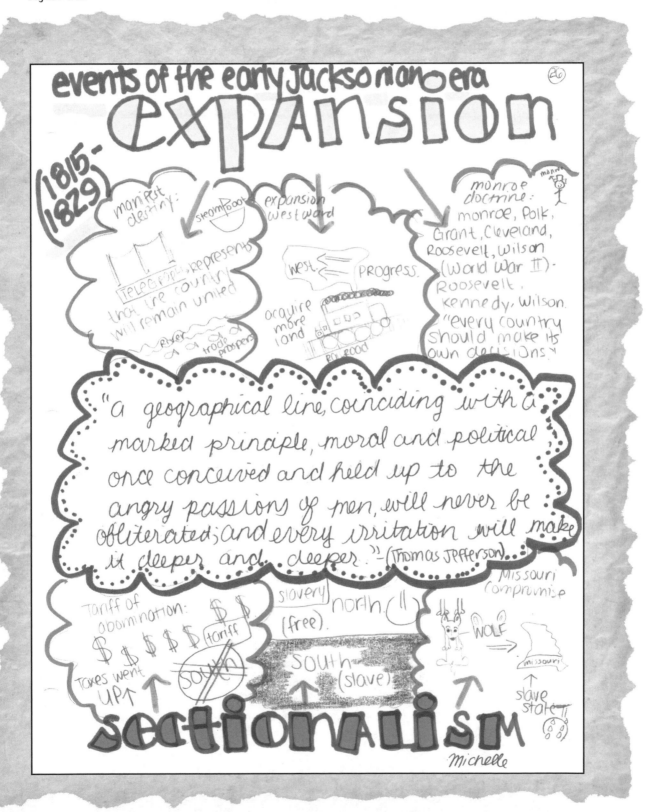

## Mapping Historical Islam: Combining Geography and History

The most meaningful projects tend to bring in multiple connections: chronology and theme in the time line, theme and historical importance in the mind map. If the project accomplishes several curricular goals at once, it seems worth the several days to a week we will usually spend on it in class. For the third and last project I'll discuss, an Islam map, I aimed to create an activity that would tap into the strengths of my visually oriented students, while at the same time making the assignment accessible for those who were not great artists. My own inclinations can be so logical, verbal, and linguistic that I wanted to go beyond my comfort zone and, in doing so, make some of my students more at ease.

The Islam map project has changed slightly over several years and is still in development because the students give me new ideas each time. Sometimes I include group work, and other times I emphasize individual assignments. Originally I asked students to complete an Islam I-Search (see Chapter 7 for a fuller description of this project). After the events of September 11, 2001, when misconceptions about Islam were swirling in the press, I wondered if I should bring in more current relevance to our historical Islam unit. Ultimately, I decided against more modern-day ties for three reasons: first, students were hearing plenty of contemporary articles about the United States' reactions to September 11 during our current events discussions, and we were covering those issues in a natural and organic way based on students' questions and interests. Second, the material about the development and flowering of Islam from the sixth century onward is so rich that we rarely do it justice in the time we have. Finally, this historical record is largely positive and inspiring, especially during the Golden Age from the eighth to thirteenth centuries. Rather than focus even more on the negative portrayals of Al Qaeda saturating the media, looking back a millennium to see the legacy of Islam seemed more appropriate and productive. However, I did resolve to tie in historical Islam to our current events discussions whenever possible, such as mentioning the circular, walled medieval city of Baghdad when we heard news reports of shellings.

The assignment involves picking events in the history or current events of Islam, describing them in the students' own words (with or without research, depending on the year and the time I have), and placing the items on a freehand map. Why freehand? Students remember maps better when they draw them, and such "tactile geography" can make maps much more interesting and meaningful. In addition, every standard in the California middle school world history list includes geography, as with "Students analyze the geographic, political, economic, religious, and social structures of the early civilizations of Mesopotamia, Egypt, and Kush" (California State Board of Education 1998, 24). Within the specific content standards for each culture, students often need to know the geographic impact of the country as well. For Islam, which had and continues to have such an influence on so many areas of the world, a map can place the religion's achievements in context. I chose a map because I wanted students to understand the global reach of this religion that developed so quickly. Because we had already studied Africa and Asia, two areas highly influenced by Islam over the centuries, I thought students would see new geographic and thematic connections by drawing the spread of the Muslim world.

Originally, I gave students the option to create a time line or a freehand map. Or, for intrepid eighth grader Chris, both at the same time! His combination map–time line covered four pieces of printer paper taped together into a rectangle, and it was by far the most thoroughly executed assignment he did all year. When I pinned it on the bulletin board, students said, "Who did that?" Chris didn't garner that kind of academic stardom very often, another testament to honoring different learning styles. In the eighth-grade early civilizations class in which I assigned it, however, most students chose the time line. I realized only too late that a time line was far easier than a freehand map. The results of the time lines were serviceable but pedestrian. There's not much exciting analysis involved in compiling a time line based on events from the textbook, even if you decorate the chart with elaborate geometric designs from the period, as Leigh did, or arrange the events surrounding a drawing of the Ka'aba, as Emma did.

Islamic bronze plate

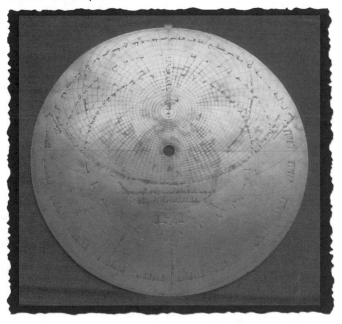

When I next assigned the project, this time letting students work with one or more partners, I limited it to a freehand map and provided poster boards. Students could compile their event descriptions and visuals on the computer, but the final map would be mostly hand-drawn so they could internalize the shapes of countries and continents as they drew them. The results were more exciting because they spotlighted students' originality. Every map looked different, from George's artistically jagged borders to Emily's painstaking lines of latitude, and the events showed the spread of Islam through Europe, Asia, and sometimes the rest of the world. Students were surprised by the geographic dispersal of the religion. To go from Arabia to Spain, for instance, was a longer journey than they had envisioned when reading these names in the textbook. Drawing the maps also brought out meaningful questions, such as whether people had traveled by land across the Sahara or by water across the Mediterranean, or whether the proximity of Arabia to the east coast of Africa had influenced trading patterns. Taking the time to create a map gave students time to think about how missionaries and traders a millennium ago had navigated these shores.

Figure 4.5 shows the brief directions for the Islam map project—brief because I really wanted students to take this as their own, and it didn't matter to me what form the finished project took. As with the mind map, I find that giving students a set of basic requirements ensures that everyone is reading and synthesizing roughly the same depth of content. At the same time, middle school students often want their projects to be unique in presentation and approach; such individuality helps them distinguish their interests and abilities from others' at a time when they are discovering what they excel in. Playing into this desire to be different academically (as opposed to being different in clothing or hair style, which many middle-schoolers adamantly do *not* want to be), gives students a relatively risk-free environment in which to sculpt their own themes.

Figure 4.5

## Islam Freehand Map

### Guidelines

With a partner or group of three, you will create a freehand map of the spread of Islam, then and now. This activity will enhance your knowledge of geography, show the vast reach of Islam, and expose you to current events about the religion. I will provide a poster board for each group. Here are the details:

- Pick six of the most important events from the chapter we've read on Islam that show the spread or influence of the religion. These events should be geographically spread out (i.e., not all on the Arabian Peninsula). A group of three will do nine events.

- Look up two current events articles from two different countries about Islam in the world today. For country ideas, see "The Population of Muslims in Modern Europe, Africa, and Asia" map in your binder.

- Print the two current events articles, highlight interesting information, and write a bibliography. (One partner will do each article. For a group of three, each person will do an article, for a total of three.)

- For each of the six historical events: Write twenty-five or more words on what the event was (brief) and why it was important for the spread of Islam.

- For each of the two current events: Write fifty or more words on what the event is and why it is important for Islam in the world today.

- Then draw a freehand map of the area your eight events cover, using the maps in your binder and your book as a guide. Include at least two illustrations, printed out or hand-drawn, to illustrate your events.

- Label the events on the map where they happened, along with their descriptions (typed or handwritten). If your descriptions really do not fit well on the map, you may put them at the bottom or on the back.

# Group Project Caveats

With long-term group projects such as those mentioned previously, I've found that I need to be mindful of several potential problems, all of which I've experienced too many times to count.

## Groups Who Get Lost in the Process Because of My Lack of Direction

It seems that the longer I teach, the longer my directions become for any project. For the projects I've designed in the last several years, I often write a day-by-day description of what students should do in class or in the library, as with the time line and Islam map assignments. Explicit directions, especially for library days, help students stay on task. Such detailed written guidance also fosters independence as they work; they can feel confident that they are not missing anything, and they realize that they do not have to check with me at every moment to make sure they are doing the project correctly. Of course, some of my favorite middle school students still want to check in frequently during a class, often just to receive confirmation that their efforts are appreciated, and I'm happy to be able to offer that.

In addition, I frequently ask students to reflect on two things that they've accomplished during the class period and two things they need to start on the following day. This five-minute assessment is their ticket out the door. That night after class, I'll often take ten minutes to glance at the reflections to get a sense of how far along they are in the process. Have I asked for too much? If so, the next day I will revise the assignment's scope, as long as I know students have been diligent in their efforts. Are there particular areas of confusion or difficulty, such as finding good book sources? If so, I might do a five-minute mini-lesson at the beginning of class the next day for everyone, or I'll pull aside a group of students with the same question to address their concerns. These exit cards help students stay focused—when I return the sheets at the beginning of class the next day, they remember where they were the day before—and let me tailor the next day's lesson to their needs.

## Dysfunctional Groups

When I assign students to groups—and I nearly always do so to avoid the painful scene of watching some adolescents wander around the classroom searching for a group to take them in—I try to include students with different strengths who work well together. Inevitably, one or two groups will have conflicts. (Haven't reality TV shows taught us this lesson?) To help everyone get along, I sometimes ask students the day before I assign groups to list three people with whom they could work productively as well as the few people with whom they should not be matched. Young adolescents are usually honest and insightful about these choices and they appreciate being asked. Even when two kids are best friends, if one of them does not complete his assignments regularly, the diligent worker will usually want to be partnered with someone else. I often give points for productive group work on the final rubric to emphasize that developing teamwork relationships can be as important, in school and in careers, as giving strong individual effort. At the same time, though, especially if I know certain people did not pull their weight, I'll ask everyone in the class to fill out a confidential sheet detailing the percentage of the group work that each person contributed. Students are nearly always generous and honest in these evaluations.

## Projects That Seem Just a Little Too Perfect Because of Help from Home

Most large projects involve significant time in class for development. I schedule such time because I want to see what the students can do themselves, jump-start students when they are stuck, and generate the creative curricular energy that comes from middle-schoolers sprawled across the floor and on desks, creating just the right poster board or PowerPoint presentation to express their ideas. In addition, doing the project in class, especially the first time through, means that I have a built-in error checker. I can fix my inevitable missteps as they occur rather than send them home and force beleaguered parents and students to deal with them at 9 p.m. the night before the project is due.

I remember the time I assigned a project on Indian sacred texts (for a description, see Chapter 5) and was watching a ninth-grade world history class humming along in pairs, finding their source excerpts on websites in the library's computer lab. I noticed after ten minutes that two students were shaking their heads, frustrated at what they saw on the screen. Their text was the *Shahnama*, a Persian national epic. Why the confusion? The site, which I had found ahead of time to help streamline their research, presented hundreds of gorgeously illustrated manuscript pages—but in Farsi, with no English translation. We spent some time looking for other sites that gave English versions, but they were not as strong as the sites for other students' texts. We finally settled on a short excerpt from one site, but it took these two students the entire period to find it, and by this time they were behind on their work. To compensate for my mistake that caused them to lose time in class, I modified the project requirements, requiring these two students only to present a summary of the text to me orally rather than write it down.

# A Culture of Discovery

Continually looking for the grand patterns of history is one of the hardest tasks we face as teachers and students. As Donald Graves writes in *Bring Life into Learning: Create a Lasting Literacy* (1999), we need to find ways to bring energy into our classrooms so that both students and teachers can remain refreshed. Offering our students the tools to make important explorations and connections is one of the most compelling ways I have found to do that.

Once we have students' attention, we can help them understand that history is important because of the themes and patterns that define cultures—trends societies tend to repeat, often to their detriment. Such common threads tie us together as people who have lived on this planet, and we falter when we fail to recognize the mistakes and successes of previous generations. By examining the patterns of the past through daily activities, longer projects, and frequent essays, we help our students see that they are one part of a vast, interconnected global history—and that they can put their newfound knowledge to work for the good in their own lifetimes.

## Chapter 5

# How Historians Think: Writing as a Way of Understanding

## What's Inside?

### Skills and Strategies

- Brainstorm and prewrite for essays
- Predict essay questions for tests
- Analyze model essays for meaning
- Weigh historical evidence
- Organize essays clearly
- Use guiding questions to comprehend larger themes

### Standards

✔ Analytical writing
✔ Logical argumentation
✔ Cause and effect
✔ Synthesis of facts

As someone who teaches both English and history, I think all the time about how much to focus on writing in history class. In my eleventh-grade classes, both regular and advanced placement, and often in my ninth-grade classes, I include an essay that counts for at least half the grade on every test. (To make the grading less onerous and encourage students to organize broad ideas cogently, I usually assign only one big essay rather than multiple small ones. Along with the essay, I include multiple-choice and sometimes matching questions to check knowledge of specific facts.) These classes become as much about constructing a historical argument as about learning the facts.

Like most teachers of analytical essays, I usually ask for a thesis, topic sentences that follow the thesis, facts that support the topic sentences, and analysis within the paragraphs that ties together the facts and relates to the main argument of the paper. (For a useful writing structure that helps students weave together facts and analysis, check out "Teaching the Multiparagraph Essay: A Sequential Nine-Week Unit" by Jane Schaffer Enterprises, which can be ordered at http://www.curriculumguides.com/engine/cart/products.aspx?cat=1. A proud disclaimer: Schaffer is my mother.)

In college recommendations that I've written for high school juniors, I find myself discussing their writing at length. Middle school is in some ways a different beast, requiring much more interactive, kinesthetic, and tactile instruction. However, I strongly believe that students can and should write often to show their comprehension: on creative and analytical homework and in-class responses, on test essays, and on the occasional take-home formal paper. Some essays are short paragraphs, especially early in the year, but on major tests I often ask for a four-paragraph essay on a key theme, consisting of a short introduction, two meaty body paragraphs, and a short conclusion. At other times, to add variety and to tap into different students' learning strengths, I will develop an objective quiz focusing on important facts and then count a project as the major assessment for the unit.

In middle school, most students are moving from being able to simply memorize and aggregate facts to being able to hold them firmly in their hands, look at them from multiple angles, and use them for their own arguments—in other words, to analyze, synthesize, and evaluate, as the top three levels of Bloom's taxonomy read. Writing frequently in history class helps students voice their emerging ideas and gather evidence for their increasingly sophisticated reasoning skills. Through writing and speaking, students become distillers and creators of knowledge, not simply imbibers and observers.

One question I grapple with is: how much are history skills separable from writing and reading skills? On the one hand, they can be quite distinct. Students can build visual and spatial understanding of cultural trends through maps and images, background in prehistoric cultures through artifacts, or chronological awareness through dates without being a brilliant writer or reader. Both students and teachers benefit from recognizing these different ways of learning.

On the other hand, history at its core rests on descriptions of events, and students must be able to understand what they read (or hear) in order to comprehend it. We can enliven the historical record through photos, videos, artifacts, skits, and many other differentiating activities, but the past will be most authentic when students can engage with a document, even a small part of one, face-to-face. History—especially modern world and U.S. history, with its plethora of written sources—

depends on people in the future reading what people in the past have written.

Similarly, to truly get into the minds of historians, students must be able to write as historians. Writing plays a role in other school disciplines, but it does not lie at the core in other subjects as it does in history and English. In science, hands-on experimentation builds data; in math, problem solving occupies the center of instruction; and in foreign language, speaking and listening skills coexist with writing and reading proficiency. Of course, writing across the curriculum helps students understand their ideas better, but only in history and English is writing *the* discipline. As a result, I often tell my students, "I can't wait to read your essays because then I will see what you have understood and what *your* spin is on the history we have looked at." Through their writing, I can see their deepest understanding and can urge them to "explain the sources of historical continuity and how the combination of ideas and events explains the emergence of new patterns" (California State Board of Education 1998, 22).

One interesting note is that I grade differently in history than in English, a tendency that became apparent when I taught the same students in eighth-grade English and then in ninth-grade world history. In history, I focus on content and organization, whereas in English, I also pay attention to style and mechanics. When I returned to teaching English after a number of years of teaching only history, I groaned at the greater grading workload, and I was right in my apprehension. My experiences with one girl, a phenomenal English writer and a good history writer, showed how different the subjects are. Her fluid writing style was similar in both classes, but at the beginning of the year in history she was not marshaling enough facts—or the correct facts—to prove her arguments. In English she had earned As and A-pluses on most of her work. In history she was earning Bs and B-pluses at the beginning of the year and As or A-minuses by the end, as she incorporated more content to support her strong thesis statements. Without realizing it, she was at first using her strong writing skills to obscure limited knowledge. As we talked about her first few essays, she realized that her spotty historical details were not supporting the promise of her visionary topic sentences and thesis statements. "I need to study more," she said. As she did, she began including many more relevant facts, and her essays improved markedly.

In English essays, teachers tend to reward innovative ideas and interpretations of literature, of course bolstered by textual evidence. In history, we also appreciate creative approaches, but they must be supported by a broader mass of facts to feel substantial.

# Stepping Up Through Scaffolding

Writing essay questions that will encourage students to bring in their own opinions can be a long process. In all essays, I aim to keep in mind the student's personal stake in writing:

- What matters to you about this topic?
- Why might this question apply to your life someday?

- How can you take the lessons you have learned in writing this essay and bring them into the rest of your life?
- Which examples of people, places, or events in the unit have moved you? How can you incorporate them into this essay?

To differentiate instruction among writers with varying degrees of fluency, it can be useful to scaffold as much as possible. Everyone in a class benefits from outlining or brainstorming essay questions before a unit test, for instance. Sometimes I give students the essay topics a week or two before a test, especially for midterm and final exams. At other times, I like to spend part of a test-review day asking students to think of possible essay topics and write their suggestions on the board. Then I apply the Goldilocks standard: asking students to rate the topics as "too general," "too specific," or "just right." For a test about the first four Chinese dynasties, a ninth-grade world history class rated these questions as follows:

a) *Which tools did each dynasty use to make art and weapons?* Too specific, with not enough room for analysis.

b) *Describe the religious, cultural, and political practices of each of the four dynasties.* Much too general and broad; impossible to do in the time given. Students are usually glad to hear they will not have to write on everything in the chapter.

c) *What influence did religion OR art OR technology have on the four dynasties we studied?* Any of these, taken alone, would be "just right" in giving students a framework narrow enough to address the question but wide enough to show their knowledge of the unit.

Students' writing tends to be more lucid if I give them enough time to outline the essay question on the test. When I teach on the block schedule, with eighty- or ninety-minute periods, providing enough time is easier than when I teach on a more traditional schedule, with forty-five- or fifty-minute periods. For a meaty paragraph, I might allot ten to fifteen minutes to write; for an essay, up to thirty-five or forty minutes, which is not enough but gives some time to think. Before every full essay, I require three to five minutes of brainstorming for which students earn points. Such prethinking invariably improves students' essay structures, though I do walk around the classroom to ensure that students are focusing on the actual writing. For students who struggle to organize their ideas for timed writing assignments, I provide multiple opportunities during the school year to practice and improve. As they strive toward this goal, I encourage them to outline any part of the essay that they did not have enough time to finish. In addition, we talk beforehand about how long they might spend writing each paragraph, and I encourage them to write down everything they remember about the topic before they start putting words on paper.

In middle school, I would rather give credit for the ideas that students do have than take off too many points for not finishing an essay. Middle-schoolers respond especially well to praise, partly because they are figuring out their strengths and weaknesses. If I reward their ideas on one test, even if these thoughts are incompletely expressed, then on the next test they might feel confident enough to expand their arguments. By the end of the year, many students who could not finish an essay at the beginning are writing fully developed papers, and incremental progress helps them grow. Of course, we sometimes take one step forward and two steps back: a student who soars on one essay might have writer's block the next, and this unevenness is to be expected. Part of our job as middle school teachers is to know that our students are works in progress—to appreciate and challenge them for who they are right now, all the while keeping an eye out for who they might become tomorrow and next year and five years from now.

Another kind of scaffolding involves giving questions ahead of time and then spending half a period in class asking students to brainstorm topic sentences or thesis statements they later list on the board. For an ancient civilizations class in which the first test focused on Greece, I gave students the following question ahead of time. They answered the same questions on the test in a paragraph of eight to ten sentences:

---

In which ways did the Greek ideal of *arête* affect and appear in the following societies: Mycenaean, Athenian, and Spartan?  Helpful resources for the question include but are not limited to:

  a.  *Polis* reading and homework response

  b.  Athens/Sparta video notes

  c.  Tyrants chart

  d.  Pericles biography

  e.  Notes on Greek accomplishments video

  f.  "Golden Age of Greece" homework reading

  g.  Homer excerpt on Hector and Andromache

  h.  Homer excerpt on phalanxes

  i.  Persian Wars battle chart

  j.  Poem, text reading, and discussion notes on women in Greek society

  k.  Socrates in-class play

  l.  Mycenaean section of Aegean Sea chart

---

Several brave volunteers wrote the following topic sentences on the board, after I looked over their suggestions, and we discussed what was strong about each idea.

- *The Greek ideal of arête, achievement or excellence, is shown in Mycenaean, Athenian, and Spartan societies in many ways.* (Straightforward and direct, especially on a timed essay. Good job defining the term.)

- *The Greek ideal of arête was very important to the culture of Mycenaeans, Spartans, and Athenians because these societies may not have survived without it.* (Interesting take on why arête was so important to these cultures. It makes the reader want to continue.)

- *Arête appeared in the Athenians' arts, the Spartans' discipline, and the Mycenaeans' wars and battles.* (Specific and clear.)

# Five Ways of Looking at an Essay

There are many different ways to build students' writing skills in middle school history classes. I have found the following five strategies particularly effective. I use them to give students regular practice responding to essay questions or prompts, with the goal of making my expectations predictable while still throwing a little creativity into the mix.

## 1. Give Specific Directions

At the beginning of the year, I tend to use straightforward questions to help students feel comfortable and know that studying pays off. For example, a test-prep question about Chinese dynasties asked, "What influence did religion and/or philosophy have on the four dynasties we have studied? If you do a four-paragraph essay, feel free to group together the Shang and Zhou in the first body paragraph and the Qin and Han in the second body paragraph."

Michael's essay was typical of the ninth-grade world history class. His writing included some facts, but it needed stronger analysis that pulled the thesis through the paper. After this first essay, I spent two periods conferencing individually with each student while the others worked on an assignment due at the end of class. I like to touch base by talking, in addition to writing comments, because then I can listen to what the student is thinking as he or she writes. These conversations also give me a chance to reiterate the more positive comments, which can inspire students to tackle the next essay with gusto. (How many of us internalize the negative while glossing over the positive?) My comments on Michael's essay appear in brackets. I usually write much more on the first few essays; this way, students can apply extensive feedback immediately and improve right away. Later in the year, I have read enough of their work that I can write briefer comments and students still know what I mean. Through the rest of the year, Michael really pushed to make his essays longer and more involved (see Figure 5.1).

After the first essay assignment about China, so many students needed help integrating facts with analysis—always a tricky balance in a history paper—that I typed up an anonymous model essay and we discussed what made it strong: topic sentences that tied into the thesis statement, commentary on the facts, and a straightforward answer to all parts of the question. With individual

Figure 5.1

## Michael's Essay on the First Four Chinese Dynasties

In a society religion and philosophy greatly influence its people. Philosophy and religion differ from each other causing conflict, however, it is what keeps the community prosperous. During the Qin and the Han dynasties [talk about the Shang and Zhou too], religion and philosophy had both positive and negative influences on china. [what kinds?]

In the Qin Dynasty, a harsh government took power. [relate topic sentence to religion or philosophy] the rulers forced labor upon peasants, burned books, and buried scholars alive. this was influenced by legalism because it favors having a strict government in order to make a happy life among the citizens. [yes—how did this produce happiness?] In the Qin dynasty, walls were made through forced labor, the ruler took weapons away from civilians, and civilians were also taught by teachers who were approved by the government. This ruler was successful because legalism also taught civilians not to rebel against the emperor. This weakened the civilians which made them easy to control. the Qin dynasty ended shortly.

[good point re: control and good facts]

the Han dynasty rose which caused the rise of education. they favored the study of confucianism and the government was less corrupt. [Michael ran out of time and so included an outline of the rest of his ideas]

- However the rulers didn't follow confucianism
- focused on profit
- confucianism showed relationship, parent to child, ruler to subject, friend to friend, older brother to younger brother and husband and wife

Figure 5.1 (continued)

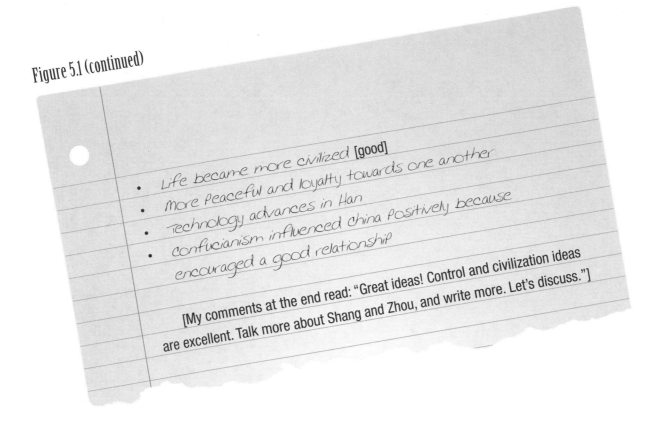

- Life became more civilized [good]
- more peaceful and loyalty towards one another
- Technology advances in Han
- Confucianism influenced china positively because encouraged a good relationship

[My comments at the end read: "Great ideas! Control and civilization ideas are excellent. Talk more about Shang and Zhou, and write more. Let's discuss."]

conferencing and this class discussion, we ended up spending two-and-a-half class periods (about 110 minutes) unpacking the first essay. This seems like a lot of time, but I find that if I don't invest in writing at the beginning, students' essays do not improve as quickly and I spend more time going back to reteach.

On a Manifest Destiny test in U.S. history, I also gave specific questions that eighth graders could choose from. Both suggested a specific time frame and certain topics. All of the terms listed were on a study sheet that I gave them two weeks before the test. Sometimes I ask students to create their own study sheets, but I often give my own so that I have the freedom to explore unusual sources without constantly fielding the question, "Will this be on the test?" I also point out that the primary sources we've gone over in detail are "free" examples because students already have a sense of the main ideas of the documents and do not have to memorize them. Figure 5.2 offers more details.

## 2. Ask for Personal Opinions

On nearly every test with a short-answer essay, I offer the chance for an individual response. After all, this is middle school, where students are nearly always glad to share what they think. In addition, a question that leads to the use of "I" can be much more interesting and revealing to read than an impersonal one. Here are two choices for a paragraph on a seventh-grade U.S. history test on the Constitution.

Figure 5.2

**Manifest Destiny Test**

**Section 2: Short Essay (40 points; 20–25 minutes)**

*CHOOSE ONE. Answer the following question clearly and concisely in about a page on a separate piece of paper. Use new paragraphs when needed to communicate new ideas. Be sure to answer the question fully and include analysis, not simply facts.*

1. There were many tensions in this period because of sectionalism. How did geographical location at this time affect people's perspectives on key issues? Pick at least two of the following (or two of your own ideas) to discuss: Jackson's presidency, the Missouri Compromise, the nullification crisis, the Mexican-American War, and Indian removal.

2. The U.S. government used a number of different strategies to deal with threats to the country during the early nineteenth century. Choose two of the following (or two major threats of your own): the nullification crisis, Indian removal, the Texas Revolution, and the Mexican-American War. For each one, briefly *explain* the strategies and *evaluate* how effective those strategies were in accomplishing the government's goals. (An example of a strategy would be using treaties to obtain land.)

a) How does the Constitution relate to your life today? Include at least four different examples. Two of these examples can come from the discussion we had on modern-day issues; the others should come from elsewhere in the Constitution.

b) Do you think the Electoral College should be abolished? Why or why not? In your response, include a brief description of what the electoral college is and why some see it as a problem.

Note that question *b* can be harder than question *a* to answer well. I often include questions that vary in difficulty so that students who are less confident can choose a "soft pitch" to hit out of the park, while students who want to impress can, like divers or gymnasts, choose a difficulty rating that makes their "routine" (essay) more interesting.

To break through the complexity of certain units, I often ask students to reflect personally on what they have learned. In a unit on ancient India, students worked in pairs while gathering background information on sacred texts such as the *Rig Veda*, *Ramayana*, and *Jaina Sutras*. With the culture of ancient India stemming so much from its divine writings, I hoped that doing a small project would make the people's emotions come alive. Students chose an excerpt from their assigned text (gathered online at the Internet Sacred Text Archive, www.sacred-texts.com) by skimming through three sections of the text and finding a segment that interested them. They created handouts containing background information, the excerpt, and an image that they then presented to their classmates, reading the excerpt aloud dramatically and asking questions about its larger meaning. Finally, students explained why the text is still relevant today.

For the essay question on the India test that followed the project, I asked students to use their notes based on classmates' excerpts to explain why the texts have lasted so long and why they are still important to people today. Answers included reflections on the importance of ritual, the need for creation myths, and the search for meaning in everyday life. In retrospect, students would have shown broader understanding by connecting all the excerpts rather than focusing so narrowly on one or another, but the ideas they wrote about were meaty. Figure 5.3 includes the essay prompts and two students' responses. Note that I gave students possible themes in the question so that they did not need to think of one under time pressure.

Indian god Ganesh

Figure 5.3

### Indian Sacred Texts Essay Question and Excerpted Responses

#### Essay Question

Write two body paragraphs (no introduction; no conclusion) about how one or two of the following terms relate to the excerpts from sacred texts that your classmates presented *and* to our lives today. Refer to at least two sacred texts in your essay, NOT including your own.

Figure 5.3 (continued)

Your topic sentences for each paragraph might take the form of: [Document] reminds us of the importance of [theme] by . . . Cite at least two phrases from the passage in your paragraph. Feel free to bring in other information if you like.

**Themes**

- Ritual
- Tradition
- Stories/myths
- Suffering
- Leadership
- The role of religion in the world
- Social norms
- An idea of your own

Following are two unedited excerpts of in-class essays, which students wrote with the presenters' handouts in front of them. Notice that Evan and Maya are beginning to connect the Indian texts' themes to their own lives.

**Excerpt from Evan's essay:**

An example of Hindu religion is the "Brahmanas." It shows us the importance of rituals and death. "from AragaPat: when relaxed . . . the vital airs departed." This shows how sacrifice connects the living and the dead. It is interesting that after the ritual, the item being sacrificed becomes a deity. It gave an importance to souls of animals that many religions don't. [I liked Evan's focus on the importance of animals and wondered what he thought the reason was for it.]

Figure 5.3 (continued)

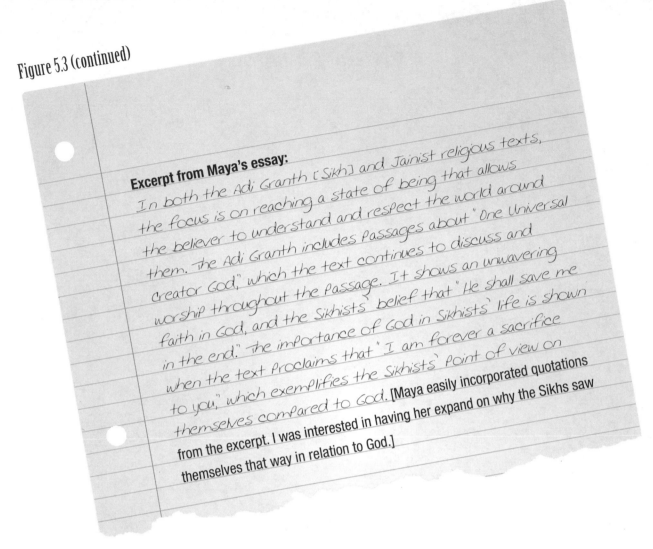

**Excerpt from Maya's essay:**

In both the Adi Granth [Sikh] and Jainist religious texts, the focus is on reaching a state of being that allows the believer to understand and respect the world around them. The Adi Granth includes passages about "One Universal Creator God," which the text continues to discuss and worship throughout the passage. It shows an unwavering faith in God, and the Sikhists' belief that "He shall save me in the end." The importance of God in Sikhists' life is shown when the text proclaims that "I am forever a sacrifice to you," which exemplifies the Sikhists' point of view on themselves compared to God. [Maya easily incorporated quotations from the excerpt. I was interested in having her expand on why the Sikhs saw themselves that way in relation to God.]

## 3. Give Students Ownership of the Question

To help students find their own perspective, I often ask them to define key terms in their own way. Figure 5.4 shows several questions that asked students to put their stamp on *transition* and *stable*. The responses varied greatly: with the Byzantine Empire question, for instance, some students saw *transition* as advancement, while others believed it meant decline. As for *stability*, some students viewed the term as positive in that it kept people safe, while others interpreted it as dangerous in that it did not allow for new opinions.

## 4. Require Students to Take a Stand

This strategy goes beyond asking students to offer their personal opinions. Instead, it encourages them to engage in historical debates that thinkers have wrestled with for decades or

Figure 5.4

## Defining Key Words

A. How was the Byzantine Empire a period of *transition*, and why was this transition(s) important? Be sure to explain what kind of transition(s) you are describing, and make sure such a transition(s) is thematically and analytically based. Include many specifics to support your broader ideas.

B. Agree, disagree, or both with the following statement: "The Middle Ages became more *stable* as the years went on." Be sure to define what you mean by *stable*. Also, make sure to use the word to refer to a variety of topics (e.g., politics, religion, and/or daily life).

C. Was the United States more *stable* by the end of the Civil War than it was in the early years of the Republic (approximately 1789–1815)? You should define *stable* at the beginning of your essay; keep in mind that it can take many different meanings, and you can choose which one works best for your purposes. Be sure to include events, people, and/or ideas from across the entire period we have studied, 1789–1865. *[This was a final exam question for the second semester of an eighth-grade U.S. history class.]*

D. Agree, disagree, or both with the following statement:  "The common person did not have much chance for a good life during the Middle Ages." In your essay, be sure to define what you mean by the term *good life* (exciting, fulfilling, rich, intellectual, protected, etc.). Here is a beginning list of items you might refer to in your response. This list is far from exhaustive—meaning that you can come up with many more ideas. Be sure to take examples from at least two or three of the readings we have done, not just one.

- The power of the church

- The feudal system

- The Crusades

- The culture of the time

- Black Death, Hundred Years' War, Papacy at Avignon, Great Schism

- Economic and social conditions of the time

- Famous battles or wars

- Monarchs' policies

centuries. As students answer questions about why a society rose and fell or why a war seemed inevitable, they can imagine themselves as chroniclers of a time long past or as political advisers to key leaders. This intimate involvement with an era requires students not only to muster facts, but also to imagine how these events affected the great questions of that time—and, often, of our time too. Here is an "old chestnut" question about the Civil War that I've asked on eighth-grade semester exams. The students became passionate about their ideas because the incidents they described were so intense and turbulent, and they analyzed the tipping points of history in the process.

A.  Looking over the period from 1789–1861, it is easy to pinpoint the conflicts that eventually led to the Civil War. But history can be astoundingly simple in hindsight. *Was* the Civil War inevitable—and if so, when did it become inevitable? Discuss important turning points in the years from 1789–1861 to prove your point. Be sure to discuss events, people, and/or ideas from across the entire period.

For a test on ancient Greece, both questions were controversial, but the second was more personal than the first. Either way, students had to consider whether Greece during its golden age was as successful as the conventional wisdom makes it out to be—a topic that, of course, can lead to discussions about whether our modern-day superpowers are as powerful as they would like to believe. While teaching AP United States history, I learned from looking at old exam questions released by the College Board that giving students a statement to agree or disagree with (or both) encourages thoughtful responses.

B.  Agree or disagree: "Greece's political, cultural, and/or military achievements outweighed its later decline."

C.  If you had been an advisor to Greece during the Dark Ages (c. 1100–c. 750 BCE), the age of colonization (750–550 BCE), and the Golden Age (c. 500–350 BCE), what would you have told its leaders to keep the same and/or to do differently to avoid its later decline? It might be helpful to organize your body paragraphs by theme.

In one contentious question about the early Americas, I was curious to see how students would weigh different factors, such as the Aztecs' sacrifices versus their astronomical achievements. Almost to a person, my students responded vigorously that the Maya, Aztec, and Inca civilizations should be greeted with near awe, even though they had some violent traditions. After I read the essays, I realized that the students had responded more glibly than I had hoped. As a result, when I returned the tests, I asked students to share a paragraph of their essays with each other and then to develop several criteria by which we can evaluate cultures. Some of their ideas included scientific accomplishments, humane treatment of citizens, diplomatic foreign policy, money for social welfare, and a powerful military. Throughout the year, I brought up some of these ideas as we studied other cultures—an effective tool because the students, not the textbook, had developed these cultural assessments.

## 5. Bring Together the Familiar in Unfamiliar Ways

Casting a new light on familiar topics often leads to essays that feel fresh and reflect the student's individual approach to learning. Options to spark students' imagination include asking them to create a metaphor for a time period; mixing terms and ideas we don't usually combine; and requiring unusual essay formats, such as haikus. Novelty primes the brain and creates neural pathways, stimulating young adolescents in their quest to understand the mystery and humor of the world around them. One question on a Middle Ages test stimulated greater engagement by making students laugh. More seriously, the assignment helped them connect the Early and Late Middle Ages by creating mental images.

*Think of an analogy, simile, or metaphor to describe the early versus the late Middle Ages. (Example: The Early Middle Ages were like an uncooked egg in the shell, while the Later Middle Ages were sometimes like scrambled eggs and sometimes like hard-boiled eggs.) Use the analogy, simile, or metaphor as your thesis statement, and use your essay to explain the comparison.*

A technique I've used in every course, from world history to U.S. history to geography and current events, is putting together key terms in thematic lists and asking students to write paragraphs connecting the terms (see Figure 5.5). These new connections give students the chance to impose their own framework on the content. As a result, they feel empowered because they, not the textbook or the teacher, decide what is most important. As a review,

Figure 5.5

### Thematic Vocabulary Essays

*Note: This set was for an eighth-grade U.S. history unit focusing on the Early Republic (1789–1815).*

Choose two of the following four lists. For each list, write a paragraph that explains how the events are related to each other thematically or otherwise. Be creative in your connections, and support your ideas with clear historical evidence. Write answers on a separate sheet of notebook paper. Good luck!

**LIST 1**
Alexander Hamilton
First National Bank of the United States
John Marshall
Hartford Convention

**LIST 2**
Thomas Jefferson
judicial review
elastic clause
Louisiana Purchase

**LIST 3**
Washington's Farewell Address
Embargo Act
impressment
War of 1812

**LIST 4**
Washington's Cabinet members
precedent
Election of 1800
"We are all Republicans, we are all Federalists."

I often ask students to make their own lists of four items, which are usually far more inventive than the ones I create.

Finally, asking for an unusual format can stimulate students' minds in new ways, giving them a right-brain spin on a left-brain series of facts. Such changeups also give students who think unconventionally a chance to shine; at the same time, unexpected essay structures challenge more linear students to think creatively, as long as we give them enough time. For a seventh-grade world history test based on Japan and China, I asked students to write a Japanese haiku about each of the Chinese dynasties, and I was astonished by how much information they fit into their more-or-less seventeen syllables. Figure 5.6 shows two examples from Sheera's test that demonstrated her multifaceted understanding of each dynasty.

# A Window into Students' Minds

Asking students to compile their ideas on paper helps us see how much they understand the content. In addition, they form new connections by constructing their own mental framework for organizing and grasping the significance of historical events. With creative approaches to analytical papers, teachers can look forward to reading students' essays because each one will offer a personal perspective. And in the process of discussing writing with our students, we can glimpse how their brains work and incorporate their individual learning styles into future lessons.

Figure 5.6

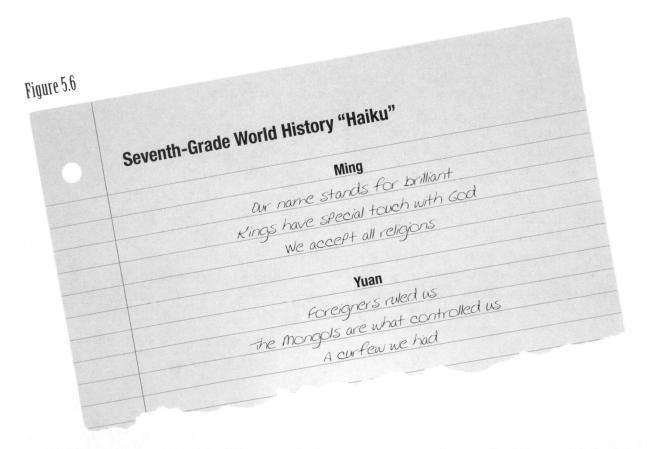

**Seventh-Grade World History "Haiku"**

**Ming**
Our name stands for brilliant
Kings have special touch with God
We accept all religions

**Yuan**
Foreigners ruled us
the mongols are what controlled us
A curfew we had

## Chapter 6

# Current Events: Connecting Past to Present

## What's Inside?

### Skills and Strategies

- Research topical issues using subscription databases
- Summarize and present news articles
- Discuss current events
- Debate political controversies
- Evaluate bias
- Write an opinion piece

### Standards

- ✔ The present versus the past
- ✔ Identity formation
- ✔ Choices and consequences
- ✔ Social institutions
- ✔ Cultural and international patterns
- ✔ Economic trends
- ✔ Public speaking

Current events can be a history teacher's ace in the hole. They create immediate relevance and help answer the questions "How does this relate to my life?" and "Why are we studying this stuff, anyway?" You don't think people pay attention to Homer anymore? Astronomers recently dissected the text of *The Odyssey* to discover the exact date when Odysseus returned home in 1178 BCE, linking a solar eclipse to one of the world's most famous epics (Maugh 2008). You're not sure whether the architectural legacy of the Anasazi still looms large in North America? People are arguing whether to drill for carbon dioxide on these Native Americans' historic lands, pitting the need for energy today and tomorrow against the preservation of sites from yesterday (Johnson 2008). Current articles prove that someone besides your teacher, your principal, and those folks who wrote your textbook actually cares about what you are studying.

We are living in a golden age of current events. Many newspapers still give away content for free on the Web, and many schools subscribe to at least one current events database, such as ProQuest Platinum Periodicals, SIRS, Newsbank, EBSCOhost, Infotrac, or Lexis-Nexis. In addition, nearly every public library provides online access to a variety of databases with a library card. When I first asked students to give current events presentations in 2000 at a Los Angeles–area school, I prepared a full-period activity on "how to read the *L.A. Times*" and even gave a quiz on the different sections of the physical paper. As much as I treasure newspapers, I now find my time is better spent with students in the library, showing them both where the librarians keep the hard copies of daily papers (those wooden dowels still hold old-fashioned allure) as well as how to navigate the best free websites and subscription databases for news. Twenty years ago, if we had asked students to bring in a recent article about China, everyone might have clipped the same piece from *National Geographic* or the local newspaper. These days, the odds are good that you will garner as many different pieces as there are students in your class, especially if you suggest that students go beyond the first set of search findings they encounter.

Beyond shedding light on contemporary problems, current events remind students that our modern-day issues are not new by any means. For as long as humans have created civilizations, we have worried about borders and resources, town squares and politics. Students can rightfully wonder why we have not solved more of these problems, and they might ask what they can do about them now and as they grow older. As consumers of today's news, our students become global citizens who can use their growing sophistication in reading and analytical thinking to draw parallels between past and present.

In this chapter, I'll discuss how we can defend spending time on current events; how to find ideas for pulling news into the curriculum bit by bit; why and how I instituted weekly current events in my classroom; and how to extend current events into two student-driven forums, a political debate and an op-ed project.

# How Can I Justify the Time?

If you and I sat down together, we could brainstorm a dozen reasons in as many minutes why young adolescents should keep up with the news. With consistent exposure to local, national, and world events, students begin to understand the mechanics of the often-imposing world around them: peacekeeping and warmongering, political allies and enemies, economic sanctions and incentives. They start to see connections between the maneuvering of today and the scheming of one thousand years ago. They gain a vocabulary, a common knowledge to draw on when they talk with well-informed adults around them: teachers, parents, siblings, aunts, and librarians. They feel empowered in their understanding, enough so that they might read articles or take action about problems they would like to solve, such as trash in the local park or education for women in Afghanistan. When these middle-schoolers turn eighteen and can choose to vote, they will know the advantages of being educated citizens.

Yet, given a list of state or national standards that seems overwhelming, how can we justify spending fifteen minutes every Friday, or five minutes here and there, on material that does not directly relate to our content—to the causes of the American Revolution or the routes of gold traders across Africa? One way is to stand firmly on a base of historical reasoning and connections. For instance, the National Center for History in the Schools (NCHS) suggests that students engage in the deepest "historical thinking" when they consider "those issues, past and present, that challenge [them] to enter knowledgeably into the historical record and to bring sound historical perspectives to bear in the analysis of a problem" (1996). If we want to investigate such tricky problems, both old and new, then we can turn to current events to see how past actions have led to our present world. The links can be as straightforward as contrasting the Athenian democracy with the United States' representative republic or as creative as comparing the city plans of ancient river-civilizations with those of today's landlocked metropolises.

Nearly every major social studies group provides strong support for current events as a pillar of the classroom by pointing out the new perspectives on historical content and skills that modern issues provide. The National Council for the Social Studies (NCSS) puts forth ten "thematic strands" that underlie that group's social studies standards, and each of them applies to current events: Culture; Time, Continuity, and Change; People, Places, and Environment; Individual Development and Identity; Individuals, Groups, and Institutions; Power, Authority, and Governance; Production, Distribution, and Consumption; Science, Technology, and Society; Global Connections; and Civic Ideals and Practices (NCSS 1994). In addition, the council supports incorporating "21st Century Skills" into history classes so that students can jump into their careers ready to tackle complex issues. Such skills include critical thinking and problem solving, media literacy, and leadership and responsibility, all fostered by studying the decisions of people in power today. (For more information, go to http://www.21stcenturyskills.org/documents/frameworkflyer_072307.pdf.) The National Geographic Society's geography standards tie in even more directly to ideas about how humans affect the earth. The subheadings, including "The Patterns and Networks of Economic Interdependence on Earth's Surface" and "How the Forces of Cooperation and Conflict Among People Influence the Division and Control of Earth's Surface" (National Geographic Society 1998–2008), evoke everyday newspaper topics such as arguments about the Kyoto Protocol and border disputes between Ethiopia and Eritrea. Finally, browsing through the history standards for most states reveals the skills that current events can address. In California, for example, historical interpretation standards for grades six through eight mention the need for students to "explain the sources of historical continuity and how the combination of ideas and events explains the emergence of new patterns" (California State Board of Education 1998, 22). Where better to find such "new patterns" than in the news of the day?

# Weaving Strands of the Past into the Present

The easiest place for teachers to find current events that relate to the curriculum is the daily newspaper. However, with the plethora of current events news services available, I often will search for links to "China" or "Ethiopia" within the past several months to find a variety of articles that might tie into the curriculum. The databases scan hundreds of newspapers and magazines at once, which means that I won't miss an important connection simply because I didn't read page A10 in last Thursday's *New York Times*.

Browsing these sites can be serendipitous. One day while I was searching for a piece that would suggest the relevance of the Maya, Aztec, and Inca cultures to today's Latin American countries, I discovered an article titled "Indigenous Americans Stake Out Identity: Descendants of Maya, Inca, Aztec Reassert Culture at Local Powwow" (Rodriguez 2003). When we read the story aloud, students realized that many people from Central and North America are interested in tracing their heritage to these ancient tribes, and ninth grader Maya said her relatives had talked about cultural rituals similar to those mentioned in the article.

Current events connections to U.S. history usually are easy to spot. For example, if the Supreme Court releases decisions or Congress debates important legislation, the tie-ins are obvious and immediate. But links to world history resources are not as obscure as you might think, especially with broad themes such as trade policy and foreign relations. One year in world history, after we had discussed the economies of medieval Africa and also looked at references to modern free trade, I brought in an article from the *New York Times* online called "Chinese Entrepreneurs Flourish in Africa Where Others Faltered" (French and Polgreen 2007); I found this article on ProQuest Platinum Periodicals by searching for "Africa economy." One person featured in the story had opened an ice cream shop in Malawi because he thought the entire country was a desert (a misconception many of my students empathized with). The accompanying photo of a Chinese man and a Malawi man working side-by-side in a Chinese restaurant in Malawi caught the students' attention. "Who would have thought of traveling to Africa to open an ice cream factory?" Peter marveled, mentally filing away this example of clever capitalism for his own life. Students had a similar surprised reaction when I brought in a newspaper article about Chinese investment in Zimbabwe's troubled economy. Both articles also related to a guiding question I had written about China's Tang, Song, and Yuan dynasties: how do governments decide how much foreign influence to allow? (See Figure 6.1 for more background on guiding questions.)

Sometimes a more analytical piece can spur meaningful discussion, helping us see commonalities in human motives and reactions throughout history. For a lesson about the Peloponnesian War

Figure 6.1

## Guiding Questions for Current Events Discussions

For each unit we study, I usually create a dozen guiding questions ranging from the specific (How did geography affect the development of Islam?) to the more general (What are the pros and cons of theocracy?). To create the questions, I go through the textbook chapter and pick out important ideas and themes; I also consult the standards to see which concepts I might have missed. On the first day of each unit, I hand out a sheet listing the key themes that will frame our studies. When I look for current events connections, I try to find articles that address these questions.

Unfortunately, it took close to a decade of teaching for me to figure out the benefits of this approach. I knew that such guidance would be helpful to students, but I didn't have confidence in my ability to hit all the major themes before I had taught them several times. Later I realized that my guiding questions don't have to be perfectly aligned with the curriculum or the particular unit. They can still serve as navigational tools for students, a way to send them up in an airplane to provide an aerial view of the textbook. In addition, students are rarely surprised by tests because the essay prompts emerge from themes in the questions.

during a unit on ancient Greece, I found a fascinating article from the *Los Angeles Times* called "Battles Change, Wars Don't" (Hanson 2005) by looking up the war's name in a current events database. The article's subhead hinted at the comparison that author Victor Davis Hanson would be making: "From ancient Greece to modern Iraq, history shows us that fear, honor and self-interest drive hostilities between the states." Within the article, Hanson insists that human nature has not changed over the years, meaning that war has not evolved very much. My students read the piece aloud in a round-robin fashion, and I asked them to underline six to eight especially "interesting or startling insights" as they read so they would pay attention throughout. Afterward, they took three to five minutes to write what was most fascinating or relevant about the article *or* whether they agreed with the author. This piece included so many shocking statements, such as the following sentences, that the students did not lack for commentary afterward.

"We recoiled in horror last September when Chechen terrorists stormed a school in Beslan and more than 150 children were killed in a bloody shootout," Hanson writes. "But in 413 BC, the Athenians unleashed their Thracian mercenaries on the tiny Boeotian town of Mycalessus." During our class conversation, Caroline wondered why Athens held a reputation for nobility when its citizens committed such an atrocity, and Megan thought that such events might have led to the society's moral decline. We recalled the term *hubris,* or overweening arrogance, from an earlier class and thought it aptly described how the Athenians might have felt as one of the two great powers in the Mediterranean world. Jesse found a simile that made the article memorable for him: "War is like water—its fundamental character remains unchanging precisely because the nature of the humans who fight it is constant over the centuries." This thoughtful essay, dressed up as a newspaper column, led to a discussion about guiding questions, including: Was it inevitable that Athens would decline? If so, at what point did it become inevitable (no right answer)?

Not every current event has to be textual. For an American history unit just before the 2003 Iraq War began, we looked at cartoons about the national bank from Andrew Jackson's 1832 re-election campaign, and the students marveled at the complexity of the images, with so many voice bubbles and characters. Then we compared these cartoons to the latest, simpler drawings from current newspapers. One 2003 cartoon by Pulitzer Prize–winning artist Michael Ramirez, for example, showed three "looters"—France, Germany, and Russia—tiptoeing into the Iraq Ministry of Reconstruction. People have less time to read the newspaper today, Billy said, and maybe that's why today's political drawings are meant to be understood in split seconds. Or maybe we are a savvier society and do not need such detail to get the gist of events, Jessica suggested. Connecting the fast pace of our culture with the often truncated way we view politics encourages students to think about what *they* care about in today's world—what they would like to see more of in the news, in TV news, or online. These young consumers were well aware of the media's influence on content, another current events skill we hope to reinforce. Figure 6.2 suggests other ideas for making engaging current events connections.

Figure 6.2

### How to Choose "Wow" Current Events Articles

Keeping in mind the young adolescent's need for novelty, fun, surprise, and suspense, we can search for:

- **Articles that raise big ideas:** For a seventh-grade geography class, I brought in an article, "Leaving the Wild, and Rather Liking the Change" (Forero 2006), which described the members of a group called the Nukak in Colombia who had lived in the forest for centuries but now decided they wanted to enter the world of commerce and urbanism. "Why would you want to leave an existence you've known forever? What would they gain from joining our world?" asked Savannah. The ensuing discussion, in which Charlie said that he'd rather go back to the jungle than deal with homework, and Alex said she'd be afraid that people would take advantage of her, added depth to the students' knowledge of world cultures.

- **The "gee whiz" factor:** "I didn't know that Istanbul's subway lines run through ancient ruins. How is that possible?" said one student after reading a *New York Times* article on the topic (Landler 2005). Immediately fascinated by this quirky

Figure 6.2 (continued)

archaeological connection, students could literally see the layers of history revealed as they reflected on how a newer city was able to overtake an old one.

- **Relevance to students' lives:** For a U.S. history class about the branches of government, I brought in an article that described "American Candidate," a proposed television show that would vet prospective candidates to run for the presidency (Poniewozik 2002). Anything that relates academics to modern media has the potential to energize students who are tethered to technology and tuned in to their own emotions.

- **Statistical tables:** Numbers can tell stories, especially for mathematically inclined students, in ways that words cannot. After we discuss the Electoral College in U.S. history, I bring in a table that lists each state, its population, and its number of House representatives. When I ask students to mark the states with the most and fewest representatives, students nearly guffaw when they see the difference between, say, Texas and South Dakota. "I'm glad I live in California," Tom says. "But what if you lived in Kansas? How would you feel about being represented in the political process?" I ask. "Lousy," he replies, and we continue with a discussion about the fairness of the Great Compromise at the Constitutional Convention.

- **Music and other audio files:** One topical U.S. history clip is National Public Radio's annual reading of the Declaration of Independence, in which news correspondents read different sentences and paragraphs in stentorian tones (to find the latest version, go to www.npr.org and search for "Declaration of Independence"). Music is another important draw. Popular songs often contain political and historical references, such as Buffy Sainte Marie's "Bury My Heart at Wounded Knee" (a song that I note is very liberal). When I play the Indigo Girls' version of this song at the end of a unit about American Indians in the late nineteenth century, students are surprised by the anger these women can muster over a massacre more than a century old, combined with what the songwriter sees as more modern atrocities by the government. A musical interlude that conveys vast geographic and cultural reach comes from cellist Yo-Yo Ma's Silk Road Project: *Silk Road Journeys: When Strangers Meet* (www.silkroadproject.org). The Silk Road Ensemble plays music from areas along the original trading routes, with song titles such as "Mido Mountain (Traditional Chinese)" and "Blue as the Turquoise Night of Neyshabur." While students listen, I ask them to write down what the songs make them think of—"a crowded bazaar at night" or "children running up mountains." In addition to showing students that people still care about the communities we have been studying along the Silk Road, the folksongs from different cultures help them imagine what traders and common people held dear long ago.

# Priming the Pump: Understanding What Students Know

In the history classroom, current events provide an inviting forum for improving reading comprehension skills because newspaper and magazine articles are often high interest and are written at a middle school vocabulary level. Early in the school year, I prompt a discussion that will give me a sense of my students' reading skills and range of interests. First, I ask students to jot down for homework which newspapers or news sources they read. For many or most students, I know the answer will be a list of entertainment or sports publications, which is a fine start. After all, how many adult newspaper readers picked up the habit by checking morning box scores? Other students list local TV news or Comedy Central's *The Colbert Report* and *The Daily Show*. For some students, the answer to what they read will be "nothing." If I sense that a majority of the class will say they don't follow the news much at all—as is the case with more than a quarter of teens ages twelve to seventeen ("Survey" 2007)—I will also ask them to poll a parent or another adult about his or her news choices.

When students bring in this "news survey" the next day, I ask them to pair and share: first read what they wrote to a partner, and then join a full-class discussion about their responses. This ten-minute discussion is a fairly nonthreatening activity for the beginning of the year, largely because most students don't keep up with the news. They are relieved to discover that they have company. I like to hear from as many kids as possible, and I poll students frequently that day to keep them involved. If one girl says she reads the sports pages in the morning with her dad, I ask everyone who reads the sports section to raise their hands. Then I ask which other sports news sources they follow. We move on similarly to entertainment, TV news, and finally newspapers. Even at the private school where I teach, only a handful of students in each class track print or online newspapers regularly, and only half to two-thirds have newspapers delivered to their homes daily. As a result, when the rare avid news followers share what they look at in a typical day—perhaps the local paper, a few stories from the *New York Times* online, and the headlines on Yahoo! News—the other students look at each other, aghast: "How do you have time to *do* all that?"

At this point, we have arrived at the real purpose of the discussion: encouraging students to consider why they might want to know about current affairs. I ask them to write for two minutes in response to "Why is it important for you to keep up with the news or to know what's going on in the world?" We make a list of reasons to put on the board: to be aware, to not look stupid, to be informed citizens, to know how to vote when I get older. I also entertain the reasons not to keep up with the news that students invariably put forth: we have too much homework and too many other activities, we can't vote yet, politics doesn't matter in our lives, we can't understand news stories anyway because we don't follow them every day.

"All of these complaints have merit," I say, "given the many legitimate pulls on your time. But, by the end of the year, I hope you will have changed your minds."

In addition, I'll often ask students to imagine themselves as historians of current events from the outset, picking headlines that they think will appear in history books in the future and explaining why. Such sorting helps them see why we include certain events in history books at the expense of others. In September 2002, for example, eighth grader Sophie chose "Bush Names Hussein Public Enemy No. 1" and commented, "America's new focus on terrorism is in Iraq. It happens to be the political head figure. Hussein leads his country by force. He is a terrorist and has his country believing in him and what he does." Her focus on an article about Hussein's intransigence foreshadowed the war that would begin the next year. When Sophie and other students shared their reflections, we wondered why the difficult topics, such as disease and violence, linger in textbooks and on the daily news. Are humans just most interested in gore and drama, or are the daily details of life just less compelling? We continue this conversation with historical and current discussions throughout the year.

# Current Events Fridays

Weekly current events presentations are my one nonnegotiable part of the middle school history curriculum because of the skills they teach, the broad themes they elicit, and the enthusiasm for past and current issues they generate. In fact, during one year when I taught only English and not history, I racked my brain to think of a way I could incorporate weekly current events into a literature-based curriculum. Unfortunately, I couldn't rationalize the time, and I missed this activity all year long.

Here's a taste of the scene:

It's Friday afternoon, seventh period. My middle-schoolers flop into the room, many of them sweaty after sixth-period PE. They begin to slouch into their seats, bracing for one last class until the freedom of the weekend—but then someone remembers it's Current Events Friday. Many regain a faint gleam in their eyes as they pull out their notes and watch several classmates write the week's headlines on the board in enormous red or blue letters.

I wish I could take credit for their sudden attention but, in fact, it is their peers' upcoming presentations that excite them. In the next fifteen to twenty minutes, two or three of their classmates will each deliver a summary of a recent news article, explain why he or she chose it, and field questions from the audience. The Q&A session is the real meat of the activity. For an article about recent violence in Myanmar, the students in the audience might start with tentative factual questions asking their classmate where the country is located and what actions its government and the international community have taken (if any) to contain the terror. Within a few minutes, however, the conversation might leap to "Why did Burma's name change?" and "Why do people have to fight so much over religion?" From here we sometimes can connect the article with whatever we have been studying in history, whether it is the border decisions in the Treaty of Guadalupe Hidalgo after the Mexican-American War or the unexpected conversion of Emperor Ashoka to Buddhism in ancient India. The present informs the past.

Today, we have a variety of local, national, and international stories. Brianna starts off by presenting a piece about water rights for a local reservoir that reported low levels this year because of drought. In her presentation she defines *acre-foot* and points to the reservoir's location on a city map. After she finishes and the students have taken a quiet minute to write down a question or comment, Matt asks where our drinking water comes from. "Let me see if it's in the article," Brianna says. It's not, and I tell her that's fine, stepping in to explain the complicated water politics of our state. "What happens if we run out of water?" one student asks, and we're on our way. In the discussion, we might refer to the role of bodies of water through the history we've studied, from the Mediterranean Sea as a conduit of goods and ideas to the St. Lawrence River as a passageway for explorers and soldiers.

Adrian is next, focusing on an article about a recall of toys made in China. Several students with young siblings write themselves a note on their homework planners (or, more likely, their hands—these *are* eighth graders) to check if they have any of the toys at home. After Adrian shows us where China is on the world map, Lee asks, "Why do we get so much stuff from China?" Adrian gives a solid answer that explains why goods are cheaper because of lower wages paid. After he finishes answering questions, I write "trade gap" on the board and ask students to think about what that phrase might mean. I also mention China's history of human rights violations and ask whether we should still do business with this Eastern economic powerhouse. On a day when we have time, this story could lead to a ten-minute discussion that includes complex ideas such as sanctions, most-favored-nation trading status, and business ethics. We could also compare these current topics with the economies of the past, from Gilded Age robber barons to Italian city-states.

Kylee completes the day's presentations with a piece about a presidential nominee to the Supreme Court, a topic we have not yet covered in this U.S. history class. The questions students ask crack open the door: How do you become a Supreme Court justice? Why does a position open up? Why aren't there limits on how long a justice can serve? Who has to approve the nomination? Kylee can answer some of these questions from her article, and I offer additional information when details become thorny. Most of the students will not remember the specifics of this discussion when we encounter Article III of the Constitution, but many of them will remember the curiosity that Kylee's enthusiasm fostered. They also will realize that our current president's nominations to the Supreme Court must be approved the same way as Washington or Adams's picks, showing continuity under the Constitution.

How did I become such a passionate advocate of weekly current events activities? During my first three years of teaching, I taught the same seventh graders for English and world history. Every once in a while I asked them to fill out a worksheet about a news article, asking for the headline, author, date, publication, and a brief summary. Current events were a sideline rather than a highlight of the course. When I was assigned to teach eighth-grade U.S. history, it seemed impossible not to incorporate current events. In a class that includes intensive study of the Constitution, I thought it would be an egregious omission to ignore the Cabinet discussions, Supreme Court decisions, and Congressional debates that were occurring right here, right now.

When I rolled out the assignment, a Current Events Friday weekly presentation, several elements worked well. The students felt ownership of the process, calling on their classmates to ask questions and often telling me with excitement about the article they had chosen for that week. They were keeping up with the news slightly more often, if only to know the name of the mayor of Los Angeles or the city where the Republican National Convention would take place. Their speaking skills were improving slowly, very slowly in some cases, as they looked at the two-part rubric—with sections for written and oral evaluation—and strived for eye contact, reasonable volume, voice modulation, and steady speed.

By the end of that first year, though, after sitting through too many painful or irrelevant presentations, I saw that I needed to improve several parts of the assignment, especially the stories students were choosing. Too many articles took the form of "145 Die in Flood" or "22 Killed in Mortar Attacks." These articles covered crucial national and world issues, but they were disheartening and narrow. By the end of some classes, I felt like I wanted to jump into a hole to avoid the misery of the human condition and wouldn't have blamed my students if they decided to join me. One extroverted seventh grader, Molly, kept telling me each Friday how depressing my class was. The next year I included a provision in the directions to "avoid stories that solely describe acts of violence; any violent acts should be in the context of a larger story or issue," and the selection of articles has been much broader since that time.

On the other end of the spectrum, I was sitting through too many presentations about lost kittens and local flower festivals, certainly important to local communities but not widely applicable to course content. I still remember Brianna's elegantly paraphrased story from the *New York Times* online about the proliferation of cupcake shops in Manhattan. (We were all hungry after that one.) I had told students that the *Times* set a journalistic standard for the country, so I couldn't blame her for picking the piece, but cupcakes were a little fluffy. However, I did not want to issue a blanket statement that students had to find "hard news" or avoid local newspapers. Often we found out personal connections from such pieces—that Cristian's aunt raised orchids, for instance, or that Rachel's sister had heroically pulled a toddler from the deep end of a pool. Thus, when I gave the directions at the beginning of the year, I asked students to check with me if they wanted to make sure that a story was important or interesting enough to be a strong contender. This informal process seemed to help. Similarly, I told students that if they couldn't find enough information in the article to create a 150-word summary in their own words, the article probably wasn't long enough. I also suggested that students did not need to read the entire article if it stretched across many pages. This provision helped with those who looked for the shortest piece in the paper.

Depending on whether the class is world geography, world history, or U.S. history, I sometimes require the current events contributions to be international or national in scope. However, it is equally interesting to keep students' options open: developing the confidence and competence to discuss topics ranging from city council issues to the latest United Nations negotiations can enrich their understanding of the world. Students often raise a hue and cry about the prohibition on sports and entertainment stories. My stock response is, "I know you'll follow them anyway, and I want you to expand your horizons."

## Directing the Discussions

To some extent, the intensity of a current events discussion depends on the class, but the relevance to the curriculum depends on the teacher. The first two years I taught eighth-grade U.S. history, I had to keep a constant eye out for verbal fisticuffs between Sophie and Alex or Austin and Danny over politics. The classes erupted with energy, possibly because they were late in the day on Friday. Such groups of students simply run themselves and require me only to rope them in so we can cover something else today, please! Most classes need more urging. To help students along, I ask them to take notes and spend a minute writing down a meaningful question or comment about the speaker's presentation after he or she finishes. This way, if no one in the class is raising his or her hand, I can call on students and know they will have at least one comment or question to put forth. If a story is complicated, perhaps about global economic policy or local legislative wrangling, many of the questions will be factual. Sometimes students bring themselves into the story through their comments, writing that they identify with a piece about cancer treatments because an uncle is battling prostate cancer, or that they recently visited an ecological preserve whose cleanup the speaker has highlighted. At other times students will ask deeper questions about political beliefs or leaders' motivations, smoothly leading into discussions about our historical guiding questions.

Current events discussions also figure in to a 5 to 10 percent participation grade I give each quarter. I know that, in our society filled with "choose your own news" from a variety of opinionated channels—cable TV, talk radio, and websites—cordial discussion about politics and current issues is unusual, and many students do not hear their parents or other adults model it for them. Thus, I see the presentations as an ongoing process of making students comfortable disagreeing with each other in a respectful way.

Toward the end of many presentations, I may step in for one of several reasons. First, the discussion might be veering toward absurdity in the level of detail of the factual questions. These are inquisitive and sometimes very literal middle-schoolers, after all. When I hear a student ask, "What do you think the president ate on the plane on his way to visit with the prime minister?" for a story about an international trade summit, it might be time to limit discussion to just one or two more comments.

Second, the conversation might be taking on so many layers that the presenter cannot answer further questions, no matter how well he or she knows the article. Many national and international stories assume extensive background that may not be immediately apparent. For instance, a piece about campaign spending limits might elliptically mention the McCain-Feingold campaign finance act without explaining what it is, or a story about nonprofit finances might mention the Sarbanes-Oxley Act and assume that readers remember it. Our middle school students may personally remember cataclysmic or headline-catching events from the past decade, such as 9/11 or a close presidential election, but even then most will not know the details. (I still remember feeling knowledgeable for recognizing the names "Ollie North," "Sandinistas," and "Iran-Contra" in middle school, yet at the same time having no idea what they meant.) As teachers we can extend the history books for our students, so that the next time they see a reference to the Balkan Peninsula or the Bush-Gore election of 2000, they will understand the context.

Finally, the discussion might be so controversial that it is not fair even to a poised presenter to expect him or her to continue to call on people fairly and maintain order. This scenario has occurred in election years with political stories and at other times with pieces about class or race. At this point, depending on the flow of the class, I either tell students we will set aside a few minutes the next week to write about the topic and discuss it further, or I open the floor to everyone and begin making a list of points for both sides on the board.

Here are two more tips to help manage current events discussions:

- Before the bell rings signaling the start of class, I look over the shoulder of that day's presenters to see which stories they have chosen. I estimate which story we might spend the most time on to ensure that each student gets ample "floor time" to do justice to his or her topic.

- I create a time-flexible activity for the minutes remaining after current events discussions. Especially when teaching multiple sections of the same class, I do not want to have to cut off discussion in seventh period simply because we had short conversations in second period. Useful activities for this purpose include those that can sponge up different amounts of time, such as annotating or acting out one or more primary sources on a topic we have been studying (a longer activity), or reviewing or previewing an element of last night's or tonight's homework through words or drawings (a shorter activity).

## Poised at the Podium

One other skill that I am always trying to develop is public speaking. I try to find time in class for a ten-minute refresher activity on a day when students have been working hard and need a mental break. After I ask students to take everything out of their hands and just watch me talk, I stand up with a few paragraphs of a newspaper article in my hands and begin reading poorly: no eye contact, slouched posture, rushed speech, body turned toward one corner of the room, volume dropping off inaudibly at the ends of sentences, voice remaining in a monotone, a singsongy "up-and-down" delivery, an apology before or after about how bad my presentation was and how I'm sorry I even had to give it. When I ask students to identify what was ineffective about the presentation, nearly every hand shoots up, eager to skewer my performance. Once we have listed all the "do nots" on the board and students have written them down, I read the same piece with eye contact, strong volume, and confident body language. We list more tips that they can glean from this version, and I ask them which presentation they would rather listen to. Of course the answer is obvious, but I remind them that it is a lot easier to critique someone than to stand up by yourself in front of the class.

After this modeling, I hand out a sheet of public speaking tips for current events. Many are straightforward suggestions that can apply to any speech, but some are particularly relevant to current events and to middle-schoolers:

- "Make sure you can pronounce names of people and cities. If you're not sure of the pronunciation, either ask someone beforehand or just do your best. Say difficult names with confidence." It can be distracting to hear the name "Ahmadinejad" pronounced five different ways within a minute. Often students whisper to me on their way up to speak, asking about the pronunciation of a difficult name. If it's obscure enough that I don't know, I tell them I'm giving it my best guess.

- "Speak slowly—far more slowly than you think you have to. Remember, if it sounds slow to you, it's probably perfect, or even a little too fast. Speaking too quickly makes your audience either strain to listen or tune out." Many students do not earn full points for slow speed for their first couple of current events. As the year goes on, the presentations become more comprehensible. If I cannot understand a student at the beginning of a presentation, I will ask him or her to take a deep breath and start again, with no loss of points.

- "Emphasize certain words in sentences. Doing this encourages comfortable pauses and helps your audience hear what's important." Based on this suggestion, students sometimes mark words they want to focus on in each sentence.

- "Most of all, do your best to enjoy yourself—or at least look like you are. 'Act as if' is a good phrase to remember. A confident attitude makes the audience feel comfortable and allows listeners to understand more of what you are saying." If we feel that the speaker is comfortable, I remind students, we will feel comfortable listening to him or her.

One of the most encouraging elements of current events presentations is that students have four chances during the year, once per quarter, to present and then improve on their previous performance. Letting middle school students know that they can practice and get better as the year progresses sends the message that we are rooting for them as learners. Through weekly current events, they not only become better speakers and readers, but they also create a modern platform from which to view historical issues.

# Elephant or Donkey? A Political Debate Based on Party Platforms

Current events are natural fodder for debates because students can see how the topics affect their lives, weighing pros and cons to see where their opinions fall on the political spectrum. But for a long time, conducting debates in class intimidated me. I'm fine with the occasional, informal back-and-forth at the end of class about whether the U.S. should have participated in the Spanish-American War or whether Confucius's ideas were more about order or harmony. But orchestrating a full-on debate involving every member of the class—ensuring that everyone participates appropriately and understands often-difficult material—seemed daunting.

Each year that I've taught U.S. history, though, students keep seeing the words *Republican* and *Democrat* and want to know what they mean. Their curiosity points to a desire for categorical understanding: How do the labels relate to the similar party titles of the nineteenth century? What does it mean that Jefferson formed the Democratic-Republican Party or that Lincoln was a Republican? One year, I briefly fielded a question about modern political parties when I was teaching four seventh-grade U.S history classes at a charter school, where students included the "doubly gifted" (academically gifted and also learning disabled) and English language learners. I decided that I wanted to see what my students could glean from looking at the political parties with their own eyes. Although I had initial doubts about readability, I decided to use short excerpts from state and national party platforms as sources. Another possibility I considered was trying to generalize from the voting records of several Democrats and Republicans in categories such as the environment, crime, and taxes. With the platforms, however, I thought that I could keep the assignment relatively simple by picking straightforward sections, and I could also build media literacy by showing students that both parties try to make themselves sound good in their own documents. (I did get questions from a few students about why I hadn't included any third parties. I said it was too complicated given the time we had, but we did look at a short list of more than a half-dozen third parties and their philosophies.)

## Targeting the Topic

Where to start? First, I skimmed through the national platforms and our state's platforms for both parties. Although these documents might seem time dependent, forcing teachers to change the excerpts for future classes, they are in fact general enough that you can use much of their language for years to come. Among the many topics, I picked ones I thought would appeal personally to my students while relating to common concerns throughout history: national security, education, criminal justice, the environment, the economy, immigration, and health care. Many other topics, such as veterans and families, would also be relevant for many populations of learners, making it easy to tailor the choices to the students you have and to the curricular themes you have covered. The day before I assigned the subject areas, I asked any students who wanted a particular topic to write me a note or talk to me after class, and a few did. From each platform topic I chose four to six paragraphs, defining difficult words in brackets within the text: *proliferation* as expansion, for instance, and *arms* as weapons.

As I introduced the platforms to my students, I explained that they would have a full block period of eighty minutes to make sure they really understood their platform excerpt before writing opening statements or preparing for the actual debate.

"You also will notice that, for some issues, the Democratic and Republican parties feel the same way," I said to one group. "I'll come around to talk about how they differ, even if their differences are not explicitly spelled out in the text. Why do you think both parties might not want to write down all the details of everything they believe?" I asked. A number of students, far savvier about spin than I ever was at their age, raised their hands.

"Because they want everyone to be on their side," Paul said.

"If they don't write something down, they don't have to be responsible for it," said Jessica.

"Good points, Paul and Jessica, and cynical too," I said, smiling. "Your job, and everyone else's, will be to try to figure out the strengths and weaknesses of the parties' arguments." While unpacking the political platforms, students would be treating them as primary documents from our own time, looking to ethical connections, emotional appeal, and logical structure to understand their content. (For more about Aristotle's rhetorical triangle, see Chapter 3.)

I placed students into groups of four to six, depending on the complexity of the topic, one group for each topic. Four members seemed to work best because each group member had more of a stake in the process. Importantly, I did not assign Republican and Democratic sides but left that to the students to choose once they had done their research. For example, in one group of four focusing on national security, Eric and Matt decided they wanted to argue the Republican side and Zach and Adam decided they wanted to argue the Democratic side. If no one in a group wanted to be on one side, they flipped a coin or decided in some other fair way which members would do what. I emphasized that, in a debate, the participants often learn more by backing up a position that they do not believe in.

Before the groups read both the Republican and Democratic platforms on their particular topic, I knew I wanted them to focus on the forest rather than the trees, so I suggested steps that would help them see the big picture. First we skimmed the passages together, taking only one or two minutes to do so. I asked students to go through this process twice, looking for key words, and to write down one or two each time.

"Economy!" cried Alejandra.

"Students with disabilities," said Matt.

"Nuclear weapons," said Carter.

This quick skim gave even the students whose first language was not English a way into the text. They found more entry points with the second direction: "Find key nouns, at least one per paragraph and eight total, that seem important to your platform." Various groups found terms such as *handgun control*, *public schools*, and *environmental protection*. Then I asked them to write down briefly what the party wants to do about half of the key terms and to rank how controversial they think each proposal is on a scale of 1 to 10. Some topics, such as encouraging parental involvement in students' education, were uncontroversial, while others, such as drilling for oil in Alaska's National Wildlife Refuge, were inflammatory.

To prepare for the actual debate, the students next brainstormed two adjectives describing the tone of each party's proposals and listed similarities and differences between the two sets of ideas. While they were doing this, I was constantly walking around, defining words and answering questions. For most groups, this process took at least one eighty-minute period and part of the next. The time commitment seemed worth it because students were grappling with important current and historical ideas about issues that never go away: the role of the government in people's lives, the need to both use and protect natural resources, and the relationships among nations. That year, when we studied Franklin Delano Roosevelt's involvement in social policy in the 1930s, John Muir's desire to create national parks in the late nineteenth century, and Lucretia Mott's trip to the World Anti-Slavery Convention in London in 1840, students would be able to relate current to past issues.

Although it was probably overkill, the next day I also asked students to list three to five ideas from their platform that they had not yet analyzed and to write ten to twenty words about each topic. I wanted to make sure that each group really understood its platform and could speak well about it. For homework students had to:

1. Print or clip at least one newspaper, website, or magazine article that relates to your debate topic (topics will be handed out today). The topics are broad enough (environment, taxes, etc.) that you should be able to find something fairly quickly in a recent newspaper. Head to the library if you need more resources.

2. List at least four interesting facts from your article *in your own words* that you might be able to use in your debate.

Bonus marchers at U.S. Capitol, 1932

After all of this in-class and out-of-class preparation, most students could decide which group members would argue which position and begin writing their opening statements with partners or groups of three. They were by no means experts; nor was I. We continued asking questions and wondering exactly what the parties meant by some of their statements throughout the entire debate process. But throughout, we were grappling with major challenges of our time and times past.

## Strong and Concise Opening Statements

I wanted the opening statements to be short, thirty to sixty seconds, so students would listen to all of the presentations and keep their own arguments concise. Figure 6.3 includes the requirements.

### Figure 6.3

**Preparing an Opening Statement**

- 200–250 words (approximately one handwritten page, single-spaced).

- Teaches and explains as well as persuades.

- Includes three to four *main* ideas with the reasons your side believes them.

- Starts off with a "grabber."

- You are now the class experts on your platform. Be creative and persuasive, and enjoy!

- Both or all three of you should work on the opening statement together, and you should divide the speaking parts roughly equally among your group members.

Having students write the opening statements together worked well. Both partners needed to have their notes based on the platforms as well as the articles they had found, and I encouraged them to mark the facts they might use when presenting their arguments.

The last task for each group was to make a name card for their team. Often, while one partner was finessing or rewriting the opening statement, the other was working on a name card (a piece of printer paper folded the long way, in a vertical "hot dog" fold) with the topic, party, and symbol. This visual representation of their ideas gave students more ownership of their position and helped us keep the sides straight during the actual debate.

On a modified block schedule, most groups needed approximately one block period or two regular periods to completely finish the opening statement. If students finished early, I asked them to start brainstorming arguments that the other side might make against their statement. As students were working or when they had finished, I glanced at all of the statements to make sure that the speeches had enough "meat" in them. By this point, students were well versed in their topics, even those whose reading comprehension skills weren't as strong, because they had considered the platform from so many different angles. The stronger readers found more difficult articles relating to their platforms, and many also talked to their parents about the information.

So far, so good. I had controlled as much of the process as I possibly could by asking students to skim the platforms twice, look for key words, explain the parties' positions on half the key words, list ideas they had not yet talked about, find articles relating to their platform, write an opening statement, and make a name card. I could have done even more to steep students in the subject, such as asking them to research what one of their representatives had said about or voted on the topic, but at this point I felt we'd spent enough time on these tasks. I was also curious to see what the students could do in the debate without further research. Now it was time to take control out of my hands and give it to the students. Figure 6.4 shows how I structured the debate to give students freedom while still maintaining order.

I like this relatively loose structure, as compared with more formal debates, because it allows everyone to participate in real time and not have to wait forever to get into the game. It rewards enthusiasm over expertise, tying into a course goal: to get students curious about the parties and expose them to themes that will appear in our historical study. I had structured the format so loosely, in fact, that on the day of the debate, when Jenny asked me what the exact debate topic was, I realized I hadn't created one. I quickly made up a generic question: "Which party is best equipped to lead the United States in the twenty-first century?" As I moderated, I checked off who was participating, and I made the rubric as simple as possible to reward risk taking and participation (see Figure 6.5).

Nearly everyone got full credit for the discussion, except for one or two students who did not write down comments or questions. Before the debate next time, I plan to spend more time discussing what constitutes civil behavior, both to educate students and to avoid hurt feelings. In the process, I will emphasize that disagreement does not mean dislike or anger and that debate should not be personal, despite what students might see or hear on television and radio talk shows. Figure 6.6 includes other ideas for expanding this process.

Figure 6.4

## Debate Structure

1. Each team gives its opening statements about the same topic, such as immigration. Students take notes, writing at least two or three major bullet points per statement. After each opening statement, ask the class for two or more factual questions to clarify students' ideas, a necessary process because so many ideas are confusing. You can give students charts for note taking (the issue at the top, with one column each for the Republican and Democratic perspectives) to help them organize their thoughts and make them feel more official. It's not necessary to collect the notes, but you can walk around the next day and give students credit for completing them. Students can add to the notes throughout the debate as other people speak.

2. After all the teams give their opening statements, students can take a break to discuss what people said, writing down at least two questions or comments that they have for one or two of the groups.

3. After five minutes, we come back together. Tell students that anyone can put forth an argument or comment on any topic, encouraging a back-and-forth dialogue. Set a goal for everyone to participate two or three times during the discussion. You might institute a thirty-second time limit for comments so that everyone can be heard frequently. If a student says something that a team wants to respond to, the team can do so immediately.

Figure 6.5

## Political Parties Debate Rubric

Name: _____

- Opening Statement (10)

    Delivered clearly: eye contact, volume, slow speed

    Covers 3–4 major points clearly: explains and persuades

    Has a relevant and interesting "grabber"

- Participation Overall (20)

    Student participates throughout the debate

    Points are relevant and on-topic

    Uses research and notes to make strong comments

    Listens to and is respectful of other speakers

Figure 6.6

## Debate Extension Activities

- **Writing:** Informal or formal written response to any or all of these questions: What did you learn about politics? Do you have a party preference? Why or why not? How did your worldview expand based on the debate? Which issues you do think are most important, and why?

- **Graphic representation:** Make a scorecard that rates the importance of each issue to your life, on a scale of 1 to 10. Write briefly why you gave each issue the score you did.

- **Current research:** Look up a state legislator or congressional representative and research what he or she has done to influence an issue that you care about.

- **Media:** Watch a recent or older presidential debate, and take notes on both the candidates' style of presentation and their positions on the issues you have studied.

- **Advocacy:** Write a letter to your congressional representative that gives your opinion on a bill relating to one of the issues you have studied.

# Making Your Voice Heard: Writing an Op-Ed Piece

A final current events project that taps into global themes and teaches organization of ideas is essentially a debate on paper: writing an opinion piece that could appear in a newspaper and then creating a "letter to the editor" about any classmate's op-ed. Compared to many analytical assignments, in which students learn from writing down their ideas but do not necessarily enjoy the process, my ninth-grade world history students said afterward that they actually had fun writing these pieces. Why? They could model themselves after real-world columnists, pick their topics, and, most importantly, use a more conversational voice and informal organization. I added the letters to the editor so that students could read each other's writing and think about how they agreed and disagreed with their classmates' ideas. Writing and then reading aloud the letters made a week before winter break something more than simply a long slog toward vacation.

I created this project one December after a semester in which we had completed five intensive units: two on ancient China, one on India, one on Africa, and one on Mesoamerica. Each week we had included current events presentations, but I wanted something more, an intensive activity through which students could see that the lessons of history have relevance today, ideally in the same regions they had studied. They chose the topic and style because I knew they would take the project more seriously this way. In addition, I hoped to tie this project to current events standards as well as to research standards, requiring students "to raise questions and to marshal solid evidence in support of their answers" (NCHS 1996). More specifically, I wanted students to practice choosing several different sources on a topic that all related to each other, partly to prepare for a larger research paper that I planned to assign in the spring semester. And I wanted most of the work to be done in class, taking advantage of our library's electronic subscription databases as well as the computer lab; students could then check their writing with me as they worked and not be burdened with excessive homework at an already busy time of year. (See Figure 6.7 for the project's goals that I shared with students.)

## Figure 6.7

### Op-Ed Project Goals

- Taking the time to find excellent sources
- Reflecting on and summarizing these sources in an annotated bibliography
- Understanding what makes an excellent op-ed piece
- Synthesizing the sources you find to write an excellent op-ed piece
- Revising your piece thoughtfully based on peer response
- Reading your classmates' editorials to learn about a variety of world events
- Writing a "letter to the editor" based on one or more of your classmates' pieces

To find op-ed models with a variety of voices, I went online to several major newspaper and magazine sites, looking for topics, columnists, local versus global range, and political perspectives. I came up with four pieces, all eight hundred to nine hundred words each, which I asked students to read and annotate for homework. The articles touch on themes of global trade, environmental awareness, governmental structure, social welfare, and new technologies:

**Op-Ed Examples**

1. Friedman, Thomas. "No, No, No, Don't Follow Us." *New York Times* 4 Nov. 2007. http://www.nytimes.com/2007/11/04/opinion/04friedman.html?_r=1&oref=slogin. Students liked the creativity of this *New York Times'* columnist's view on a $2,500 car made in India.

2. Liu, Melinda. "Communism by the Numbers." *Newsweek* (Web exclusive) 27 Oct. 2007. http://www.newsweek.com/id/57663. Some students appreciated the numeric organization of this online *Newsweek* columnist's rundown of Chinese leaders, while others thought it was too contrived.

3. Banks, Sandy. "A Small Triumph for Children in Foster Care." *Los Angeles Times* 10 Nov. 2007: B1. http://articles.latimes.com/2007/nov/10/local/me-banks10. Many students appreciated the personal perspective this columnist took on an important local issue, and they wished they could tie in such a personal view to their pieces on world affairs.

4. Will, George F. "An Inconvenient Price." *Newsweek* 22 Oct. 2007: 68. http://www.newsweek.com/id/43352. I was surprised by my largely liberal class's reaction to this conservative pundit's piece arguing that global warming is not as dire as people are making it out to be. Many disagreed with his points but said they liked his terse style and strong facts.

I could have picked dozens of other articles, but these provided some diversity of philosophy, gender, and race. Incidentally, opinion pieces by women on foreign affairs were harder to find than I anticipated. (See Figure 6.8 for a rubric that guided the project.)

# Creating Engaged Citizens

By pulling in relevant current events—whether through informal, round-robin readings of news articles, clips of meaningful music, formal current events presentations, a structured yet informal political debate, or a student-driven op-ed piece and letter to the editor—we can help our students become more involved citizens. The skills of writing, synthesis, reading comprehension, and public speaking take on greater meaning because students are commenting on and understanding their own world. At the same time, students are drawing thematic comparisons between present and past that illuminate the intentions of people who lived hundreds or thousands of years ago. In Chapter 7, we'll look at another skill, research, to see how students can effectively dig for information that enhances their understanding of both the modern and ancient worlds.

Figure 6.8

## Op-Ed Project Rubric (60 points)

1. **Sources and Annotated Bibliography (30)**                         _____

   • Articles are of high quality and cover the issue thoroughly (5)

   • Summaries thoughtfully cover the entire articles (~150 words per article) (7)

   • Summaries are IN YOUR OWN WORDS (7)

   • Thoughtful responses to *Why did you choose each article? Why is it a quality source?* and *What is the tone?* (~50 words per article) (5)

   • The three articles, attached and with key info highlighted (3)

   • No typos or grammatical errors (3)

2. **Op-Ed Piece (22)**                                                _____

   • No fewer than 600 and no more than 900 words (2)

   • Includes information from all three articles (2)

   • Describes the problem clearly, even for someone unfamiliar with the issue (3)

   • Grabs the reader's attention and proves to us why we should care; proposes an interesting solution or a novel approach to the problem (4)

   • Shows creativity in ideas and style (4)

   • Includes at least two significant revisions based on peer or self-response (2)

   • No typos or grammatical errors (3)

   • Emailed to Ms. Cooper by Dec. 17 at 8 a.m. (2)

3. **Letter to the Editor (8)**                                        _____

   • 150–250 words total for one or two letters (2)

   • Logically and clearly expresses reasons for agreeing/disagreeing with op-ed (4)

   • Has zest, pizzazz, and passion! (1)

   • No typos or grammatical errors (1)

**Grand Total (60)**

Chapter 7

# The Power of Information: Igniting Passion Through Research

## What's Inside?

### Skills and Strategies

- Locate print and online sources for research papers
- Learn bibliographic format
- Define a viable research topic
- Write a thesis statement
- Compose and organize note cards
- Paraphrase information
- Synthesize multiple sources
- Cite sources
- Question the ethics of power

### Standards

- ✔ The research process
- ✔ Synthesis of facts
- ✔ Evidence gathering
- ✔ Media literacy
- ✔ Historical issues

Research helps students open up the world and become historians. They hold the past in their hands, turning it this way and that, investigating its sharp angles, putting their distinctive stamp on events from decades and centuries ago. With interest in a topic and strong research skills, students can understand any field that requires discernment of quality information.

For middle school students, especially, discovering a topic they care about enables them to see themselves in the context of history. For a project seventh-grade world history students did on the history of Islam, for example, Ashley drew a mosaic of Islamic tile patterns, while Sarah created an illustrated time line of three religions' claims to the Temple Mount in Jerusalem, and Sabrina baked cookies with Islamic calligraphy inscribed in frosting. All three students did rigorous research relating to their topics, but they used their preferred learning styles (visual for Ashley, analytical and logical for Sarah, kinesthetic and visual for Sabrina) to make the investigation their own.

When I begin a research project, I like to ask students to find their own stake in it: who or what do they want to live with for the next several weeks or months? Often they make a case on paper for their top three topics, and the most persuasive argument wins. For a project about world dictators, Jacob wrote that he wanted to focus on Haile Selassie because of the stories his uncle had told him about Rastafarianism, and Tara wrote that she preferred Slobodan Milosevic because her father is from the Balkans and she wanted to understand the complicated conflicts there.

Middle-schoolers are the perfect age to do research because they are curious about nearly everything. In addition, research taps into their natural desire to understand the world's mysteries and to see how their emerging view of the world meshes with or diverges from historians' opinions. Including a creative component can inspire all students, especially unconventional thinkers, to synthesize the information they have read in a new and personal way, making history their own. Yet encouraging young adolescents to sustain a long research project can be like asking them to swim in an icy pool: if we toss them in without warning, they often shriek and shiver before they can focus on the assignment. If we introduce them to the process gently, dipping in one toe at a time, they warm up quickly and can see each task clearly.

Much to my disappointment, the research paper has fallen out of favor in recent years (Hayasaki 2003). The reasons are understandable to all of us: the omnipresent threat of cut-and-paste plagiarism, mitigated but not eliminated by sites such as TurnItIn.com; the labor-intensive grading process that can make a paper seem interminable; and the need to cover content standards while also leaving time for stacks of note cards and detailed outlines.

As history teachers, however, we know that research lies at the heart of our discipline. Reading a textbook is to doing history as watching a videotape of game performance is to playing quarterback on a major-league team. National and state standards feature research prominently, arguing that "true historical understanding" compels students to "raise questions and to marshal solid evidence in support of their answers," as well as to "create historical narratives and arguments of their own" (NCHS 2008). When students pose questions about information in their textbook, they are not only soaking up knowledge but are challenging the historical record, examining what has been left untold so they can tell it in their own voices. When students construct their own arguments about history, they transform from witnesses to architects of the historical record, a process that gives them power and understanding.

While the vast majority of our students will never become historians, they will enter careers that require them to recognize quality information, build a case, and then persuade colleagues of their position. One analytical state standard requires students to "distinguish relevant from irrelevant information, essential from incidental information, and verifiable from unverifiable information in historical narratives and stories" (California State Board of Education 1998, 21). This concept of finding the best facts sounds deceptively simple. However, learning to sift the wheat from the chaff in books and Internet sites takes repeated examination of many sources. Considered from a career-minded, real-world perspective, research becomes a media literacy imperative that can help students comprehend the often-jarring images and words they see all around them. At many schools, the English department shepherds students through the research process, largely because proper citation format requires prodigious attention to detail; at other schools, research falls under the science department through science fair preparation. I believe that research fits most naturally into the history curriculum because it is the bread and butter of the historian's craft. When we engage students in projects that ask them to explore many different facets of a civilization and then share their findings with the class, we create patterns that reinforce global themes in the curriculum, from human geography to human rights.

In this chapter, I will focus on making research personal and individual to students. First I will discuss the skills students need in their "historian's toolbox" to embark on this process incrementally and with confidence: writing a strong thesis statement, brainstorming key words for searches, paraphrasing information successfully, creating note cards, and organizing those note cards into an outline. (Many research programs, such as Big6, offer an excellent structure for guiding students through the research process.) At the end of the chapter, I'll give examples of small, creative, and informal projects to whet students' appetite for research.

# Filling the Historian's Toolbox by Tackling the Research Paper

## Why the Research Paper? And How Can We Fit It In? (Hint: Enlist Help)

What's reasonable for the middle grades? With their growing capacity for synthesizing several sources at once, young adolescents are capable of constructing a formal research paper, perhaps two to four double-spaced pages for sixth and seventh graders and three to six pages for eighth graders. In doing so, they "frame questions that can be answered by historical study and research," as the California historical skills standards for middle-schoolers suggest. This process of finding a broad topic, narrowing a thesis, evaluating and choosing sources, scanning books and electronic media for information, compiling a bibliography, paraphrasing sources, taking notes, organizing note cards, making an outline, and revising multiple drafts builds patience and perseverance in middle school students. When teachers help students encounter the process step-by-step, giving mini-lessons at each curve of the road, we also set the stage for their success. By the time they have written their paper, they can look back and realize that, though it may have seemed overwhelming as a whole, it was doable in parts, and they have accomplished more than they thought they could. In middle school, this sense of slow and steady achievement can be as important as the research skills students learn because they discover the value of persistence in addition to talent. Of course, completing a research paper once is not enough to cement such skills in students; they benefit from returning to the same concepts throughout middle and high school.

For me, assigning a research paper always means focusing on one element at the expense of another because there is never enough time to check in with every student on every detail. As I grade the papers, I inevitably groan about elements I did not teach well enough during this go-round. In one eighth-grade early civilizations class, I met with each student twice about two sets of note cards, and these notes ended up being thorough and interesting. However, I neglected to meet with the students as they moved from note cards to a thesis statement, and their arguments suffered because I had not given them the attention they deserved. Another year, for a ninth-grade world history research paper, the thesis statements were super, but many of the outlines (which I had not checked) related poorly to their thesis statements. Every year I hope that this is the year that I will manage to teach every step as fully as it deserves, but every year I still find many areas to improve. Sometimes I feel like I'm standing in front of the Whac-a-Mole game at Chuck E. Cheese, taking care of the critter in one hole only to find that the other three moles have surfaced, screaming for me to pay attention.

To make myself feel better and to surrender to a necessary reality, I've decided that, with a process as complex as a research paper in a middle school class, what is most important *is* the process. Are our students trying to make their bibliographic citations complete, even if they've missed a colon here or a database name there? Are our students attempting to weave information from multiple sources into one paragraph, even if their writing includes too-large blocks of text from one book? If students are engaged in the process enough that they are learning something— and are not committing any academic sins such as plagiarism—then I console myself that we are doing well enough, for the moment, and that they can finesse their work each year as they move toward senior year of high school.

Because the research process takes years to polish, vertical teaming within a history department can yield huge benefits. Unfortunately, in the four schools where I have taught, only one has had a research scope and sequence that every teacher followed at each grade level. At that school, if you teach eighth grade, you know that your students will have written a paper the year before that is two to four pages in length and integrates two to three sources, and you know that your students will be familiar with the library's online catalog. Skills still vary among students, and teachers need to catch up the new eighth graders who might have missed that instruction, but the strength of exposing everyone to the same framework each year makes planning meaningful lessons much easier. In schools without such a firm research scope and sequence, which is far more the norm, I have done informal preassessments: asking the class who has written a bibliography before, or having students take ten minutes to write what they know about creating a thesis statement. Even in a class where most students say they know how to do a bibliography or create note cards, I always give models. All of us, including teachers, forget the many nitty-gritty details involved in research if we do not immerse ourselves regularly in the process.

Collaborating with other departments also can be invaluable in developing our students' research skills—we really do not have to do this alone. In one school where I've worked, the middle school science teachers present bibliographic citation format while introducing science fair projects in the fall. The science department agrees to use Modern Language Association (MLA) format for their initial research, even though the usual science format would be American Psychological Association (APA), so that we can achieve consistency across disciplines. The teachers agree that it's most important for students to understand citation formats in general than know how to use a particular citation format for a specific discipline. The English department then reinforces MLA citation with a dictators project in the winter (see p. 158 for the project), and the history department follows up with a library research project of its own in the spring. (Thanks to science teacher Laura Kaufman and history teacher Kristina Kalb for their collaboration.) In an ideal world, every school district would craft a research scope and sequence that recommended what every department, including art and foreign language, would teach students about research. Then students could see that research, like writing, is crucial and cross-curricular.

## Building the Assignment: To Structure or Not to Structure?

A research paper in which students can select any topic from the ocean of history has many merits, and I have used such an assignment a number of times. Had I not done so, I never would have learned about Frances's interest in her Scottish clan lineage, Taryn's fascination with Japanese culture, or Evan's obsession with the Vikings. If I assign this broad prompt—"pick any topic from the time periods and locations of the material we're studying this year"—I make sure to schedule at least several days of topic finding in the library and conferences with me before students have to commit to a subject. I also ask students to do prewriting before they arrive in the library on an idea that might interest them. Many databases, including Gale's History Resource Center, have browsing features, which allow students to search in a particular time period for events and people. In addition, librarians can direct students to specialty encyclopedias, such as a history of warfare or technological developments.

One librarian suggested a wonderful idea for testing the viability of a topic: search a large public library catalog to see how many books are listed. If at least three appear, that topic should be viable; if not, students can look for another subject that will yield more fruit. (Thanks to librarian Meryl Eldridge for this idea.)

At other times, I like to give a little more structure on the paper topic. A problem-solution paper for a current or historical event can work well, as can any variant on the I-Search model, which encourages students to take a personally meaningful question and answer it creatively (Macrorie 1988). Dr. T. Roger Taylor's framework of eighteen different approaches for an I-Search puts any teacher through his or her paces in creating an assignment (Taylor 2006). With such categories, Taylor's structure leads us to choose topics that lie outside our comfort zone as learners, encouraging students and teachers to view history with new lenses. When I followed Taylor's paradigm for an I-Search on Islam, I included this idea for the "Visualization Skill" category: *Where Three Faiths Coexist:* Study the Temple Mount in Jerusalem: what does it consist of, and what archaeological finds are reputed to be underneath? Why is the area so disputed? Drawing or modeling the area could be an interesting project." In response, Sarah created her illustrated time line of the site over three millennia from the perspectives of Islam, Christianity, and Judaism. For "Examples of Change," I suggested this topic about the annual pilgrimage to Mecca: "*The Hajj:* Find at least two firsthand accounts of the hajj through the ages: how has it changed? Start with material in your notebook on the steps of the hajj, then find firsthand accounts from long-ago and modern travelers." Bobby located a source from Muslim traveler Ibn Battuta and compared it to newspaper accounts of the pilgrimage today. Often, giving a list of specific topics that the teacher has thought through can help students find more immediate success with sources and a thesis statement.

To decide how prescriptive to make an assignment, I think about what I want my students to learn and how much I want their topics to overlap. If I do give a list, I ask students to rank their top three or four choices and write fifteen to twenty or more words on why they want each topic. This motivational strategy can spark reluctant writers to explain their ideas fully and clearly. Of course, I still receive many "I want to do the Maya because they were really cool and violent" justifications, but such statements are part of the delight of teaching middle school. If I receive a response like that and I think students would really benefit from exploring the topic anyway, I'll sometimes go back to them and ask, "What interests you about the fact that they were violent? What else about them is cool for you?" Then the students have a chance to expand their thoughts, and I can match such curiosity with a topic in which I believe the students will invest themselves.

# Owning the Thesis Statement

The most important caution when helping students build research papers is that your first thesis is not your final thesis. Much of a research paper involves serendipitous discovery, and writing an unchangeable thesis statement at the beginning of the process cuts off much of that search. I often compare writing a thesis statement for a historical research paper to writing a hypothesis for a scientific experiment: we are posing an idea, but we might be proven wrong, and we need to stay open to alternative interpretations and new facts.

I introduce thesis statements to middle school students because otherwise a research paper is simply a report, with no interpretation or involvement by the student. Organizing information in categories without an argument has its place, especially with weaker readers, but I fully believe that every student is capable of explaining his or her own spin on the subject. Even if that point of view is simple or general, it constitutes a start at independent thinking.

With younger students or less fluid writers, I will often give "thesis starters," sentences that students can fill in so they can grab a foothold in the process. Students should fill in the blank with opinion or analysis, not facts. Some teachers like to require that the blanks at the end of the sentences include two or three different statements for a two- or three-pronged approach that helps with organization. If students find that structure helpful, I'm glad, but I don't require them to include two or three points because one point is sometimes sufficient to cover an entire essay.

### Examples of Thesis Starters

- (This civilization) succeeded/declined because _____. (*The early Maya culture succeeded because of its organization and imagination.*)

- (This famous person) made a difference in his/her world by _____. (*Nineteenth-century Progressive reformer Jane Addams made a difference in her world by showing that the poor deserved respect.*)

- (This place, ritual, object, or document) was important to the people of (its society) because _____. (*The Magna Carta was important to the people of England because it allowed them to challenge the king.*)

Whether or not students use these sentence helpers, I usually look at their thesis statements several times during the process of completing note cards to ensure that the arguments are accurate and analytical. To make time for this one-on-one instruction, I give students another assignment, such as analyzing a document in partners, to be completed by the end of the period. Then I'll walk around the room and look at each student's thesis statement, sometimes taking two days to do so, asking questions as I go.

Consider the typical process of writing a thesis statement on a common middle school interest, the Vikings. Evan comes in on the day students must have their topics (general topics, not thesis statements) and says he wants to write a research paper on the Vikings. "That's great!" I say. When I ask him what interests him about the Vikings, he says he wants to find out about their ships. I write down "ships" on his topic sheet, which so far has "The Vikings" written on it. "What do you know about their ships?" I ask him. "Um, I think they were built really well," he says. "That's true," I say,

and write down "built really well" on his topic sheet. "Let's go with that in your research. As you take notes on sources in the library tomorrow, try looking for information on how the ships were built and why they were built that way." This is enough for now, before Evan has done any research, because I want him to find out more information that can lead him to a fuller analysis of the ships. The answer to how the ships were built is factual; however, by the time he browses through some sources, he can start thinking about the whys behind such master craftsmanship.

Viking tools: spears, rudder, shield, and dragonhead

A week later, after Evan has completed his first set of note cards, we meet again. "What did you discover about the ships?" I ask, flipping through the cards and seeing topic headings such as "Wood" and "Masts."

"Well, the ships were built with wood planks that overlapped each other," Evan said, "and they could be sailed from both front and back."

"Wow, how interesting," I say. "Why do you think they overlapped the wood?"

"So the ships would be stronger while they sailed." I write this down on his topic sheet.

"How about sailing from both front and back—being 'double-sided,' one of your note cards says?" I ask. "What advantages would that give the Vikings?"

"Um, it would let them turn around easily if they needed to."

"Why might they need to?"

"If they were being attacked."

"Great, so we have that the Vikings made their ships strong and—what's a word for being able to turn around easily?"

"Quick? Flexible?" Evan puts forth.

"Okay, flexible, that's good. Let's try writing a possible thesis for your paper. I know we've talked about only two facts, but we can make a start. Hmm, how about: 'The Vikings built strong ships that were flexible in the water because . . .' As you finish your final set of note cards, keep thinking about the 'because' part, and I'll check this one more time next week."

As I walk by Evan's desk the next week, I see his final thesis statement: "The Vikings built strong, quick ships because they wanted to explore the world and get new lands."

"I didn't really like 'flexible' after all," he said apologetically. "It made me think of stretching during PE."

After I laughed, I said, "That's great; I think you've made the sentence better. And I really like that you have two parts to the rest of the sentence, both exploring the world and getting new lands."

Evan's thesis statement is by no means original, but it works for a middle school research paper. Why? It contains analytical words and helps him organize his paper around an argument. It also shows cause and effect: the Vikings built their ships to accomplish a goal. Ideally, as Evan writes the paper, he might think about goals he wants to accomplish in middle school and how he can achieve them: not by building strong, quick ships, for instance, but by practicing basketball three-pointers with his brother each day so he can take some risks in an intramural game, or by working with a computer program to speed up his typing skills so that he can finish his homework faster. Completing these thesis starters can also lead students to think about themselves: how can they make a difference in their world, for instance, or contribute to the success of their country?

You might be thinking that this is a whole lot of time to spend with every student discussing a thesis statement and note cards. It absolutely is. I've arrived at this labor-intensive process only after too many years of assigning a research paper, glancing at a thesis statement maybe once, and then reading paper after paper that looked slapped together, with no through line or visible thought. Usually I spend about two minutes per student with the initial topic choice and then a minute in the subsequent conversations; the conversations could obviously take much longer if I allowed more minutes and took more class periods. Working with students on their thesis statements is worth every minute for a number of reasons:

a) I can watch students' minds turning and encourage their thinking.

b) Students are working as analytical historians.

c) Plagiarism becomes more difficult because the student and I have devised a thesis that is based on their note cards, and they must attach all such brainstorming papers to their final drafts for full credit.

d) Students realize that research matters and that someone cares enough about their topic to meet with them and check in about it. Engaging in such conversations can turn the research paper from a dull, solitary process to one in which students know they will get to talk about what they are learning. For the same reason, I often take three minutes at the end of a research period for students to share the two most interesting facts they learned that day with a partner. For middle school students (and most of the rest of us), socializing about a topic makes it more interesting, relevant, and personal.

# Learning the Library

Libraries vary as much as the schools in which they are located. I have always enjoyed library time because it shows students how many exciting subjects they can choose and because it creates camaraderie with the librarians. For major research papers, I usually require that half the sources be books, when possible, so that students can have experience looking through an index and finding information manually. In addition, when they find pertinent books on a topic, they often realize that the Web's resources, however dazzling, do not always compare to the depth of information in a relevant book. In recent years, I've sometimes modified this book requirement for papers based on current topics; in those cases, articles on electronic databases such as ProQuest Historical Newspapers or websites about current topics can give the most up-to-date information. But books will remain important, and I want to show my students that, in a world of push-button searching, roaming the old-fashioned way can often yield deeper results. Here are some questions you might consider as you think about how and when to bring your classes to the library to look for both books and electronic database articles:

• How do I sign up on the librarian's calendar of class visits?

• Can I schedule a visit with the librarian to see which books she could put on reserve for my class? When I am writing a research project, I often will base topic lists on the resources the library has, and seeing the books in person helps my brainstorming.

- How would I like to partner with the librarian while my students are in the library? Would she like to give a three-minute overview of the most fascinating reserve books, do a presentation on relevant databases on a Smartboard, or help kids sign up for a wiki she has made on the topic? Can we create a lesson plan together that combines her knowledge of the library's resources with my recent mini-lessons on research skills?

- Are there enough computers anywhere on campus (library, laptop cart, computer lab) for my students to be 1:1? If not, I often assign half or a quarter of the class to work on the computers and rotate the rest through relevant books. Not having enough computers can actually be a benefit in encouraging this "Google generation" to dive into print.

- How many days do I think my students will need to be in the library to find sources? I often multiply my estimate by 1.5 or 2 so that no one feels rushed. If students finish early, they can always work on other parts of the assignment, such as note cards.

- What is due to me from the students at the end of each day in the library? With a hard-and-firm check-in point, students tend to work more productively. If I say something as general as, "Your goal today is to find one good source, write a bibliographic citation, and get started on your second source," such a direction gives me something to ask about and to check off at the end of the period. This quick "how are you doing?" can also take the form of a daily participation grade. Sometimes students work faster and harder if I use the language of "This is your goal, and I will talk to each of you about it before you leave today," rather than "This is what is due at the end of the period"—though the effectiveness depends on the student and, perhaps, whether we are meeting last period on a Friday.

# Sussing Out Spectacular Sources

Many fine online rubrics exist for helping students assess the validity of websites. Yet when my middle-schoolers begin a research paper, I hope they will not need to go to the free Internet at all or will do so only at the tail end of their research. Among the many excellent history databases available, either through a district's subscription or through the public library, and the glory of well-researched books, most students should find enough information.

## Clever Keyword Searching

I have endured many frustrating periods in the library—the result of poor planning on my part. Too late I realized that students need time to think about how to find information before they log into a library catalog or a subscription database. One tool I now commonly share with students is how to brainstorm keywords effectively before a print or electronic search. The day before we visit the library, I take ten minutes at the end of class to ask students to work with partners and come up with keyword ideas. They need to think of at least four different terms that will enable them to elaborate on their topics: not just "Vikings," but also "Norse warriors" or "longboats." If we have time I'll ask students to put the terms on the board and add to each other's lists. Finding terms before we reach the library helps avoid some of the "I can't find anything!" frustration of novice researchers. For those students who are having trouble thinking of terms, I ask them to go to their textbook, find a paragraph or section on their topic, and then list words they could look up. If they still have trouble, I ask them to work in partners and look through each other's textbook sections, suggesting several phrases that might lead to helpful searches. On the other hand, for those students who brainstorm a list of terms quickly, I'll ask them to make a mini-outline of how those terms might fit into the tentative thesis they've already written. This process helps quick-but-not-always-deep thinkers sort out what might and might not be relevant to their arguments. I've also done this exercise on a day when we're already in the library computer lab. Those students who make a list right away can start their searching, and those who need more guidance can work with me at the board in the library classroom until they're ready.

Without such keyword preparation, many students justifiably spend half the period in the library waiting for me to get around to them to help narrow a search, complaining meanwhile to their friends that they have 110,000 hits on "Ming Dynasty" and just don't know where to start. Given such reasonable annoyance on their part, students do their best, but I chalk up the period as a wasted hour. To build success once we enter the library on later days of research, I encourage students to use a book or article they previously found to help them create a list of terms to search. I tell them that this is like "good" cheating—you're using what you already know to help you get ahead. In terms of online sources, I ask students to go to Google only after checking several of our online databases and after consulting with the librarians about print sources. Students can use Wikipedia as a starting point, but I discourage their citing it as a source because of its changeability. Happily, some databases help students narrow their topics automatically. For instance, searching ProQuest Platinum Periodicals for "China" and "infrastructure" yields not only a list of articles, but also "Suggested Topics" such as "China AND foreign investment" and "China AND international trade." Students merely click on one of the suggestions to further target their search.

## Finding Relevant Books

To help students look for useful books, I pretended I was writing a research paper and jotted down every step I took to create a handout for students on discerning valid book sources (see Figure 7.1). As many admirable qualities as our tech-savvy students possess, print is not their native medium. Though I am an inveterate reader, I am sometimes newly astonished at how much better a book is than a database on a particular historical topic—how much more surprised, then, might our students be? Such a "how to read" guide encourages students to delve beyond the cover or title page of a book in looking for information.

To adapt this guide for struggling readers, I have done an "act-it-out" in the library with them for Section D, "INSIDE a book." We all take a book and follow the steps together as I read them aloud. Such kinesthetic and aural learning can help all students, not just those whose reading comprehension skills are limited. I also encourage students to read only the first sentence of each paragraph until they decide whether a source is useful. This way, they do not become bogged down in text and can keep moving to different options. Similarly, I emphasize that you do not need to use an entire chapter of a book, or even an entire page, for the book to be a good source. Sometimes one or two paragraphs are the most relevant to your paper, and everything else can fall by the wayside while you focus on one key nut of information.

Finally, I tell students that, when all else fails, ask a librarian. Several years ago, I worked as a faculty-library liaison at my school, helping connect faculty with the librarians while they were doing research projects. In conjunction with that role, I spoke to a dozen college and high school librarians about teaching research. Nearly everyone I spoke with cited the same number one research skill they would like students to have upon entering college: being willing to ask a librarian for help!

Figure 7.1

### Finding Good Book Sources: The Holy Grail of Research

**Important:** As you go through this process, be open to digging for information. Don't give up too easily! If you throw up your hands early on, you might deny yourself the opportunity to have an "aha" moment while doing research.

#### A. BEFORE you look in the library catalog for books

1. Take ten minutes to consult a general source, such as Encyclopaedia Britannica Online, to find out basic information about your topic. You will generally *not* cite such a source in your works cited list because it is so general.

2. Based on this initial browsing, write three to five "search terms" you could look for in an index or a table of contents about your topic.

   Example: If your topic is the Watergate hearings of 1973, you could list as search terms *Richard Nixon, Committee to Re-Elect the President (CREEP), Deep Throat, Bob Woodward,* and *James McCord.*

#### B. AS you consult the library catalog

1. Try entering all the search terms you have brainstormed. As you go, write down (a) the author, and (b) Dewey Decimal or Library of Congress number for books that look useful.

2. Write down call numbers that keep coming up. For example, if you are writing about Watergate, the most common Dewey Decimal number will probably be 973.924. Many subjects will have two or three common numbers because they

**Figure 7.1 (continued)**

are represented in two or more sections: religion is covered in the 200s but also in the 300s and 900s, for example, and history is covered politically in the 900s but sociologically, psychologically, and philosophically in the 100s and 300s.

### C. IN the "stacks" (bookshelves) of the library

1. Go first to the two or three books you find most interesting. While in these sections, browse the titles of all other books within the *specific* call number of your book (973.924, for instance, NOT the entire 973 section).

2. Do the same for the other call numbers you wrote down for your topic.

3. Also look in specialized encyclopedias or series of books, such as a book series about American decades or a multivolume encyclopedia about the history of science and mathematics. *Ask a librarian* if you are unsure which such series or encyclopedias would be most useful. You will save untold time by doing so.

### D. INSIDE a book

*Do not start on page 1 and read straight through.* Instead, be a savvy skimmer by doing the following:

1. Once you have found a book that looks promising, first look in the INDEX at the back for *at least three* of your search terms. Some guidelines:

   a. Go to one or two page numbers for each of your search terms. Find the term on the page listed and read the paragraph it is in. Ask yourself, "Is this related to what I want to talk about in my paper?" If yes, then look at the other pages in the index on your search term. If not, try one more reference on each search term and then decide whether another book would be stronger.

   b. Page references that span two or more pages are often the best; if only one page is listed, your term may just be a brief mention on that page.

   c. Italicized page numbers usually mean that page has a photo or illustration relating to your topic.

   d. If you look up an enormous topic, such as "Richard Nixon," the book might list fifty or more references. Try looking farther down in that listing to more specific references, such as "Nixon—trip to China" or "Nixon—Election of 1968."

2. If the index references look promising, turn to the TABLE OF CONTENTS at the front of the book. Some guidelines:

Figure 7.1 (continued)

a. Find a chapter or section that looks most relevant to your topic OR a chapter for which you found many references in the index for your search terms.

b. Then SKIM several pages of the chapter by looking at the first sentence of each of the paragraphs. Ask yourself, "Is this the kind of information that would be useful or interesting for my particular paper topic?" If yes, then you've probably found a good source—congratulations! If not, try one more chapter and ask yourself the same questions.

c. Keep in mind that you sometimes need only a few pages from a source, especially for smaller topics.

3. Other details that can be useful for evaluating books:

a. For a book you like, look at the book's own bibliography and find some of the books listed. This method also works well for the bibliographies at the end of each chapter in many textbooks.

b. Look at the date of publication on the copyright page (back of the title page). For a paper on the most recent developments on DNA research, you will want a very recent book or journal article; for a paper on Washington's presidency, much older books will be fine.

c. Look at the publisher if your teacher tells you about strong publishers in your field, such as a university press.

**E. AFTER you have decided a book is a good source**

1. Record the information on the title page and copyright page (back of the title page) by:

a. Making two photocopies, one of the title page and one of the copyright page;

OR

b. Writing down the information you will need for your bibliographic citation. See our school's "MLA Citation Guide" for details on citing sources for most classes.

2. Check out the book or, if it is a reference book, copy the pages you need. Make sure the page numbers are not cut off on the copier, as you will use them for parenthetical citations or footnotes in your paper.

3. Before you return a checked-out book, copy the pages for which you took notes if your teacher has asked you to attach them to your final paper.

# Fine-Tuning Note Cards

Like you, I've seen every kind of sloppy note card that exists: those that didn't paraphrase enough, those with no page numbers, those with no title, those with so much information that the student started writing vertically up the margins in infinitesimal print, and those with so little information that the student might as well not have written the card at all. Needless to say, most of these errors occurred after note-taking lessons in which I didn't spend enough time modeling how to move from a source to a note card. Although note cards can vary in format, I tell my students that this step is one place where detail and consistency are important. You can slide by in many areas in life, I say, but with bibliographic entries and note cards, you just have to grit your teeth and do it right.

Why note cards? Every year a student asks if he or she can simply highlight text from a photocopy of a book and then work directly from these pages rather than making note cards. I explain that real historians use note cards or a similar system to keep themselves honest, to steer as far from inadvertent plagiarism as they can. Working directly from a text can make even the best writers think that they are synthesizing an author's ideas in their own words when, in fact, they are not. And I remind the students that, even though everyone will be writing note cards using the same format, their own voice and style will emerge when they take these cards and meld them into their own creation. Note cards also:

- help students make a topic their own because students pick the information that is most meaningful to them, not to someone else;

- encourage students to select only the most relevant information because the space limits the amount students can write down;

- remind students of academic honesty by requiring specific citation information for each fact;

- foster integration of sources because the cards can be shuffled physically and easily, leading to new, often personal connections not always evident in the pages of just one source.

At one excellent school where I've worked, the middle grades history teachers require students to write research note cards quoting exactly what the source said: in other words, to list the facts verbatim. Having always been a member of the "paraphrase note cards" club myself, I was surprised by this approach. By quoting directly on note cards, students do need to take an extra step to paraphrase when they actually write the paper. However, the method makes sense for two reasons: first, students know exactly what the original text said; and, more importantly, I can hold a note card next to a paraphrased page and pinpoint any inadvertent plagiarism. (See the next section for ways to help students practice paraphrasing throughout the year.)

Regardless of whether students paraphrase or quote verbatim, I give them a handout that models what the bibliography cards and note cards should look like (see Figure 7.2). I ask students to put just one or two facts on a card; with such small bits of information, students can more easily move around their cards to fit facts into different paragraphs. If students include five or six sentences on a card, they are far more likely to plagiarize the author's sentence order and organization of material. (For note cards quoted directly from the source, I tell students that they may write out the quotation or make a photocopy and then paste it onto the note card.) If a few diligent students really want to put more

Figure 7.2

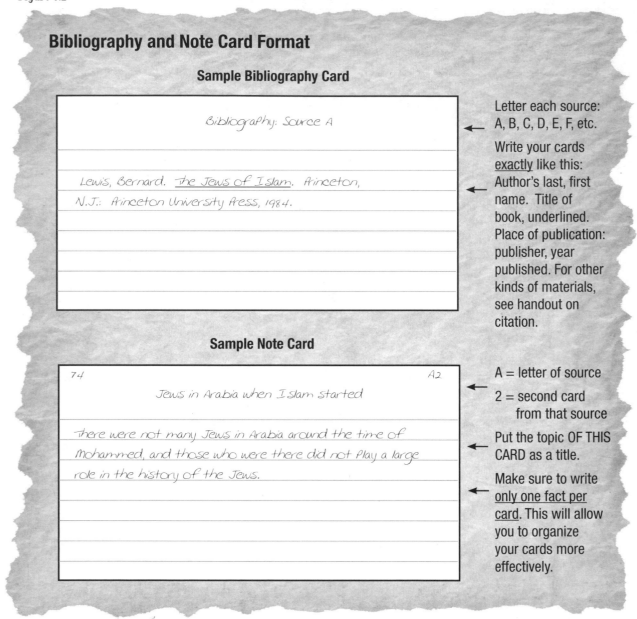

**Bibliography and Note Card Format**

**Sample Bibliography Card**

> *Bibliography: Source A*
>
> *Lewis, Bernard. The Jews of Islam. Princeton,*
> *N.J.: Princeton University Press, 1984.*

Letter each source: A, B, C, D, E, F, etc.

Write your cards <u>exactly</u> like this: Author's last, first name. Title of book, underlined. Place of publication: publisher, year published. For other kinds of materials, see handout on citation.

**Sample Note Card**

> *7-4*                                              *A2*
>
> *Jews in Arabia when Islam started*
>
> *There were not many Jews in Arabia around the time of*
> *Mohammed, and those who were there did not play a large*
> *role in the history of the Jews.*

A = letter of source

2 = second card from that source

Put the topic OF THIS CARD as a title.

Make sure to write <u>only one fact per card</u>. This will allow you to organize your cards more effectively.

information on a card ("Please, Ms. Cooper, I work so much better this way!"), then they can highlight the sections of each card that they used before they turn in the paper.

To encourage students to further individualize the information on the note cards, I ask for specific topic headings, such as "Stern Rudder" or "Definition of Viking" for Evan's paper on the Vikings. With such clear subjects, Evan can then see at a glance which cards relate to each other as he begins sorting them and constructing an outline. For a four-page paper, students might have more than fifty note cards if they include only one fact per card, but I tell them it's okay because such expansiveness will help them solidify their thesis statements later. Of course, middle-schoolers love to use colorful school supplies that will distinguish their projects from their peers'. So some will use pink cards for one source and yellow for another, or blue for one topic and green for another, or silver ink for one topic and green glitter ink for another. This is one place in the research process where I can delight in encouraging absolute freedom: whatever works for them works for me, as long as I can read their information.

# Paraphrasing with Panache

When I ask students to paraphrase on the note cards, I let them practice a summarizing activity for homework, either before the research paper or earlier in the year. Students read part of a current article and recast it, paragraph by paragraph. If I can pick a story that makes them think about their own lives, so much the better. One standby is a *Los Angeles Times* piece, "Schools Roll Out Programs to Help Crack Down on Bullies" (Garrison and Hayasaki 2001), because it addresses a raw middle school issue in an unemotional way. Any similar article would work well, especially one about a relevant current issue such as virtual online worlds or social networking sites. For the handout, I pick five or six paragraphs from the story (usually just a sentence or two each because newspaper paragraphs are short), number them, and give students the directions in Figure 7.3.

The assignment itself is not the exciting part, but rather the discussion that comes the next day. I ask several brave volunteers to share verbally or write on the board what they produced for numbers 1–4. As we look at the summaries, questions arise. Is there a good synonym for *major* in a sentence about a "major campus objective"? Yes: *main, primary,* to name a couple. Is there a good synonym for *bullying*? How about *fighting, battling,* or *picking on people*? Well, these aren't quite the same as *bullying,* one girl says. Why not? Because bullying includes so much more, she points out. The students agree: *bullying* is not a word we can change without altering the story's meaning or making it incomprehensible. The same goes for *zero-tolerance,* but we can certainly find substitutes for *terrorize* in this context: *intimidate, frighten.* One student asks if she can paraphrase a quotation by a school district official without giving his name at the end. No way, I say. How would you like someone to list one of your brilliant ideas without giving you credit? All right, how about keeping the same order of one of the article's sentences but just changing a few words? No again, I say. The author retains rights to the structure of the sentence as well as the content; try starting in a new way. By the end of the discussion, students sense that they have to be far more careful than they thought when putting someone else's words into their own.

Of course, paraphrasing is one of those unwieldy skills that demand frequent revisiting during the course of a year and throughout an entire middle and high school education. Just when I think my students understand that they cannot cite something without putting it in their own words or using quotation marks, I read a series of current events presentations that seem lifted from the newspaper or glance at a sheet of bullet-point notes that read like the encyclopedia. At these moments, I backtrack and put together another mini-lesson on plagiarism, perhaps bringing in an article about recent accusations of historians' own blunders or about students expelled for plagiarism at a local university. In our Web-based world, where six different sites on the topic can sometimes

Figure 7.3

**Paraphrasing "Students Roll Out Programs to Help Crack Down on Bullies"**

For 1–4 below you will be paraphrasing, or putting in your own words, the newspaper story above on bullying. In paraphrasing, aim to use different words than the original does, but do not agonize over or spend too much time deciding which words to use. Do your best, and we will discuss this tomorrow. The sentence below is one example of effective paraphrasing. Use this example as a model for your work.

*Original text:* "Belvedere Park is a prize to those who live in East Los Angeles—an oasis of ball fields and swing sets amid the urban sprawl" (Garrison and Hayasaki 2001).

*Sample paraphrase:* For residents of busy East L.A., Belvedere Park provides a relaxing place for them to play sports and enjoy themselves.

1.  Write the main idea of paragraphs 1 and 2 in your own words (10–20 words).

2.  Write the main idea of paragraph 3 in your own words (approx. 10 words).

3.  Write the main idea of paragraphs 4 and 5 in your own words (10–20 words).

4.  Write the main idea of paragraph 6 in your own words (20–25 words).

read like identical sextuplets because the webmasters all copied their text from each other without documentation, the fight against plagiarism is ongoing and stiff.

# Integrating Information

Sometimes, to shock my students into citation, I show them an article from a historical journal and ask them to look at how many endnotes or footnotes the author has used. "You mean we really have to include this many, not just one per paragraph? This is insane!" Yes, it is crazy, I tell them, but it is also the only way to ensure that you are giving proper credit to the people whose intellectual property you are borrowing. Streamlining the note cards into a research paper can be a brutal process of organization and attention to details. Three activities can help students navigate this swamp.

First, students look at a handout with three or four sample "note cards" that the teacher prepares on one topic; everyone has the same samples, so the teacher has to make only three or four cards. After reading through the cards and writing down the main idea in their own words, students work in groups to integrate the information into a well-formed paragraph. (Thanks to Joan Black at the Bishop's School in La Jolla, California, for this fantastic idea.) Some of the cards feature conflicting information that students must sort out. The paragraph must include references to at least three of the sources in endnotes, footnotes, or parenthetical citations. This activity can take several days, but it is well worth the investment of time because of the questions students ask about citation, such as what they should do when sources differ and how to use each source sufficiently.

A second option is to give students a model paragraph that shows them exactly where each endnote comes from. Even after I went over how to write endnotes one year with my seventh graders, students were still confused enough that I recognized I needed to show them what I meant. Discussing a model paragraph about Venice's sinking buildings eliminated my sense that students were, well, sinking under the weight of having to do so much at once. Most effective was showing them exactly which sources went with which endnote and how much we needed to change the sentence structure to safely paraphrase the article. If I were using MLA parenthetical citations, I would change the handouts to include parentheses rather than endnotes. (See Figure 7.4 for the model paragraph handouts.)

Figure 7.4

## Sample Paragraph with Endnotes

### Venice, Italy: With Sea Levels Rising, Will the City Survive?

This is a sample body paragraph for your paper. It would be paragraph #2 after an introduction. Your word-processing program will place endnotes automatically at the end of the paper.

### Sample Body Paragraph

Flooding and high water levels have always been a problem in Venice, but the issue has gotten worse recently. For example, St. Mark's Square is one of the lowest places in the city. One hundred years ago, the square was underwater fewer than ten times each year. Now that number is six times higher, with approximately sixty floods per year.[1] One famous flood in 1966 filled St. Mark's Square with one-and-a-half feet of water, which was not unusual. The high tide did not go down, however, and half a day later another tide caused the square to be underwater by a few more feet, causing rats to seek high ground.[2] A second flood like the calamity in 1966 "may only be a matter of time," according to the *Economist* magazine.[3] Floods of all sizes are simply a part of daily life in this city.

---

[1] "Saving Venice," *Economist*, 27 Sept. 2003, *Lexis-Nexis Scholastic Universe: News*, Lexis-Nexis, 2006 <http://web.lexis-nexis.com/scholastic>, 1.

[2] Robert Kunzig, "Turning the Tide," *U.S. News and World Report*, 7 Oct. 2002, *Lexis-Nexis Scholastic Universe: News*, Lexis-Nexis, 2006 <http://web.lexis-nexis.com/scholastic>, 2.

[3] "Saving," 1.

**Figure 7.4 (continued)**

**Venice Paragraph Note Cards**

Note Card for Endnote 1

"Saving" St. Mark's Square flooding

Page 1

"To grasp the problem, the popular tourist destination of St Mark's Square is an excellent place to start. One of the lowest, and oldest, points in the city, it is home to treasures such as St Mark's Basilica and the Doges' Palace. In the first decade of the 20th century, the square flooded less than ten times a year. By the 1980s it was flooding 40 times a year, and today it floods some 60 times a year."

Note Card 1 for Endnote 2

Kunzig Flood of 1966: First tide

Page 2

"As a young woman, Rizzoli [Paola Rizzoli, oceanographer at M.I.T.] lived through the event that has shaped the debate ever since—the flood of the century. On the morning of Nov. 4, 1966, the tide registered more than 4 feet above the 0 point on the gauge at Punta della Salute, across the Grand Canal from St. Mark's. That was enough to put a foot and a half of water in the famous square—the lowest point in Venice—but it was nothing historic. What happened next was historic. Whipped up by sirocco winds that blew ceaselessly up the Adriatic, the tide refused to ebb."

**Figure 7.4 (continued)**

Note card 2 for Endnote 2

Kunzig Flood of 1966: Second tide

Page 2

"The next tide, 12 hours later, piled right on top of the first. At 6 P.m.,
it crested at more than 6 feet. Virtually the entire historic center of
Venice was under several feet of water. Rats were running up the walls;
power failed and ruptured oil tanks spilled their contents into the flood;
furniture floated out of apartments. 'We couldn't leave the house for
three days,' Rizzoli recalls. 'There were people driving motorboats in St.
Mark's Square. This was the wake-up call.'"

Note card for Endnote 3

"Saving" St. Mark's Square flooding

Page 1

Another disastrous flood, such as the one the city suffered in 1966,
may only be a matter of time.

Figure 7.4 (continued)

**Venice Paragraph Bibliography**

**Bibliography**

Kunzig, Robert. "Turning the Tide." *U.S. News and World Report* 7 Oct. 2002. *Lexis-Nexis Scholastic Universe: News.* Lexis-Nexis, 2006. <http://web.lexis-nexis.com/scholastic>.

"Saving Venice." *Economist* 27 Sep. 2003. *Lexis-Nexis Scholastic Universe: News.* Lexis-Nexis, 2006. <http://web.lexis-nexis.com/scholastic>.

Finally, to help students pull together the information they have culled from disparate sources, I devote one or two days in class to an "organize-your-note-cards party." After students finish their note cards, ask them to bring in their rubber-banded stack. A rule of thumb is about a dozen per assigned page because students will realize that some cards are irrelevant once they start writing. If you teach on the block schedule, this is a perfect activity for a long stretch. Play some music and bring treats if you like, and tell students to follow the directions on "Turning Your Note Cards into a Research Paper" (see Figure 7.5). By organizing the cards into categories, students are effectively compiling their information in paragraphs; by ordering the cards within each category, students are structuring the sentence order in their paragraphs. Categorizing their cards in class means that students do not feel overwhelmed at home while sorting through the massive amounts of information they have gathered, and this activity creates camaraderie. The teacher can zigzag from person to person suggesting new ways to organize, and the students who finish early often revel in helping others succeed in the process. Megan, an eighth grader, talked for a week about how she had helped Evan figure out a good structure for his paper. To do so, she had looked at the categories he had created, suggested topics that might fit together, and helped him decide on a logical order for the topics.

The most difficult part of organizing note cards is moving from general paragraph topics, such as "Raids" for a paper on the Vikings, to an analytical topic sentence for that paragraph. To help students with this analysis, I talk to them about their topic sentences after they have completed an outline based on the cards. Evan had written the following topic sentence for a paragraph on "Raids": "The Vikings raided many cities along the coasts." I asked him the catchall question: "Why?" "Because they wanted riches," Evan said. Then I asked, "How?" "By using their ships and men to make people fear them." "All right, let's put that 'why' and 'how' together," I say, and write down: "The Vikings raided many cities along the coasts, using fear, because they wanted riches." Again, this is not original or earth-shattering, but it shows that Evan is thinking, and it gives clear direction for the facts he will include in his paragraph. With such one-on-one instruction, each student is challenged at his or her current level, ideally resulting in truly individualized teaching and learning.

Figure 7.5

## Turning Your Note Cards into a Research Paper: Six Easy Steps

1.  Spread out your note cards on a flat surface.

2.  Place note cards in three to ten categories, depending on the size of your paper.

3.  Top each category stack with a fresh note card or sticky note; write the name of the category on the card. Paper-clip cards in a category together, if you like.

4.  Once cards are in categories, order the cards in *each* category in a logical way—in the order you want to write the information in your paper.

    *   Don't be afraid to set aside note cards that do not relate well to any category; often you'll have a few strays that just don't fit.

5.  Put the categories in the order you want to write about them by stacking the cards together. It can often work to put the most general categories first and follow up with more specific categories. Put a rubber band around your cards for safekeeping.

6.  Begin writing your outline based on your note cards.

    *   Each paragraph should contain one to three categories of cards.

    *   Each paragraph must have an analytical topic sentence.

    *   Again, feel free to set aside cards that no longer seem to fit in.

# Whetting the Appetite: Making Research Appealing

Before I assign a large research paper in any middle school class, I aim to build up the research techniques described above—and make the process seem friendlier—through smaller, creative assignments. Activities focusing on identity, biography, and ethics draw students into the research process without their even realizing they are preparing for deeper investigations later on.

The assignments that follow are all eminently flexible. Teachers can ask for more or fewer articles, require more or fewer sources, include fewer parts of an assignment for a class that needs more scaffolding, or require more for a class that can run on its own. Much of the joy of these relatively informal, creative projects lies in their adaptability to your and your students' needs.

## Identity: It's All About "Me"

Who hasn't Googled themselves? We can take this ego-surfing into the research age by requiring students to look up their name or that of a relative on an electronic subscription database: a current events resource, such as Gale's Infotrac, EBSCO, or ProQuest Platinum Periodicals, or a historical database, such as ABC-CLIO's World History or ProQuest Historical Newspapers. I originally put together this lesson to expose students to our library's electronic subscription databases in a nonthreatening way and to emphasize that history can be as local and personal as investigating themselves and their classmates. If students cannot find their own full names, they can try just their last names. Usually students will not see themselves listed, but they enjoy reading about the exploits of people who share their names or those of relatives.

After they find two interesting articles, students can list similarities and differences between themselves and the person in the article or write about which elements of that person's life they would like to incorporate into their own goals. Such reflection drives students to consider questions of identity, "remembering past achievements and projecting [themselves] into the future" (NCSS 1994). More practically, with middle school students, such discussion of goals helps them clarify their talents and shows them that they, too, can make headlines in the future with their accomplishments.

The giggling and laughter during this activity are pleasurable to hear: "Can you believe that I was an astronaut in 1977?" "I wonder if this military general was my relative!" More seriously, in introducing the lesson I can teach about keyword searching (see p. 138 in this chapter); narrowing one's search by chronology or relevance on databases such as ProQuest Platinum Periodicals by typing in dates or clicking on "most relevant"; and skimming the first several paragraphs of a story to see if it is useful. Research-based ego surfing is an excellent getting-to-know-you activity during the first several weeks of school, especially when students share their findings with a classmate the next day.

## Context: The News Back Then

Online newspaper databases generate excitement for nearly any era in American history, modern world history, or geography. They also directly connect students to events of 20 or 120 years ago by linking them with primary sources that were once found only in archives. By analyzing these articles, students can assess point of view and compare newspaper accounts with current textbook or encyclopedia descriptions of events; they can also imagine what it would have been like to read these articles over the breakfast table in, say, 1862, and to have discussed them with their siblings and parents in a world without computers or iPods.

My school subscribes to ProQuest Historical Newspapers, which includes every article, fully searchable, from a variety of American newspapers from their inception to the present, such as the *New York Times* from 1851 to 2004 and the *Hartford Courant* from 1764 to 1994. Whenever I mention this resource to students, parents, or teachers, their eyes justifiably widen in wonder. The database's search function looks through every word of every article and spits out the applicable ones immediately. The articles appear in their original form, scanned in from newspapers, showing minutiae such as cracks in the newsprint. It sure beats the old way of poring over microfiche, the thought of which makes my students shake their heads in pity when I recount tales of dark hours in the college library basement.

In the middle of a unit on the Civil War, I might ask my eighth graders to find two articles about the same general or battle from two different newspapers, such as the *Atlanta Journal-Constitution* and the *Chicago Tribune,* and then write about the tone of each piece. To scaffold the instruction, I ask them to find two significant phrases from each article, paraphrase them, and write an adjective or two describing tone. They also write a sentence or two about how the newspaper's location in the north, south, or border states affected its point of view.

Similarly, to coincide with an interdisciplinary unit on evolution and *Inherit the Wind* by the science and English teachers, my students find two articles from 1925 from the actual Scopes trial. They then write a brief summary of the story, list important quotations, and write a question they still have about the story or the trial. The headlines, such as "Man Is a Machine, No More, Darrow Says" (1925) and "We Might As Well Be Monkeys If We Act Like Them" (Rogers 1925) pique the interest of students who have little previous knowledge of the trial and set the stage for the drama that follows in English class. Eighth graders Patrick and Andrew found especially fascinating the list of scientists whom the judge barred Defense Attorney Clarence Darrow from calling as witnesses: "Why would somebody do that? Doesn't it go against free speech?" they ask. Exactly! We continue discussing the importance, as well as the inconsistency, of eyewitness accounts: they give us a window into the past but also feature the prejudices and assumptions of the time. The activity takes approximately two library days, plus time the next day in class to present and share. (See Figure 7.6 for directions and sample library worksheet.)

## Figure 7.6

### You Are There! *Inherit the Wind* and the Scopes Trial: Historical Newspaper Research

**Background:** During the next two days in the library, you and a partner will find and write notes about newspaper articles from either the year of the Scopes Trial (1925) or the year that *Inherit the Wind* appeared (1955). We have an amazing database called ProQuest Historical Newspapers that includes *every article* from the *New York Times, Los Angeles Times,* and many other papers from the 1800s to the present. It's astounding!

**Your Mission:** Find two substantial, interesting newspaper articles on your assigned search topic. Summarize them on the sheet provided. In class the next day, you will do a brief oral presentation on what you have found. You and your partner should participate equally in finding the articles. *You will be given a grade in the library each day for being on task.*

Figure 7.6 (continued)

**A. Step-by-Step Directions for Finding Articles**

1. Log in to your computer in the library. (All of this also works at home.)

   > Go to: www.ProQuestk12.com
   > Enter username and password
   > Click on "My Products Page"
   > Click on "ProQuest Historical Newspapers"

2. Type your search phrase on the top line exactly as it appears on page 2 of this packet under "Search Topics" (e.g., Scopes Trial and Bryan).

3. BEFORE you click on "Search," go to "Date Range."

4. Click on "Between" and type in 01/01/1925 to 12/31/1925.

5. Now click "Search."

6. Once you have your results, click on "View All" at the bottom of the page. Then go to "Sort Results By" on the right side of the screen and pull down to "Most relevant." Wait for the page to reload.

**B. Sorting Through Your Search Results**

Now you have a huge set of search results. To sort through them:

1. Click on and SKIM *at least four articles* from *at least four different search pages* (e.g., one can be from results 1–10, a second from results 11–20, a third from results 51–60, etc.).

2. Decide on one article that you like. DO NOT PRINT. You will do all your note taking in class without printing.

3. Fill out the newspaper worksheet on page 3 based on the first article you found.

4. Do steps 2 and 3 for a second article: ideally, one that is substantially different in focus or topic from the first.

**Search Topics**

You and your partner will be assigned one of these topics. Type them into the search box exactly as they appear here. You will present what you discover in class next week.

Figure 7.6 (continued)

1. Scopes Trial and Bryan
2. Bryan and Evolution
3. Scopes Trial and Darrow
4. Darrow and Evolution
5. Scopes Trial and Tennessee
6. Scopes and Evolution

### Citation Format for Proquest Historical Newspapers

Author (last name, first name—if given). "Headline of Article." *Name of Newspaper* Date of publication: Page number(s). ProQuest Historical Newspapers. Date of Access in Proper Format <www.ProQuestk12.com>.

Rockwell, John. "Bruce Springsteen Evolves into Figure of Rock Expression." *New York Times* 16 Jul. 1974: 43. ProQuest Historical Newspapers. 11 Oct. 2006 <www .ProQuestk12.com>.

### Articles Summary
#### NEWSPAPER ARTICLE 1

1. Citation (see page 2 of this packet for format):

2. Read through the article with your partner.

3. Summarize the main event or idea of the story in 20–30+ words:

4. What are two of the most interesting *quotations or facts* from this story that you would like to share with your classmates? List them below. Put quotations in quotation marks.

   a)


   b)


5. What is a question you still have about the story or the trial itself?

## Biography: Meeting People from the Past

Before embarking on an era, I usually ask students to briefly research the time period so they can find a hook for greater interest. I added this pre-research stage after too many days of introducing what I thought was a fascinating unit and getting only blank stares in response. I was metaphorically tap dancing in front of the whiteboard, nearly breaking a sweat to foreshadow the stupendous Songhai civilization or the grand Gilded Age while my students sat back in their chairs, mildly amused but not involved. When students build their own context, they connect with the material more; I wanted *them* to do the work so that I was not the only one excited or informed about the unit to come.

One informal way of jumping in is to ask students to spend a day in the library researching a figure from the period we are about to study, whether the Progressive Era in U.S. history or the Golden Age of Greece. *People* are often the easiest to begin with, rather than an *event* or a *social trend*, because students can personally relate to the subject's goals and challenges. In addition to having students find four significant sources of information about the person and imagine why he or she was important, I also ask them to find a "wacky fact," a detail they can share with their classmates that will also enliven the unit. This way the people become more than just a list of political accomplishments late in life. For instance, Danielle discovered that Theodore Roosevelt published a book called *The Naval War of 1812* when he was only twenty-four years old, and Justin found that muckraker Ida Tarbell majored in biology in college. "They were young once, too," said Caitlin quietly, finally looking up from doodling in her notebook.

Although this biographical activity seems simple, it gives students ownership of the period and shows them historical patterns. With the Progressive Era, for example, it quickly becomes evident that many reformers were trying to change the way that big companies operated; with the Golden Age of Greece, students allude to themes of intellectualism (Demosthenes, Socrates) and foreign relations (Persian Wars, Peloponnesian War). During these two-day library ventures, students establish the main ideas of the chapter on their own through their presentations. To help students see overarching themes, I ask them to take graded notes on their classmates' presentations. At the end, they work with partners to list two or three themes they might encounter in the unit, such as *change*, *optimism*, or *military preparation*.

For such projects, I ask the librarians ahead of time to set aside reserved resources on the topic and, sometimes, to make a list of relevant articles and websites. At the beginning of the year I show students a copyright page, table of contents, and index, and I remind them that they need to search by last name when a list is in alphabetical order. These book skills are second nature to teachers, but I well remember the first time I told a seventh-grade class to look something up in an encyclopedia and half the students searched by first name! (See Figure 7.1 for more about teaching students to search through books.)

Sometimes I do a more formal variation of this assignment called "prereading explorations" for classes with especially self-directed students. At the beginning of a unit, I assign each student a person or major concept from the textbook chapter they will be reading. For homework or in class, each student finds two sources, including one from a subscription database, and creates an attractive letter-sized poster about the term that includes an image and three paraphrased facts with parenthetical citations. Students also attach a bibliography and sources, highlighting the information that they used for their paraphrases. Before we start the reading, students present their findings and I put the posters on the wall. This activity plays into the students' love of creating fun visuals and sharing information with each other; at the same time, it lays the groundwork for longer research projects. Many students use the bullet-point notes to help them begin to review for a chapter test.

Ida Tarbell

During a typical prereading discussion, I sit in the back while students present the most interesting facts they can find. One day while sharing explorations on medieval Chinese dynasties, Kristin showed a map of the ancient city of Chang'an, emphasizing its gated walls and dozens of Buddhist and Daoist monasteries. "Why did they have so many monasteries in a trading city? Was religion really important in the Song and Tang dynasties?" Jeff wondered. "It will be, definitely," I said. "Keep in mind the city's sense of religion as you read through this chapter." When Nathan presented his visual reference link to Kubla Khan from the Yuan Dynasty, his subject was familiar to most students, but few had heard the first lines of Samuel Coleridge's "Xanadu," which Nathan then shared: "In Xanadu did Kubla Khan/ a stately pleasure dome decree." Jennifer wondered if there really was a "pleasure dome," and if so, what did it look like? In response, Nathan described the opulence of the Mongol court. From this point on, whenever students encounter Chang'an and Kubla Khan in the chapter to come, they will be able to trigger their prior knowledge that their classmates have shared.

## Ethics: The Power of Power

The most exciting research projects I've found are those that cross disciplines and create transferable understandings. One activity I did in conjunction with an eighth-grade English class study of George Orwell's *Animal Farm* gave students a deep and abiding knowledge of the characteristics and motivations of dictators. On the day I handed out the list of possible dictators and asked the class to take five minutes to look them over, adding that students could choose those not on the list if they checked with me, hands shot up. Students could not wait to pick their own personal dictators to investigate.

"Ms. Cooper, who would you say is a really terrible dictator, I mean really bad?" Andrew asked. "Well, what do you mean by 'bad'?" I replied. "Who killed the most people?" he said, illustrating a middle school fondness for extremes. "I don't know who killed the most, but Stalin was pretty awful, and I think you'd like him based on what you liked in *Animal Farm*. How about it?" I asked.

On the other hand, Sarah said she'd like to find a "nice" dictator, and her friends around her immediately started laughing. "Sarah, they're *dictators*!" Kimberly said. "They're not supposed to be *nice*!" I stepped in, suggesting that, even though no dictator was really nice, she might like the more moderate, reform-minded Nicolai Ceausescu.

For this longer project, I required several sources: an entry from Encyclopaedia Brittanica online or a book to give an overview of the dictator; a newspaper article from ProQuest Historical Newpapers or ProQuest Platinum Periodicals to show contemporary opinions of the person; and a piece from a Gale database, such as History Resource Center or Virtual Reference Library (a school-specific collection of e-books, such as *History Behind the Headlines*), to give critical commentary or additional biographical background. Students also had to turn in their highlighted sources; a bibliography to cite their sources; a chart comparing the dictator with a character in *Animal Farm* to relate to the English literary analysis requirement; and a creative response to synthesize the hard research they had gathered. For this project I gave considerable time in class over two weeks to work, both so students would not feel rushed and so I could help them at each stage.

The leeway for creative expression at the end of the project fired them up. As students looked over the imaginative possibilities at the end of the research project, such as a courtroom drama or a political cartoon, their imaginations began to swirl—at least for those who weren't trying to figure out how to earn the most points for the smallest amount of work. Many were excited by the chance to put their research into a product of their choice, to communicate in a way that showcased their talents. And I was glad that such creative synthesis produced analysis, "revealing and explaining connections, changes, and consequences" of their dictator's choices in life and impact on posterity (NCHS 1996).

In listening to the two-minute presentations at the end of the project, students perceived patterns that they had not fully grasped even after a thorough reading of Orwell's novel. "Why aren't any of the dictators women?" "Why did so many dictators not get along with their fathers?" "What makes someone want that much power?" "Do you have to have a military coup to become a dictator?" "Would I end up wanting as much power as these dictators if I had the chance?" Some questions I could answer and some I could not—they were ethical conundrums that I lobbed back at the class to discuss—but all cut to the root of what makes history fascinating. With the significant research that students had done, they became experts on the uses of power.

The next year when I taught many of the same students whom I had guided in eighth grade, *Animal Farm* and the dictators project became shorthand for what drives tyrants to govern. When we looked at how and why Shi Huangdi exerted absolute power in the Qin Dynasty, or why the North Korean totalitarian state has gone largely unopposed by its people, students remembered the commonalities they saw among dictators. In doing so, they explored global concepts such as whether absolute power corrupts those who have it and why certain leaders possess authority in a society, even when their decisions do not benefit the people. (For examples of students' creative work, see Figures 7.7a, b, and c.)

# Wrapping Up the Loose Ends

One of my favorite statements about research pops up from at least one student every year: "Doing research is a lot of work!" By its nature, research involves trying to resolve an infinite number of questions. Your students will always be able to find one more reference or another captivating story, and you will always be able to make one more suggestion on their papers. The elusive "perfect" source will always lie just around the corner. When I finish a paper or project with my students, I ask myself whether they learned useful skills and showed excitement along the way. I also ask whether I was able to connect with each student multiple times over the course of the research, from hammering out a thesis statement to squatting in the stacks to suggesting a new paragraph based on the note cards laid out on the desk. If the answer is yes, then I feel satisfied—at least until next year!

Figure 7.7a

**Tara's Poster on Slobodan Milosevic**

Figure 7.7b

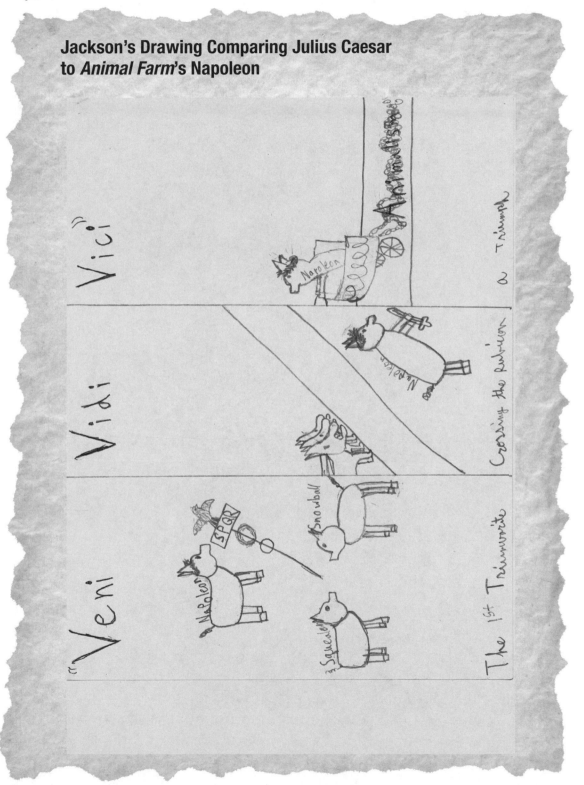

**Jackson's Drawing Comparing Julius Caesar to *Animal Farm*'s Napoleon**

Figure 7.7c

## Chapter 8

# Global Citizenship: Learning to Evaluate Ethics and Solve Problems

## What's Inside?

### Skills and Strategies

- Discuss and debate character issues
- Consider the power of individual and collective action
- Write about and illustrate values
- Simulate a town hall meeting on ballot propositions
- Analyze political commercials
- Record an oral history
- Engage in service learning

### Standards

✔ Decision making

✔ Problem solving

✔ Ethics and moral values

✔ Rights and responsibilities of citizens

By the time you arrive at the end of the school year, your students ideally will have learned the majority of the skills and strategies that you aimed to teach them: how to dissect primary and secondary sources, view the past broadly to see recurring patterns, relate history to current events, and compile research to create strong historical arguments.

But beyond meaningful content and analytical skills lies something more elusive: the hope that students will apply historical lessons, bringing the past to bear on modern ethical dilemmas. It raises a thorny question: Can we explicitly teach values? Many excellent character education programs say yes. Middle school is a critical moment to reinforce the ethical principles that elementary schools and parents have taught, at a time when students are just realizing how complex human relationships can be. Schools that verbalize and follow through on the importance of key values—such as honesty, kindness, generosity, and respect—tend to engender these ideals in their students.

While advisory groups and all-school assemblies can be useful venues for discussing such character traits, history classrooms can provide intimate settings that promote frank conversations about important human decisions. The past offers an unending supply of case studies about leaders who have risen above pettiness or succumbed to arrogance, common people who have distinguished themselves through self-sacrifice or heroism, and governments that have held to noble ideals or yielded to corruption. History provides a dramatic stage for teaching about ethics, values, morality, leadership, and problem solving.

Young adolescents long to understand such conundrums. They tune in to conflict all around them, on TV and the Web and in their own homes, and they pay careful attention to role models when solving ethical issues. *Turning Points 2000*, the gold standard vision for effective middle school education, suggests that a fifteen-year-old who has been "well served" in middle school will epitomize these five qualities (Jackson and Davis 2000, 22):

- An intellectually reflective person

- A person en route to a lifetime of meaningful work

- A good citizen

- A caring and ethical individual

- A healthy person

Discussing ethics in history class enables us to address the first four criteria and meet our responsibility to help students imagine becoming citizens of an increasingly interconnected planet.

How do we talk about character education without stepping on toes or imposing our own values on students and their families? One way to avoid being bombastic is to stick to historical facts and ask students to draw their own conclusions, especially with current political debates in which we are sorely tempted to champion our own views. When I taught high school, I felt more comfortable sharing some of my political opinions because high school students can sense which way the wind is blowing. However, middle school students are far more literal in their thinking and far more influenced by their parents than older teens; they do not always realize that a viewpoint we espouse may be biased. So with middle school classes I try to provide multiple perspectives on an issue, unless the event is something irrefutably horrific, such as the Holocaust. I've gone so far trying to be neutral that I have ended up playing devil's advocate if I think I am slipping too far to one side.

At the same time, we help our credibility with students when we show them that teachers, too, look to the past to assemble role models for our lives. One year after I taught the U.S. Constitution, I received a card on Valentine's Day from "James Madison." My exuberance over this founder's drive to preserve the Constitutional Convention in hundreds of pages of notes had led eighth grader Grace to create the tongue-in-cheek greeting. Perhaps I went overboard in idolizing our fourth president, but I hope such enthusiasm inspires students to find several figures in history to hang in their personal hall of heroes.

In the first section of this chapter, I'll focus on daily activities that help us raise questions about character traits and moral quandaries. These self-contained investigations encourage students to place themselves back in time, imagining the choices they might have made under similar circumstances. If I use a document to support such an activity, I often think not only of its language or historical content, but also of the values it implies. Then our analysis of the source does triple duty in the curriculum by helping students review reading comprehension skills, further their historical observation skills, and confront ethical issues. In the second part of the chapter, I'll unpack a project that extends students' problem-solving skills through a town meeting on local ballot propositions. Finally, I'll suggest several ways that students can take their interest in global and community activism outside the classroom.

One more note: When designing activities and projects that examine ethics, values, and the rights and responsibilities of citizenship, we can and should assess for evidence of thoughtfulness, thoroughness, and creativity in students' presentations. But keep in mind that the full impact of these ethical investigations may not show up in typical assessments. If a student says, "I'm going to vote when I'm eighteen" after a unit on the political process, we can delight in this clear connection to citizenship and encourage her enthusiasm. But we cannot include in her history grade this year her presence at the polls when she's eighteen. We measure what we can, which is considerable, and do our best to prepare students for the future.

# Where Do Values Fit Within the History Curriculum?

Certain units naturally reveal related ethical discussions. Along with laying out the skills and content I want students to understand by the end of a chapter or unit, I also write down a few values that might tie into these broad ideas. To come up with such themes, I read through the textbook and note the conflicts people are having: what issues lie at the root? For instance, the Revolutionary period in U.S. history suggests conversations about authority and risk taking, while the Constitutional period leads to talk about compromise and teamwork. In world history, feudal Europe can raise issues of security versus freedom, while Alexander the Great's conquests can prompt discussions about tolerating foreign customs. Every unit will not spur engaging conversations about morality, but every chapter can stimulate problem solving. For example, Mesopotamia and ancient India can spur students to think about the difficulties people faced when they built early river-civilizations, and the Great Depression can motivate students to consider when and how a government should aid its people during an economic crisis. Figure 8.1 suggests some possible resources for ethics-related primary sources, along with activities that highlight values and problem solving.

While some of the following five lessons refer to supplemental documents that your students can read, all of them can be based simply on a tale from the textbook—spiced up, if you like, with additional information from a book or the Internet. A common thread in these activities is asking students to imagine themselves in the roles of policymakers, which empowers them to make decisions that could change the world for future generations.

## Figure 8.1

### Resources to Guide Ethical Observations in History

Many helpful resources provide role-playing ideas and case studies for ethical discussion and problem solving. Here are several to get you started:

- Lockwood, Alan L., and David E. Harris. *Reasoning with Democratic Values: Ethical Problems in United States History.* 2 vols. New York: Teachers College Press, 1985. These books contain stories and follow-up questions that will capture your students' imagination about all periods of U.S. history, such as John Adams's decision to defend British soldiers after the Boston Tea Party. This is a must-have for any U.S. history teacher; you'll find new stories to tell your students, too.

- "TCI Brings Learning Alive." http://store.teachtci.com/Shopping/Program.aspx. Teachers' Curriculum Institute. 2008. TCI's units, some directed specifically at middle-schoolers, include thoroughly researched, creative, and ready-to-use role plays and simulations.

- Social Studies School Service. www.socialstudies.com. 2008. Type in "simulation" or "role play" to find dozens of activities for all branches of social studies.

# Respect and Tolerance for Community:
# The Reasons Behind Rules

## Values and Rationale

The monastic societies of medieval Europe governed themselves by some of the most intricate rules ever created. Investigating one of these rulebooks, the Benedictine Code, encourages students to consider why we make certain laws or have laws at all.

This lesson, which asks middle-schoolers to compare the rules under which they live to those governing monks 1,500 years ago, considers the values of respect and tolerance for others in a community. Such a comparison can also spur questions about why Benedictine monks volunteered to live so ascetically: Would any of us be so sparing in our ways? Does our society have fewer rules than those in the past? Why or why not? What impact does this have?

Given that every culture has rules, the rationale behind them—such as stability and order—can transfer to other units. We can also ask the question of whether individual loss of freedom is worth the trade-off of communal security. In response to this question, many middle-schoolers initially say that they would willingly enter a society where rules did not apply. When others point out that they would not be protected from anyone, many students change their minds, leading to discussion about the lengths to which societies will go to feel protected.

## Lesson

Consider asking students which rules they need to follow at home or school or both, and the reasons behind the rules. Compile a list on the board. Then, for a unit on medieval Europe, you could read aloud a paragraph or two from the Benedictine Code, rules for one of the most famous medieval monasteries. (For relevant excerpts, see the Medieval History Sourcebook at http://www .fordham.edu/halsall/source/rul-benedict.html.) I originally chose this source because the textbook mentioned the code in a section on medieval monasteries, and it seemed like a relevant document for middle-schoolers, who often like to question authority. The code delineates restrictions that governed every aspect of a monk's life, including the admonition to not sleep with a knife, thus preventing the monk from accidentally harming someone in his sleep.

For an assessment that ties into medieval motifs and encourages comparisons between then and now, students can make a short "illustrated manuscript." In it, they might write and illustrate a rule from the Benedictine Code (or another medieval society) on one page and a similar rule from their own life on the facing page. After students share their rules with each other, they can debate whether they think a society needs to have rules.

As your students continue studying history, they can draw on this conversation to understand the motives behind leaders' choices. This lesson, complete with artistic expression based on the culture you are studying, could be applied to any other set of rules, such as India's *Brahmana*, which explains the details of rituals set forth in the sacred Hindu *Vedas*.

# Mercy and Compassion: The Lessons Victors Leave Us

## Values and Rationale

Sometimes a negative example of a value can be even more powerful than a positive one because it shocks students into remembering the consequences of events. One of the most appalling actions by victors of war was the Roman decision to plow salt into the fields of the defeated Carthaginians after the Third Punic War, thus ruining the soil for many years. (Some say this is a legend; regardless, there is no dispute that the Romans, under General Scipio Africanus—also called Scipio Aemilianus—destroyed the city and killed thousands of its inhabitants.) The Romans acted out of vengeance. In the Senate in the years leading up to the war, Cato the Elder illustrated this hatred by repeatedly ending his speeches with the phrase, "Carthage must be destroyed." Showing students the lengths to which winners will go to avenge an economic feud makes war seem more real, not simply a list of battles, strategies, and dates. As a result, students might be less likely to valorize the process of war, even while they understand its necessity at times.

Asking half the class to take the role of the Romans forces them to imagine what might have gone through these people's minds, and hearing the perspective of the Carthaginians from the other half of the class can evoke the mercy that the Romans did not show in history. Middle school students, especially boys, respond ardently to gross or disgusting stories, perhaps because they themselves vacillate from one extreme emotion to another almost hourly. If the gory details help them remember this example, then the Romans' treatment of the Carthaginians will be a tool in their arsenal of thinking about how to treat victims humanely—whether the victim is an acquaintance battling cyber-bullies or a refugee struggling in a far-off land.

## Lesson

Once I've shared the story about the Romans' plowing salt into the fields of the Carthaginians and decimating Carthage, I split the class into two groups that represent the Carthaginians and the Romans. Within these larger groups, I ask students to form pairs or trios; each set of students needs to come up with at least three reactions to or three reasons for the Roman actions. Then I ask the Romans and the Carthaginians to stand up, facing each other. The two sides alternate back and forth, offering reasons and reactions, until every student has had a turn. (You can also split the class in half for a fishbowl discussion, with half participating and the other half taking notes.)

Afterward, students can choose a response to the debate: writing a journal entry from the perspective of the Romans or the Carthaginians about the effects of the war, drawing a picture of the destruction that shows the victors' or victims' emotions, creating a memorial plaque about the Punic Wars (Teachers' Curriculum Institute includes several such memorial plaques in its lesson plans, www.teachtci.com), or an idea of their own. Through these reflections, students can empathize with either side to understand that the ravages of war, whether physical or psychological, affect everyone.

You can add fuel to the fire of the Carthaginians' indignation by telling students what the Roman general Scipio did upon watching Carthage burn, according to the historian Polybius: "At the sight of the city utterly perishing amidst the flames Scipio burst into tears, and stood long reflecting on the inevitable change which awaits cities, nations, and dynasties, one and all, as it does every one of us men." (I found the quote on Paul Halsall's Internet Ancient History Sourcebook, http://www.fordham.edu/halsall/ancient/polybius-punic3.html. To locate this document, I went to Halsall's site, which I know is a top-notch source of world history documents, and scrolled down to "The War with Carthage.") Noting that the Romans regretted their destructive actions even as they were performing them provides a painful lesson about the psychology of revenge. Students were at first astonished and perplexed by Scipio's comment: Why in the world would he burst into tears? He just won the battle! After some discussion, we established that watching the destruction made him reflect on his own mortality and the potential collapse of even the great Roman Empire. Just as every civilization rises, every civilization eventually declines. Statements such as Scipio's humanize such vast and impersonal trends.

A similar lesson plan could also be used for General William Tecumseh Sherman's march through Georgia at the end of the Civil War or for the nuclear attacks on Hiroshima and Nagasaki at the end of World War II. Contemplating the morality of annihilating an enemy applies to any "total war" situation.

# Courage and Independent Thinking: Disobeying Immoral Commands

## Values and Rationale

Students are sometimes surprised by the idea, set forth at the Nuremburg Trials of the Nazis after World War II, that "following orders" is not a justification for committing evil acts. The knowledge that we are responsible for our own behavior, no matter who is telling us what to do, kindles further intellectual independence in these young adolescents. At the same time, however, such freedom can be intimidating: How do we know when we should not trust someone who is giving us directions? In one seventh-grade discussion, Abbie wondered whether, when she became an adult, she would know when to disobey an authority figure. In response to such questions, we can pull in examples of how older teens and adults react to this dilemma: the collapse of companies such as Enron, for example, where many employees wondered about the ethics of their actions but still followed the orders of the CEO; or, on a more personal level, the difficulty in finding the courage to talk to a trusted adult about abusive parents or boyfriends. A conversation about the "banality of evil," to use Hannah Arendt's famous phrase (Arendt 1963), applies to historical periods across time and poses the universal question that Daniel Goldhagen asked in his extremely controversial *Hitler's Willing Executioners: Ordinary Germans and the Holocaust*: How do generally decent people commit indecent actions under the orders of others? And what kinds of leaders inspire such rigid obeisance in their followers?

Part of the cowling for one of the motors for a B-25 bomber is assembled in the engine department of North American [Aviation, Inc.]'s Inglewood, California, plant (Library of Congress Prints and Photographs Division. U.S. Office of War Information, Alfred T. Palmer, photographer, October 1942.)

Investigating the evildoers of history raises another question: Should we encourage students to do in-depth research on "bad" leaders, or is such extended time with villains better spent on heroes instead? This is a dilemma that I've answered both ways, depending on the motives for the assignment and on the class. For one culminating end-of-year research project in a seventh-grade U.S. history course, my answer was no because I intended for the project to give encouragement, not drag students down, as they left my class and entered summer vacation. Throughout the year, we had spent most of our time on difficult subjects such as slavery, and we ended the curriculum with the Civil War; as a result, I hoped to show them that positive agents for change existed in recent times.

On the other hand, for eighth-grade students who had just read *Animal Farm* in English, a research project about modern dictators in history class seemed an appropriate way to cement their understanding of how a dictator like Orwell's Napoleon could rise to power without the citizens protesting. Transferring Orwell's fairy tale vision to real life was a natural next step to link the global concepts of totalitarianism, absolute power, and rule by fear. Although the cumulative dictators presentations left us feeling disheartened and pessimistic, the message this project communicated made the experience worthwhile. Students understood that many dictators share commonalities in their rise to power, such as disbanding the legislature or holding sham elections, and that we need to be alert to such ugly tactics in countries around the world. (For details of the dictators project, see the end of Chapter 7.)

## Lesson

This lesson starts with a personal thought question, continues with skits about decision-making scenarios, and ends by linking the skits to whichever controversial historical leader you are studying. The beginning thought question strikes at the heart of middle-schoolers' desire to question authority and determine their place in a confusing world: What would it take for you to disobey the wishes of a parent, teacher, or other leader? When have you not followed the wishes of someone in charge, and what happened as a result?

After we discuss their thoughts as a class or in small groups, we turn to kinesthetic and oral learning through skits that the students create themselves, based on possible real-life scenarios. Students can become even more engaged in this activity by coming up with the skit topics themselves, either in pairs or through a class discussion. The scenarios describe situations in which a leader tells a follower to perform an action that the follower might not believe is right. For example: "You and your partner are a coach and an Olympic athlete having a private conversation. As the coach, you are encouraging the player to use steroids." Through such role playing, students realize how hard it can be in real life to stand up to someone who has power over you. In addition, students are building emotional intelligence and empathy, qualities we hope our future leaders will have.

After the skits, we turn back to historical figures who confronted ethical dilemmas when asked to follow authority, such as the Qin dynasty's book burners, the Nazis' underlings during World War II, or Southern slaveholders' families before the Civil War. Students can talk with each other or compose a reflection paragraph about how the skits informed their understanding of these historical conundrums: Would you have challenged authority? Why or why not? The answer to these questions before we do the skits is usually yes, but their response often changes after they realize how much courage such iconoclasm requires. By stepping into modern-day roles of leader and follower and then applying these lessons to history, young adolescents place themselves along an ethical continuum that spans generations and affects people from all walks of life. Ideally, the next time they witness an injustice, they will have more strength of character to challenge the abuse.

# Enlightened Leadership: Treating Followers Kindly

## Values and Rationale

Studying and imitating the noble actions of famous leaders is a tried-and-true way of locating role models in history. This lesson goes a step further by asking students to imagine what they would do as leaders to secure the well-being of their people. Middle school students often are especially keen observers because they spend so many hours watching and listening to teachers, parents, and coaches in action. Tapping students' brains for their extensive knowledge of how adults in their own lives are effective and ineffective helps our young adolescents assess the actions of historical leaders. A phrase in a world history book sparked the idea for this lesson about ancient India: Emperor Chandragupta Maurya II, who served in fourth-century India, encouraged the "spiritual growth and public welfare" of his people *(Empires* 1987). It is useful to challenge the perfect nature of this statement—after all, no leader is all good or all bad—but these qualities are so broad that they give students wide latitude to interpret with respect to other leaders. This lesson could be used for dozens, if not hundreds, of inspiring leaders in history.

## Lesson

As with the lesson about challenging authority, this one also begins with a thought question. But this time, we focus on enlightened leadership, which urges students to think from the perspective of the leader rather than the follower. I give students five to ten minutes to freewrite on the following question: what would it look like if a leader encouraged the "spiritual growth and public welfare" (health and well-being) of his or her people? The ideas that students mention during the follow-up discussion—including "provide protection with an army," "allow people their own religion," "equal rights," "employment," "public hospitals," "a system of laws," and "education"—hint at what the rest of the section will cover.

Then we return to the personal so students can see that historical and current leaders share important characteristics to which everyone can aspire. I ask: Which qualities do good teachers and parents share with enlightened political leaders? Which qualities do good teachers and parents possess that are different from those in politics? Such questions can generate conversation about whether leadership is affected by the number of people one governs or by the public or private nature of such governance. You could also ask students to take home the question to discuss with their parents or another trusted adult, extending this ethical discussion of leadership beyond the classroom.

By the end of the class conversation, students have created lists of qualities that define strong political leaders. They can use these compilations as yardsticks by which to measure any other leader's success. Not every student will agree with every characteristic. In their disagreement they can act as historians, marshaling evidence to show that strong leaders act in a particular way. To reinforce these ideas visually, each student could also illustrate and describe one quality; the bulletin board could then be a "wall of qualities" that students could consult as they encounter other historical leaders. (For models of drawing and writing about qualities that you can share with your students, please see J. Ruth Gendler's *The Book of Qualities* [1988]. Thanks to dance teachers Hilary Thomas and Caterina Mercante for sharing this book with my students and me.) You could also follow this lesson with a chart that assesses several historical leaders based on the qualities that students have brainstormed: showing compassion, ensuring security, and providing for people's needs.

# Intrepid Exploration and Risk Taking: Charting New Paths

## Values and Rationale

In our increasingly interconnected, global society—a world in which employers often reward innovative approaches to work—students benefit from considering the benefits of risk taking. Explorers, both intellectual and physical, appear in nearly every chapter of every textbook. Think of Clara Barton, bringing aid to wounded soldiers in Cuba during the Spanish-American War, or Ibn Battuta, traversing Asia and Africa to chronicle Muslim customs for his readers.

While I was teaching about Thomas Jefferson in U.S. history one year, I wanted to delve into the experiences of Meriwether Lewis and William Clark beyond the usual geographic description of their arduous journey through the new Louisiana Territory that Jefferson purchased from France in 1803. I thought that entering into the minds of these explorers as they started their trip might help students understand the courage needed to embark on such a journey. In addition, the lesson could encourage students to think about "the interactions among states and nations and their cultural complexities" (NCSS 1994), as well as consider the flora and fauna and tribes and cities that Lewis and Clark would encounter while they served as both ambassadors and explorers.

To find a document that hinted at the psychology of the trip, I followed a colleague's recommendation to the amazing HistoryTeacher.Net site, which lists dozens, if not hundreds, of primary documents for each time period. Under "Jeffersonian Republicanism," I found Thomas Jefferson's instructions to Meriwether Lewis from 1803, the year of the Louisiana Purchase (http://www.historyteacher.net/AHAP/Weblinks/AHAP_Weblinks6.htm; the site leads you to the actual document at http://www.mt.net/~rojomo/landc.htm). This document not only previewed the challenges that the duo might face on their long trip, such as surviving climate changes and navigating river tributaries, but it also helped us understand President Thomas Jefferson as micromanager, someone who wanted to put everything on paper because he would not be able to join the team himself. His words provide an unusually clear depiction of a leader's hopes for the future. As students read Jefferson's meticulous instructions, they could anticipate forthcoming events on the journey with an insider's eye. Curiosity whetted, they could follow the historical trail with greater enthusiasm and start to ask themselves, "What would I have done?"

## Lesson

You can choose several paragraphs of Jefferson's directions to Lewis and Clark from 1803. The most effective sections to stimulate middle-schoolers' concrete thinking can be found in the middle of the document, where Jefferson lists everything he would like the explorers to note as they traverse America's recently expanded territory.

Consider having small groups of students pick one topic from the list—such as minerals or diseases—and discuss how difficult or easy they believe it would be to find information about this topic on the journey. Then each group can stand at a different place around the perimeter of the room with a drawing that illustrates the specific quest. The class as a whole can rank the topics from easiest to most difficult, either compiling a written list on the board or physically representing the continuum from "most difficult" to "least difficult." For the items that might be tough to assess quickly on a long journey (such as "peculiarities in [people's] laws," for instance, "or the remains . . . of any [animals] which may be deemed rare or extinct"), students might make an action plan—in the form of a flow chart, a list, or even symbols—of how they would approach the problem. Finally, students can illustrate half a dozen of Jefferson's priorities on a piece of paper. What does the drawing show about what is important to the president? How might Lewis and Clark's interests diverge from Jefferson's as they travel? Such questions bring into focus the difference between desk politicians and outdoor explorers, as well as the need for individuality and quick decision making when one is forging new paths.

# Creating an Informed Citizenry: The Ins and Outs of Lawmaking

Once we have established connections between history and our students' lives by investigating values such as compassion, risk taking, and leadership, we can use these insights to help us solve modern problems. Taking in the broad sweep of the political spectrum, as with the party platform debates in Chapter 6, is a useful process for giving students a sense of our country's and the world's major concerns. For a more specific, hands-on case study, we need look no further than the topics that vex every community: local and state ballot measures. By examining representative government through the lens of a school referendum or a local utility's request for a rate increase, students can understand how voters' decisions influence the quality of technology in their classrooms or the constraints on their family budgets.

This project's prop, the gray newsprint ballot booklet that voters receive in their mailboxes, communicates immediately to students that they will be asked to consider real problems instead of make-believe scenarios. When this annual or semiannual list of initiatives and measures lands in my mailbox, I know I need to set aside several hours to read the state's descriptions and consult local newspapers, the League of Women Voters' nonpartisan summaries, and often several other websites. Some students have seen these booklets at home, so they groan when I put them on display; they have heard their parents weigh and complain about the issues. Some students have no idea what the booklets describe because their parents do not or cannot vote. I tell students that they are going to wrestle with issues that most grown-ups don't understand and that, when they are done, they will be able to tell their parents how to cast their ballots. Students usually giggle at this thought; such generational table-turning lends credibility to their academic work because they will be able to use their knowledge to teach an adult.

Giving students real-life subjects to address through ballot propositions serves several purposes:

- It helps them see that citizens can solve problems by consulting a variety of sources. We do not have to fix everything by ourselves, nor should we. Resources exist to help us be wise participants in democracy.

- It communicates that we are confident in our students' growing ability to consider complex choices.

- It provides immediate relevance—"Oh, that's what all those serious-sounding television commercials are about!" This process also demystifies media coverage of local propositions so students can cut through the blather and form their own opinions.

- It places them in the role of political commentators and analysts so they can become local, state, and national leaders in years to come.

- It conveys important information about the process of lawmaking. Students will be able to apply this knowledge when they are asked to sign a petition outside the grocery store or when they want to place a proposition on the ballot themselves.

To accomplish these goals, students begin by reading through and briefly summarizing at least four short sources of information about their ballot measure. (For nonpartisan explanations that students can understand, go to the League of Women Voters' Smart Voter site, www.smartvoter.org.) Students then share their interpretations with a partner or group and clarify any misunderstandings with their peers or with me. Part of the beauty of this assignment is that the teacher is not the final voice of wisdom. My students see that I am challenged by the questions they are asking and that I do not always have all the answers—but I will make my best effort to find them.

On Election Day, we take a class vote on the propositions that the students have presented. The next day, we hold a town meeting to consider how the measures' success or failure will affect students' lives. During this discussion, when we put the desks in a circle and talk about how each proposition fared, I hear words I never expected to hear in a middle school classroom: "Ms. Cooper, can you believe that Measure 89, about the legislature's power to tax, lost by less than one percent?" Taylor asks. Stacy said she was angry that Measure 6, about changing the source of our water supply, didn't pass: "Don't people realize that we need to improve our ways of getting water or we won't have enough in twenty years?" Gabriella, pondering the election from a financial perspective, observed: "It's amazing that the opponents to Measure 99 spent so much money on commercials, but it still didn't pass. I guess the people of this state can see through false advertising."

In this conversation marked by pride in their research and annoyance at what they sometimes see as foolish decisions by adult voters, students are using the knowledge they have gathered to voice their opinions on the political process. As organizations such as Rock the Vote have discovered, bringing relevant issues to young people can give them a reason to care about the political process.

When we tell middle-schoolers that they are capable of understanding the issues that adults find confusing, they will often surprise us—and themselves—with their tenacity and thoroughness. And, when they do vote at eighteen or begin their careers at twenty-two or twenty-five, we can hope that they will remember how competently they analyzed the political system when they were eleven or fourteen. Finally, we can dream that they will become involved citizens who understand how the democratic process works and eventually seek to improve it.

Extensions of this lesson could include widening the audience of the presentations, thus giving even more credence to the students' work and informing parents and other adults about the ballot in an enjoyable way. We also could schedule the presentations for a small assembly or class meeting and then take a mock vote of the audience. A parents' group might be especially receptive to the students' work, and such scrutiny would inspire the students to polish their work even more.

# Connections Outside the Classroom: Engaging with the Real World

The possibilities for engaging students in discussions about the rights and responsibilities of citizens, decision making, governmental accountability, and thoughtful problem solving are nearly limitless. Beyond the bedrock of meaningful conversations about history and current events, one of the best ways to help our kids think about the world they will encounter as adults is to venture outside school. In the process, students meet people who have real history to share. Being taken seriously by organizations outside campus also boosts middle-schoolers' self-confidence and encourages them to create more connections with their communities in the future. One event that can tie in directly with classroom research is National History Day (www.nationalhistoryday.org), a contest that highlights the role of primary sources and encourages students to think critically. Following are three more suggestions for helping students look beyond their self-interests, understand their communities better, and, perhaps, make a lasting contribution to historical scholarship and current issues.

## Oral History Projects

Many cities sponsor oral history projects: repositories of tapes and transcripts that tell how life was years ago. When I interviewed local luminaries for my city's project, I found new perspectives on construction work in the 1930s, architectural innovations in the 1950s, and court-ordered school desegregation in the 1970s. As our students talk with relatives or strangers about experiences decades ago, they hear stories of the past from someone who lived it. In the process, they often realize that history can be told from as many different perspectives as there are people on Earth. The students are acting as historians themselves, contributing valuable information for future researchers and considering how they would have reacted to the same tribulations.

One year I asked students to participate in the Veterans History Project (http://www.loc.gov/vets) sponsored by the Library of Congress, which collects information, tapes, and transcripts on all American wars. The project provided a free trainer who came to school and talked with students about how to interview effectively. About half the students interviewed relatives or family friends, and the others found interview subjects through references from teachers or family members. On the day when students shared bits of their taped interviews with the class, the atmosphere was nearly reverential. To hear stories about Korea, Vietnam, the Persian Gulf War, and even World War II from real people who lived through the conflicts was to stare war in the face. The students imagined themselves trudging through the snow in Germany or wading through a rice field in Vietnam, and they wondered whether they would have panicked or kept their cool. Such a project takes considerable in- and out-of-class time, as well as frequent check-in points; however, I've found that the immediate identification with the process and problems of history makes everything else we study more meaningful.

Oral histories are one history-related example of a much larger category of projects: service learning, in which students perform curricular-related volunteer work in the community for academic credit in their classes, often during their school day. For more information, you can look to these resources:

- Roberts, Pamela. *Kids Taking Action: Community Service Learning Projects K–8*. Portland, ME: Stenhouse, 2002.

- Kaye, Cathryn Berger. *The Complete Guide to Service Learning: Proven, Practical Ways to Engage Students in Civic Responsibility, Academic Curriculum, and Social Action*. Minneapolis: Free Spirit, 2003.

- National Youth Leadership Council. www.nylc.org. 2008.

- Learn and Serve America. www.servicelearning.org. 2005–2008.

## Model United Nations and Speech and Debate

Middle school students can address real-world problems with their own imaginative solutions through two well-established forums: model United Nations conferences and speech and debate tournaments. For Model UN, students from one school usually assume the role of one or more countries, with different people serving on different committees as representatives of that country. Beforehand, students research the country's relationships with the rest of the world; during the conference, they act as UN representatives by sponsoring and writing resolutions and lobbying for their cause. Through caucuses and compromises, they mimic their real-world counterparts, reinforcing how messy and exciting diplomacy can be. Middle-schoolers usually compete in Junior Model UN conferences. (For more information, please see "Model UN Headquarters" [2002].)

UN General Assembly Chamber in New York

The National Forensic League sponsors a junior branch for middle-schoolers who want to compete in speech and debate tournaments. Events can include extemporaneous speeches about current issues and team or individual debate competitions focusing on domestic and foreign policy topics. Speech contests provide an outlet for students who wish their history teacher would talk about current events every day, and they can also give confidence to shyer students who want to enter with a memorized, prepared speech in a less impromptu category. (For more information, please see National Forensic League [2007].)

## Field Trips

With lean school budgets, a dearth of chaperones, and the challenge of encouraging students to be on their best behavior in public, field trips can seem like too much trouble. However, visiting a historical museum or site gives students a hands-on exploration of the past in a way that few other experiences can match. Many larger museums offer discounts for students and school groups, and some venues are free with a reservation. When I've taken my students to a local architectural treasure or historical site, I've noticed that they view that history more seriously when we return because they realize that real people were confronting thorny issues in real time. (Field trips also give us the chance to require students to write thank-you notes afterward, not a skill that you see in the standards but certainly one that will serve them well for life.)

Out-of-school excursions go over best with other teachers and school administrators when the events have a multidisciplinary focus, such as the trip I took with our school's eighth grade to the Japanese American National Museum in Los Angeles. The visit helped students understand Jeanne Wakatsuki Houston and James Houston's *Farewell to Manzanar* in English class, supported by a background on World War II in both English and history. Interdisciplinary trips help justify the expense and time away from school because more people are involved, and such interconnectedness also encourages teachers from other disciplines to help arrange chaperones, organize activities, and prepare students.

The Japanese American National Museum staff offered a variety of activities during our visit. Among the compelling connections: tours through the permanent collection about the internment camps, conducted by people who lived in the camps during World War II; participatory origami and *taiko* drumming to showcase traditional Japanese arts; and a video that explained the legacy of the internment camps in U.S. history. The field trip became a touchstone throughout the school year, including the time I said, "Remember when you saw the actual letter from the first President Bush that gave reparations to the former internees in the 1990s? Now we're going to talk about other groups, such as descendants of African American slaves and Holocaust survivors, who are still seeking such redress." Observing history's trail adds resonance to the curriculum and encourages students to look beyond their everyday experiences to the world ahead.

# Rolling Up Our Sleeves to Touch History

When we make our classes more authentic by directly connecting historical topics to contemporary problems and politics, our students gain the context they need to make judicious decisions today. They realize that their ancestors, though living in different times without light-speed technology and accelerated schedules, encountered similar ethical dilemmas. Stressing our common values and concerns links people across cultures and eras and helps students gain respect for the communities they will shape in the future.

# Epilogue

Teachers rarely take time to savor a good day. Parents will occasionally send cards at the end of the school year thanking us for teaching their sons or daughters well, and students will sometimes write appreciation notes of their own. (In the middle grades, gratitude might be presented in unexpected formats, such as the language of cell phone texting: "You are the best teacher! Thanx for everything. Have a gr8 summer, and don't 4get me!")

Kudos recognizing our cumulative influence can feel terrific, but good teachers also care about daily impact. Yesterday we engaged our students—but what new and exciting plans do we have for them today? No matter how student-centered our courses are, we must deliver five or six strong performances a day, 180-plus days a year, and the pressure to be inspiring can overwhelm us.

Once in a while, we have to step back and congratulate ourselves when a week has gone particularly well. I remember one day when I looked at my lesson planner and noticed that I had addressed a range of historical issues and skills during a two-week span, differentiating the instruction to give students multiple entry points into the subject. We had compared the strengths and weaknesses of the Qin and Han dynasties in ancient China with the United States today, trying to decide which civilization was most successful. In our current events discussions about a recent presidential debate, I had encouraged students to argue the side they didn't agree with to help them understand key issues from multiple perspectives. We had inferred details about the influence of Mongol culture by looking at art from Iran during the fourteenth century, noticing in particular the Chinese magical symbols of a dragon and a phoenix. During one class period, I had consulted with all the students about their first essay test, pointing out examples of strong analysis and suggesting places where they could shore up their facts. My students also had chosen topics for a creative research project about India and would spend three days in the library the following week. Each day,

I knew we could have gone deeper. But looking back, I realized that we had done well, and before moving ahead I needed to take a moment to pat myself on the back.

If we're fortunate, our students might congratulate us too. My second son was born in March one year, a perfect "teacher baby" birthday that allowed me to take off most of the second semester. On the last day before maternity leave, my long-term substitute for ninth-grade world history said that, even though I had planned current events presentations and a preview of the upcoming unit on Greece, he had a surprise in mind. For the next fifteen minutes, each of my students, most of whom I had also taught in eighth-grade English, told me what they liked about my teaching. I share this story with you because their tributes went to the heart of what I want to do—what we can *all* do as middle school history teachers. The students' comments focused on two main ideas:

First, they felt a personal connection to history. They recognized the influence of real human beings whose actions, motivations, and leadership resonate through the ages. And they could see themselves leaving a similar mark on future generations.

Second, they believed that I cared about them individually, not just as a group of history students.

By the time their tributes ended, all I could say was how privileged I was to teach them. Most importantly, I was privileged to know them. (I was reminded of a teacher friend's comment that while she loves math, working with numbers is just an excuse to know her students.)

Teaching history is a joy because we have a ringside seat at the showcase of humanity's greatest conquests, tragedies, and dilemmas. If we make this subject personal and compelling for our students, their understanding of the generations that came before them can positively shape the world they have inherited. As a middle school history teacher, I can think of no greater role than making sure their hearts and minds are up to the challenge.

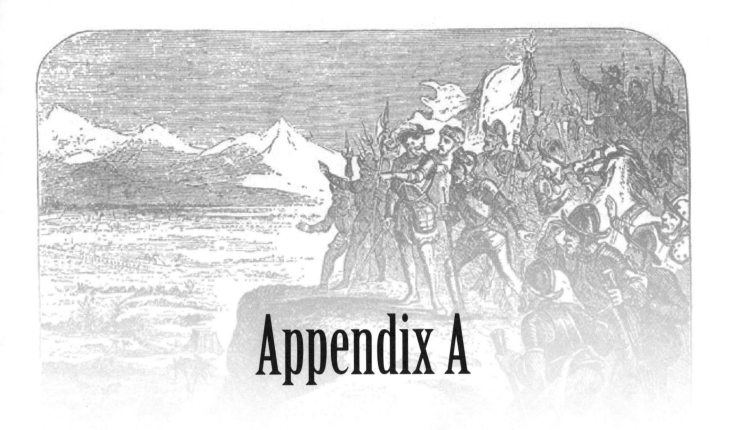

# Appendix A

## Rich Historical Narratives

Here is a starter list of some of my favorite titles that feature compelling historical narratives or geographical descriptions. I know I've left out many wonderful books. Often I'll use only one page or paragraph with my classes, enough to give students a sense of the historian's style without overwhelming them.

### American History and Current Events

- Catherine Drinker Bowen, *Miracle at Philadelphia: The Story of the Constitutional Convention, May to September 1787* (Boston: Little, Brown, 1966).

- Dee Brown, *Bury My Heart at Wounded Knee: An Indian History of the American West* (New York: Holt, Rinehart, and Winston, 1970).

- *Cobblestone* magazine, Carus Publishing Company. 2008. http://www.cricketmag.com/ProductDetail.asp?pid=15&type=.

- John Demos, *The Unredeemed Captive: A Family Story from Early America* (New York: Alfred A. Knopf, distributed by Random House, 1994).

- Barbara Ehrenreich, *Nickel and Dimed: On (Not) Getting by in America* (New York: Metropolitan Books, 2001).

- Joseph Ellis, *Founding Brothers* (New York: Alfred A. Knopf, 2000); on the formation of the United States government.

- Bob Greene, *Once Upon a Town: The Miracle of the North Platte Canteen* (New York: W. Morrow, 2002); on World War II.

- Erik Larson, *The Devil in the White City: Murder, Magic, and Madness at the Fair That Changed America* (New York: Crown, 2003); on Chicago World's Fair of 1893. I avoid sharing the often-grisly alternate chapters that describe a murderer at large in the city at the same time as the fair.

- Edmund Morris, *The Rise of Theodore Roosevelt* (New York: Ballantine Books, 1979). Also *Theodore Rex,* the sequel (New York: Random House, 2001).

- *Opposing Viewpoints* books and electronic subscription databases. Gale Group. http://www .gale.cengage.com/OpposingViewpoints.

- Eric Schlosser, *Fast Food Nation: The Dark Side of the All-American Meal* (Boston: Houghton Mifflin, 2001); on current events.

- Jay Winik, *April 1865: The Month That Saved America* (New York: HarperCollins, 2001); on the Civil War.

## World History and Geography

- *Calliope* magazine, Cobblestone Publishing. *Cobblestone* magazine, Carus Publishing Company. 2008. http://www.cricketmag.com/ProductDetail.asp?pid=14&type=.

- Jared Diamond, *Collapse: How Societies Choose to Fail or Succeed* (New York: Penguin, 2005). See discussion of teaching strategies in Chapter 2.

- Jared Diamond, *Guns, Germs, and Steel: The Fate of Human Societies* (New York: W. W. Norton, 1999).

- Bruce Feiler, *Walking the Bible: A Journey by Land Through the Five Books of Moses* (New York: Morrow, 2001); on ancient societies in the Fertile Crescent.

- Ross King, *Brunelleschi's Dome: How a Renaissance Genius Reinvented Architecture* (New York: Walker, 2000).

- Emma Larkin, *Finding George Orwell in Burma* (New York: Penguin Press, 2005).

- Ellen Levine, *A Fence Away from Freedom: Japanese Americans and World War II* (New York: G. P. Putnam's Sons, 1995); on oral histories.

- William Manchester, *A World Lit Only by Fire: The Medieval Mind and the Renaissance* (Boston: Little, Brown, 1992).

- *Opposing Viewpoints* books and electronic subscription databases. Gale Group. http://www .gale.cengage.com/OpposingViewpoints.

- Oliver Sacks, *Oaxaca Journal* (Washington, D.C.: National Geographic, 2002); a search for ferns and history in Mexico.

- Peter W. Schroeder and Dagmar Schroeder-Hildebrand, *Six Million Paper Clips: The Making of a Children's Holocaust Memorial* (Minneapolis: Kar-Ben, 2004); suggested for grades 4 through 8.

- Dava Sobel, *Longitude: The True Story of a Lone Genius Who Solved the Greatest Scientific Problem of His Time* (New York: Walker, 1995).

# Appendix B

## Primary Source Pointers

How do we decide which documents to use among the hundreds available, especially in the print-rich sources of American history? I suggest the following criteria:

- The document is so important to the historical period that it can help students see major themes of that time in a new light.

- The document presents an argumentative strategy that students can try to emulate when writing or speaking.

- The document helps students understand a key historical concept—such as leadership, civic ideals, economic principles, or cultural identity—from a human perspective.

## How Do We Use the Source to Connect Students to History?

1. **Make it personal.** Especially with a document that might not seem immediately relevant, I often tell my students to imagine how they would be affected by the conditions described. How would they rule if they were judging John Brown's trial for the Harper's Ferry raid?

How would they solve the problems of insane asylums that Dorothea Dix describes in front of the Massachusetts legislature? Such a personal connection makes history immediate and thrusts our students into the moral and human issues of the past.

2. **Choose words judiciously.** I rarely use all of a primary text, especially if the subject is weighty or the passage long. One or two paragraphs is usually sufficient to convey the document's essence and allow for interesting close reading. I often choose the sections with the most concrete imagery and humor.

3. **Strive for variety.** Use different kinds of documents as much as possible: speeches, acts, proclamations, letters, diaries, trial proceedings, military orders, newspaper articles, handbills, song lyrics, poetry, photographs, and diagrams. Some students will gravitate to one kind of source more than another, and these changeups also keep the teacher interested.

4. **Pick sources that tell a different story than the textbook version.** For some sources, such as the Northwest Ordinance of 1787, unpacking the actual document probably won't give students much more flavor than reading the description in their textbook. For other sources, however, the document tells more than the book: for instance, George Washington's 1793 "Proclamation of Neutrality" shows his strong desire to remain above the European fray.

5. **Troll a variety of sources for primary documents.** I often look to anthologies for short excerpts, such as Norman F. Cantor's *Medieval Reader* for the Middle Ages or William Safire's *Lend Me Your Ears: Great Speeches in History* for all times and areas. The Internet is also an excellent source for all kinds of documents, especially those from 1922 or before that are thus in the public domain. (See number 7 in this list on fair use policy for educators.) Often I will see a reference to a proclamation, source, or piece of art in the textbook and then type in the title on Google to see if I can find a usable piece. Many government and museum sites, such as the National Archives (www.archives.gov) and the Library of Congress American Memory site (memory.loc.gov), offer a wealth of resources. A few companies that sell fine primary source compendiums are Jackdaw, with folders filled with facsimiles of original primary sources, and Social Studies School Service (www.socialstudies.com), which offers a wide variety of materials.

6. **Look for artifacts, too.** Going beyond the written text to artistic and archaeological pieces can tap into students' different learning styles. Many museum websites have excellent exhibits containing artifacts, often with superb free teachers' guides. I find these sites by using a search engine and typing in my current topic, such as "terra-cotta soldiers." For instance, the British Museum website has a teacher resource pack on the Qin Dynasty's terra-cotta soldiers from a 2007–08 exhibit (http://www.britishmuseum.org/whats_on/all_current_exhibitions/the_first_emperor/for_schools_and_teachers.aspx), and the Metropolitan Museum of Art hosted an exhibit from later China titled "China: Dawn of a Golden Age, 200–750 AD" (http://www.metmuseum.org/explore/china_dawn/index.html). The National Center for History in the Schools sells teaching units that include primary source photos and artifacts; examples are "Ghana: Medieval Trading Empire of West Africa" for world history, grades 5–8, and "Mexican Immigration to the United States, 1900–1999"

for U.S. history, grades 8–12. (To order, go to http://nchs.ucla.edu. Many guides are also available as e-books for immediate purchase and use.)

7. **Keep in mind fair use guidelines.** As teachers, we are allowed to copy small portions of certain documents for temporary classroom use. However, there are many restrictions, notably how often and how much of a text we use and whether our use of it will deprive the publisher of profit. An example of what we cannot do is create a course pack or anthology without securing copyright permissions for everything included. Education World, an excellent website for all things teaching, has a five-part series about copyright and fair use that I've found helpful in sorting through this confusing issue: http://www.education-world.com/a_curr/curr280.shtml. You can also go to the government site on copyright and fair use at http://www.copyright.gov/fls/fl102.html.

A slightly different version of these tips was originally published as "10 Techniques for Teaching with Primary Source Documents," by Sarah Cooper, in the UCLA History-Geography Project Newsletter, Spring 2002.

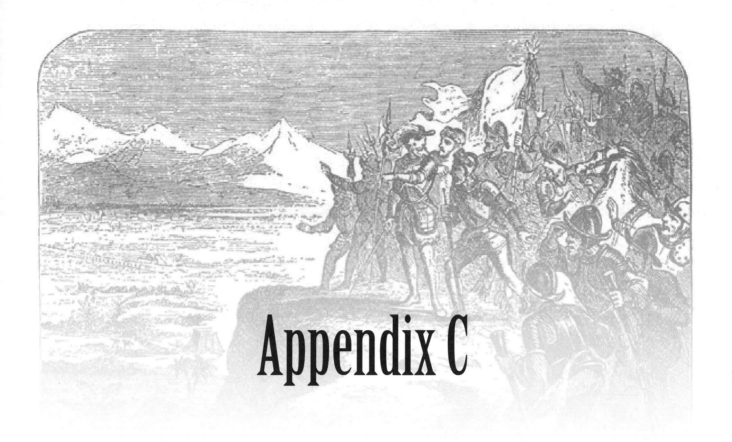

# Appendix C

## Ways to Probe Primary Sources

### First, Ask These Questions

When trying to gather evidence from a primary source, first try to answer these basic questions. (You may not have enough information to do so.)

1. What is it?

2. Who wrote or made it?

3. When was it written or made?

4. Where was it written or made?

5. How was it written or made?

6. What evidence does this source contribute to my research?

### Then Ask, What Is the Meaning of This Primary Source?

1. Why was this document/object written or made?

2. Who was the intended audience/user?

3.  What questions does this source raise? What don't we know about this source?

4.  What other information do we have about this document or object?

5.  What other sources are like this one?

6.  What other sources might help answer our questions about this one?

7.  What else do we need to know in order to understand the evidence in this source?

8.  What have others said about this or similar sources?

9.  How does this source help me to answer my research question?

10. How does evidence from this source alter or fit into existing interpretations of the past?

Reprinted with permission from http://dohistory.org/on_your_own/toolkit/primarySources.html.

# Appendix D

## Resources for Primary Sources

The most useful places to begin looking for primary sources are your history textbook or your students' language arts anthology because both books are close at hand and targeted toward middle school interests and comprehension levels. In addition, the websites that accompany most textbooks often offer excellent and relevant selections. Many primary sources, poems, songs, and other documents are also easy to find on the Internet, and I frequently use a search engine to locate famous sources, such as the Declaration of Independence or a fragment of Confucius's *Analects*.

The following sources—just a tiny sampling of what is out there—offer appealing pathways into the rhetorical realm of history.

## U.S. History

- Susan M. Pojer, HistoryTeacher.Net. www.historyteacher.net. 1998–2009. An astonishing compendium of primary sources, in addition to quizzes and other study materials, that is so good it has been featured in the *New York Times*. A New York social studies teacher has maintained the site for more than a decade as a labor of love. For reams of U.S. primary sources organized by time period, scroll to the bottom of the home page and click "American History AP," then "Web Links."

- Diane Ravitch, ed., *The American Reader: Words That Moved a Nation* (New York: HarperCollins, 1990). A fine mix of the tried-and-true with some lesser-known choices.

- Linda R. Monk, *Ordinary Americans: U.S. History Through the Eyes of Everyday People* (Alexandria, VA: Close Up, 1994). Used copies of this out-of-print book are available through online bookstores. Monk's collection provides invaluable and fascinating social history documents arranged chronologically.

- Henry Louis Gates, Jr., and Nellie Y. McKay, *The Norton Anthology of African American Literature* (New York: W. W. Norton, 1996). Although this is a literature anthology, it has historical documents in its earlier sections and relevant literary pieces from more modern periods, such as the Harlem Renaissance.

- Caroline Kennedy, *A Patriot's Handbook: Songs, Poems, Stories, and Speeches Celebrating the Land We Love* (New York: Hyperion, 1993). This book offers a wide assortment of pieces arranged under themes, such as the rights we hold under the Constitution.

- *The Primary Source Document Series* (Logan, IA: Perfection Learning, 1987, 1988). You can find this on www.socialstudies.com. The seven books in this series each focus on approximately a dozen documents, and reproducible questions lead students through each selection. This book might not be for everyday use because the questions can focus on tiny details, but it is helpful to lead students through a deeper exploration of key documents.

## World History

- Paul Halsall, ed., "Internet History Sourcebooks Project," 10 Dec. 2006. http://www .fordham.edu/halsall. This phenomenal website's three main sourcebooks are Ancient History, Medieval, and Modern. From these, Halsall has compiled sub-sourcebooks on African, East Asian, global, Indian, Islamic, Jewish, and women's history and the history of science.

- Jeanne Larsen, trans., *Willow, Wine, Mirror, Moon: Women's Poems from Tang China* (Rochester, NY: BOA Editions, 2005). This collection from a variety of poets beautifully shows the creativity of the Tang dynasty.

- Norman F. Cantor, *The Medieval Reader* (New York: HarperCollins, 1994). You will learn a lot about the Middle Ages just by browsing through the table of contents to see the book's huge array of sources.

- Clarice Swisher, ed., *The Spread of Islam* (San Diego: Greenhaven Press, 1999). This book is mainly a collection of essays, but I like it best for the clear maps and accessible primary and secondary source excerpts embedded throughout.

- Ronald Mellor and Amanda H. Podany, *The World in Ancient Times: Primary Sources and Reference Volume* (New York: Oxford University Press, 2005). This book is directed toward middle school students and includes introductions, definitions, and excerpts for 76 primary sources, from the Egyptian *Book of the Dead* to a sermon by the Buddha.

- Lewis Copeland and Lawrence W. Lamm, *The World's Great Speeches*, 3rd enlarged edition (New York: Dover, 1973). This old-fashioned book includes many twentieth-century political speeches from America and elsewhere, as well as a core selection from ancient Greece and Rome.

# Resources

Amos, H. D., and A. G. P. Lang. 1982. *These Were the Greeks*. Chester Springs, PA: Dufour Editions.

Appiah, Anthony, and Henry Louis Gates, eds. 1999. *Africana: The Encyclopedia of the African and African-American Experience*. New York: Basic Civitas Books.

Arendt, Hannah. 1963. *Eichmann in Jerusalem: A Report on the Banality of Evil*. New York: Viking Press.

Ayodele, Thompson. 1992. "Free Trade Will Help Africa." In *Africa: Opposing Viewpoints*, ed. David L. Bender and Bruno Leone. San Diego: Greenhaven.

Banks, Sandy. 2007. "A Small Triumph for Children in Foster Care." *Los Angeles Times*, Nov. 10: B1. http://articles.latimes.com/2007/nov/10/local/me-banks10.

Barton, Nancy. 1982. "It Almost Didn't Happen." *Cobblestone*, September.

Berkeley, Bill. 2001. *The Graves Are Not Yet Full: Race, Tribe, and Power in the Heart of Africa*. New York: Basic Books.

Bransford, J., A. Brown, and R. Cocking. 2000. *How People Learn: Brain, Mind, Experience, and School.* Expanded ed. Washington, DC: National Academy Press. As cited in Metiri Group, Cisco Systems, Inc., 2008. *Multimodal Learning Through Media: What the Research Says.* San Jose: Cisco Systems, Inc. http://www.cisco.com/web/strategy/docs/education/Multimodal-Learning-Through-Media.pdf.

Brecht, Bertolt. 1947. Trans. H. R. Hays. *Selected Poems.* New York: Harcourt Brace Jovanovich.

British Museum. 2008. "The First Emperor: China's Terracotta Army." May 3. http://www.britishmuseum.org/whats_on/all_current_exhibitions/the_first_emperor/for_schools_and_teachers.aspx.

Brummett, Palmira Johnson, et al. 2000. *Civilization Past and Present.* Vol. 1, 9th ed. New York: Longman.

California Democratic Party. 2008. "2008 Platform Committee." http://www.cadem.org/site/c.jrLZK2PyHmF/b.1196347.

California Republican Party. 2008. "Republican Party Platform, 2008–2011." Feb. 24. http://www.cagop.org/index.cfm/about_party_platform.htm.

California State Board of Education. 1998. *History—Social Science Standards for California Public Schools: Kindergarten Through Grade Twelve.* http://www.cde.ca.gov/be/st/ss/documents/histsocscistnd.pdf.

Cooper, Sarah. 2002. "10 Techniques for Teaching with Primary Source Documents." Spring. UCLA History-Geography Project Newsletter.

———. 2003. "My Dinner with GW: Eighth Graders Learn History Through Current Events." *Common-place* 4: 1.

Dalton, Rex. 2006. "Awash with Fossils." *Nature* 439: 14.

Davidson, Basil. 1959. *The Lost Cities of Africa.* Rev. ed. Boston: Little, Brown.

The Democratic Party. 1995–2008. www.democrats.org.

Demosthenes. 1973. "The Second Oration Against Philip." In *The World's Great Speeches*, ed. Lewis Copeland and Lawrence W. Lamm. 3rd enlarged ed. New York: Dover.

Diamond, Jared. 2005. *Collapse: How Societies Choose to Fail or Succeed.* New York: Penguin.

———. 1999. *Guns, Germs, and Steel: The Fates of Human Societies.* New York: W. W. Norton.

"The Dinner Party by Judy Chicago." 2004–2008. Brooklyn Museum. http://www.brooklynmuseum .org/exhibitions/dinner_party.

DuBois, W. E. B. 1903. *The Souls of Black Folk.* Chicago: A. C. McClurg. http://www.bartleby .com/114/.

*Empires Ascendant: Time Frame 400 BC–AD 200.* 1987. Alexandria, VA: Time-Life Books.

"Evaluating Ballot Measures." 2000. League of Women Voters Education Fund. Jan. 19. http:// ca.lwv.org/lwvc.files/mar00/pchelp.html#bonds.

Fischer, David Hackett. 1994. *Paul Revere's Ride.* New York: Oxford University Press.

Forero, Juan. 2006. "Leaving the Wild, and Rather Liking the Change." *New York Times*, May 11. http://www.nytimes.com/2006/05/11/world/americas/11colombia.html?_r=1&scp=1&sq= leaving%20the%20wild%20forero&st=cse&oref=slogin.

Franklin, Benjamin. 2003. "On the Federal Constitution." In *The World's Famous Orations*, ed. William Jennings Bryan. New York: Funk and Wagnalls, 1906. http://www.bartleby .com/268/.

French, Howard W., and Lydia Polgreen. 2007. "Chinese Entrepreneurs Flourish in Africa Where Others Faltered." *New York Times*, Aug. 18: A1.

Friedman, Thomas. 2006. *The World Is Flat: A Brief History of the Twenty-First Century.* New York: Farrar, Straus and Giroux.

———. 2007. "No, No, No, Don't Follow Us." *New York Times*, Nov. 4. http://www.nytimes .com/2007/11/04/opinion/04friedman.html?_r=1&oref=slogin.

Garrison, Jessica, and Erika Hayasaki. 2001. "Schools Roll Out Programs to Help Crack Down on Bullies." *Los Angeles Times*, Sep. 6: B6.

Gendler, J. Ruth. 1988. *The Book of Qualities.* New York: Perennial.

Goldhagen, Daniel Jonah. 1996. *Hitler's Willing Executioners: Ordinary Germans and the Holocaust.* New York: Knopf.

Graves, Donald H. 1999. *Bring Life into Learning: Create a Lasting Literacy.* Portsmouth, NH: Heinemann.

Halsall, Paul, ed. 2006. "Internet History Sourcebooks Project." Dec. 10. http://www.fordham.edu/halsall.

Hanson, Victor Davis. 2005. "Battles Changes, Wars Don't: From Ancient Greece to Modern Iraq, History Shows Us That Fear, Honor, and Self-Interest Drive Hostilities Between the States." *Los Angeles Times*, Oct. 20: B11.

Harness, Tiffany. 2007. "An Inspiration for Independence." *Washington Post*, March 7: A10.

Hayasaki, Erica. 2003. "2 Rs Left in High School: Out of Choice or Fatigue, Many Teachers Have Abandoned the Term Paper, Leaving a Hole in College-Bound Students' Education." *Los Angeles Times*, May 19: A1+.

Helgren, David M., and Robert J. Sager. 2000. *World Geography Today.* Austin: Holt, Rinehart, and Winston.

"How to Write a Letter to the Editor." 2003–2007. *Minnesota North Star Chapter of the Sierra Club*. http://www.northstar.sierraclub.org/involved/letters/tips.html.

Jackdaw Publications: Primary Source Documents. 1999–2009. May 8. http://www.jackdaw.com.

Jackson, Anthony W., and Gayle A. Davis. 2000. *Turning Points 2000: Educating Adolescents in the 21st Century.* New York: Teachers College Press.

Johnson, Kirk. 2008. "Energy Boom in the West Threatens Indian Artifacts." *New York Times*, Aug. 2: A13.

Joint Committee on Geographic Education of the National Council for Geographic Education and the Association of American Geographers. 1984. "The Five Themes of Geography." National Geographic. http://www.nationalgeographic.com/education/themes.html.

Kunzig, Robert. 2002. "Turning the Tide." *U.S. News and World Report*, Oct. 7. Lexis-Nexis Scholastic Universe: News. Lexis-Nexis, 2006. http://web.lexis-nexis.com/scholastic.

Landler, Mark. 2005. "A Subway Bores into the Ottoman and Byzantine Eras." *New York Times*, Aug. 2. http://www.nytimes.com/2005/08/02/international/europe/02istanbul.html?scp=4& sq=landler%20subway&st=cse.

League of Women Voters. 2008. "Smart Voter: Nonpartisan Election Information." http://www .smartvoter.org.

Library of Congress. 2008. "American Memory." May 6, 7. http://memory.loc.gov.

Liu, Melinda. 2007. "Communism by the Numbers." *Newsweek* (Web exclusive), Oct. 27. http:// www.newsweek.com/id/57663.

Macrorie, Ken. 1988. *The I-Search Paper*. Portsmouth, NH: Boynton/Cook.

"Man Is a Machine, No More, Darrow Says." 1925. *New York Times*, Dec. 11: 8. ProQuest Historical Newspapers. www.ProQuestk12.com.

Massachusetts Historical Society. 2008. "The Adams Family." May 3. http://www.masshist.org/ adams/manuscripts_1.cfm##.

Maugh, Thomas H., II. 2008. "Astronomers Hit a Homer with *Odyssey*." *Los Angeles Times*, June 24: A1+.

McPherson, James M., and William J. Cooper. 1998. *Writing the Civil War: The Quest to Understand*. Columbia: University of South Carolina Press.

Mellor, Ronald, and Amanda H. Podany. 2005. *The World in Ancient Times: Primary Sources and Reference Volume*. New York: Oxford University Press.

Metropolitan Museum of Art. 2008a. "China: 2000–1000 B.C." 2000-2008. http://www.metmuseum.org/toah/ht/03/eac/ht03eac.htm.

———. 2008b. "China: 1000 B.C.–1 A.D." 2000–2008. http://www.metmuseum.org/toah/ht/04/eac/ht04eac.htm.

———. 2008c. "China: Dawn of a Golden Age, 200–750 AD." 2000–2008. http://www.metmuseum.org/explore/china_dawn/index.html.

"Model UN Headquarters." 2002. UN Cyber School Bus. http://www.un.org/cyberschoolbus/modelun/index.asp.

Morris, Edmund. 1979. *The Rise of Theodore Roosevelt*. New York: Ballantine Books.

National Archives. 2008. May 8. www.archives.gov.

National Center for History in the Schools (NCHS). 1996. "Overview of Standards in Historical Thinking." http://nchs.ucla.edu/standards/thinking5-12.html.

———. 2008. UCLA. May 6. http://nchs.ucla.edu.

National Council for the Social Studies (NCSS). 1994. "Curriculum Standards for Social Studies: II. Thematic Strands." http://www.socialstudies.org/standards/strands.

National Forensic League. 2007. "The National Junior Forensic League." http://www.nflonline.org/AboutNFL/NJFL.

National Geographic Society. 1998–2009. "Geography Standards." *National Geographic Expeditions*. http://www.nationalgeographic.com/xpeditions/standards/matrix.html.

National History Day. 2008. www.nationalhistoryday.com.

Partnership for 21st Century Skills. 2007. July 23. "Framework for 21st Century Learning." http://www.21stcenturyskills.org/documents/frameworkflyer_072307.pdf.

Pink, Daniel. 2006. *A Whole New Mind: Why Right-Brainers Will Rule the Future.* New York: Riverhead Books.

Pojer, Susan M. 1998–2008. HistoryTeacher.Net. www.historyteacher.net.

Poniewozik, James. "Political Reality: Can TV Make a President?" *Time*, September 30.

Republican National Committee. 2008. www.gop.com.

Robinson, Simon. "The Saga of Ghana." *Time*, March 19.

Rodriguez, Yolanda. 2003. "Indigenous Americans Stake Out Identity: Descendants of Maya, Inca, Aztec Reassert Culture at Local Powwow." *Atlanta Journal-Constitution*, Nov. 5: F1. ProQuest Platinum Periodicals. www.ProQuestk12.com.

Rogers, Will. 1925. "We Might as Well Be Monkeys if We Act Like Them." *Washington Post*, July 19: SM2. ProQuest Historical Newspapers. www.ProQuestk12.com.

Roosevelt, Eleanor. 1960. *You Learn by Living.* New York: Harper & Brothers.

Rowe, Mary Budd. 1987. "Wait Time: Slowing Down May Be a Way of Speeding Up." *American Educator* (Spring): 38–47.

Safire, William, ed. 1992. *Lend Me Your Ears: Great Speeches in History.* New York: W. W. Norton.

"Saving Venice." 2003. *Economist*, Sep. 27. *Lexis-Nexis Scholastic Universe: News.* Lexis-Nexis, 2006. http://web.lexis-nexis.com/scholastic.

Social Studies School Service. 2008. May 7. http://www.socialstudies.com.

Spencer, Leon P. 1992. "Free Trade Will Not Help Africa." In *Africa: Opposing Viewpoints*, ed. David L. Bender and Bruno Leone. San Diego: Greenhaven.

Starr, Linda. 2004. "The Educator's Guide to Copyright and Fair Use." Education World. Dec. 17. http://www.education-world.com/a_curr/curr280.shtml.

"Survey Finds Young Americans' News Use Is Half That of Older Adults: Teens' Daily News Use Is Even Lower Than That of Young Adults," based on a report by Thomas E. Patterson. 2007. John S. and James L. Knight Foundation. July 10. http://www.knightfoundation.org/news/press_room/knight_press_releases/detail.dot?id=130362.

Taylor, Dr. T. Roger. 2006. *Curriculum Design for Excellence, Inc.* www.rogertaylor.com.

Teachers' Curriculum Institute. 2009. www.teachtci.com.

Ulrich, Laurel Thacher. 1991. *A Midwife's Tale: The Life of Martha Ballard, Based on Her Diary, 1785–1812.* New York: Vintage.

U.S. Copyright Office. 2006. "Fair Use." July. http://www.copyright.gov/fls/fl102.html.

"Using Primary Sources." 2008. DoHistory.com. Film Study Center, Harvard University, and Center for History and New Media, George Mason University. May 20. http://dohistory.org/on_your_own/toolkit/primarySources.html.

Valle, Sabrina. 2007. "Losing Forests to Fuel Cars: Ethanol Sugarcane Threatens Brazil's Wooded Savanna." *Washington Post*, July 31: D1. ProQuest Platinum Periodicals. www.ProQuestk12.com.

Washington, Booker T. 1901. *Up from Slavery: An Autobiography.* New York: Doubleday, Page. http://www.bartleby.com/1004/.

Wiggins, Grant, and Jay McTighe. 2001. *Understanding by Design.* Upper Saddle River, NJ: Prentice Hall.

Will, George F. 2007. "An Inconvenient Price." *Newsweek*, Oct. 22: 68. http://www.newsweek.com/id/43352.